BARGAIN SHOPPING

Online

BARGAIN SHOPPING Online

Kate Shoup Welsh

McGraw-Hill

New York   San Francisco   Washington, D.C.   Auckland   Bogotá
Caracas   Lisbon   London   Madrid   Mexico City   Milan
Montreal   New Delhi   San Juan   Singapore
Sydney   Tokyo   Toronto

McGraw-Hill

A Division of The *McGraw-Hill* Companies

2 3 4 5 6 7 8 9 0   DOC/DOC   8 7 6 5 4 3 2 1 0

ISBN 0-07-135894-3

Design by Michael Mendelsohn at MM Design 2000, Inc.

Printed and bound by R. R. Donnelley & Sons Company.

McGraw-Hill books are available at special quantity discounts to use as premiums and sales promotions, or for use in corporate training programs. For more information, please write to the Director of Special Sales, McGraw-Hill, Professional Publishing, Two Penn Plaza, New York, NY 10121-2298. Or contact your local bookstore.

If you have an idea for a book you would like to publish, please send your proposal to or contact:

Michelle Reed
Editor
michelle_reed@mcgraw-hill.com

For Grandpa White,

who passed on to me the bargain-hunting gene;

and for Ian,

who showed me that using a computer

doesn't necessarily make one a dork.

Acknowledgments

It always amazes me how many people must work together to produce one measly book; I'd like to thank everyone who had a part in this one, especially Michelle Reed, a fine editor and an even better friend. Thanks go, too, to Mark Wilson for the use of his super-fast machines. Finally, thanks to my husband and family for putting up with me both during this project and, well, just generally.

Introduction

Raise your hand if this sounds like you.

You're not sure who the sixth President of the United States was, but you recall with precise clarity exactly how much you paid (or, more importantly, didn't pay) for your vintage Saks Fifth Avenue purse at that flea market nine years ago. You always nose out the best deals on everything you buy. You arrive at yard sales before the sun rises. "Retail" is not a term you use except to scoff those who pay it.

If your hand is up—and sports at least one ring that you bought deep-discount—then you've bought the right book (and if you managed to find it on sale, more power to you). Why? The advent of the Internet has brought bargain shopping to new heights. These days, you can buy everything your heart desires at great prices, without ever leaving the comfort of your own home; this book shows you where to go to find the discounted goods you want.

No more setting your alarm for pre-dawn hours to be the first in line for that big sale (I won't even MENTION the fact that you don't have to pay for gas to get to the mall, not to mention battle those mall-walking people for a parking space). Sleep late, leave your bunny slippers on (you know, the ones you bought right after Christmas last year), and dial in! You'll be amazed at the deals you can uncover.

By the way, if you stumble across a site I haven't included here (or, for that matter, the name of the sixth president of the United States), drop me a line. I'll see about including it in the next edition.

Happy Hunting!

Kate Shoup Welsh
kateshoupwelsh@earthlink.net

CONTENTS

CONTENTS

Key

☆ Kate's Pick

Cost of shipping:

$	inexpensive
$$	moderate
$$$	expensive

⊕ **Ships internationally**

🔨 Indicates an auction site

Ease of navigation:

👍 Good

✋ Average

👎 Poor

BARGAIN SHOPPING Online

Fashion

Apparel for Men

A Denim Shop
www.denimshop.com

Find denim shirts, pants, jumpers, jackets, and more for men.

Shipping: **$ $**   ⊕   Navigation:

Alloy
www.alloy.com

Save up to 60 percent on your fave Gen X clothes in Alloy's Bargain Basement.

Shipping: **$ $ $**   ⊕   Navigation:

Apparel Concepts for Men
www.apparelconcepts.com

Buy wardrobe basics by makers you've actually heard of, at below wholesale. Free shipping on orders over $100!

Shipping: **$**   Navigation:

Amazon Auctions
www.amazon.com

Click the Auctions tab and choose Clothing & Accessories. You'll find a variety of clothes for men. Shoes and vintage clothes are also for sale! Shipping rates vary depending on who's selling the item you want to buy.

     Navigation:

Auction Nation
www.auctionnation.com

Click the Clothing link to see what apparel items are up for sale. Note: Shipping costs vary depending on who's selling the item you want to buy.

     Navigation:

Bargain News Auctions Online

www.bnauctions.com

Click the Jewelry & Fashion link to see what men's togs are on the auction block. Delivery charges vary by seller.

 Navigation:

Big Dogs

www.bigdogs.com

Internet shoppers receive special deals and free gifts at this site, which features casual clothing for men.

Shipping: **$ $** Navigation:

Bluefly

www.bluefly.com

Save 25 to 75 percent on shirts, pants, ties, and more by designers like Ralph Lauren and Tommy Hilfiger. This site totally rules.

Shipping: **$ $** Navigation:

Boxlot

www.boxlot.com

You'll find a little of everything on the auction block here —including apparel for men (vintage, too!). Note that shipping rates vary by seller.

 Navigation:

Bugle Boy

www.bugleboy.com

Click the Clearance Sale link for great prices on Bugle Boy togs. Shipping's a little steep, but prices on goods may be low enough to make up for it.

Shipping: **$ $ $** Navigation:

Burlington Coat Factory Direct

www.coat.com/bcfdirect

Find some nice deals on clothes and (surprise!) coats for men. You'll also find luggage, and tons of other stuff here!

Shipping: **$ $ $** Navigation:

Classifieds 2000
www.classifieds2000.com

Click the General Merchandise link and choose Clothing & Accessories to find thousands of auction and classified ads. Shipping charges vary by vendor.

Navigation:

CyberShop
www.cybershop.com

Up to 80 percent of original prices! Click the Departments tab and select Apparel to find the deals. Click the CyberBargains link for the best prices on a variety of items.

Shipping: $ $ Navigation:

Cyber Sweaters
www.cybersweaters.com

All sweaters are $39.95; buy two or more, and save $10 on each sweater.

Shipping: $ $ Navigation:

DesignersDirect.com
www.designersdirect.com

Save up to 75 percent on clothes by Levi's, Nike, Fila, Tommy Hilfiger, and more.

Shipping: $ Navigation:

DesignerOutlet.com
http://designeroutlet.com ☆

Save 35 to 75 percent on clothes for everyone but the family pet. You'll find goods by (drool) Prada, Cynthia Rowley, DKNY, Versace, and Ralph Lauren, to name a few. Be sure to click the Specials button for the best deals.

Shipping: $ $ Navigation:

Dockers.com
www.dockers.com

Click the Hot Deals link for some bargains on Dockers (Note: you must register to view the bargains). Free shipping for orders over $60!

Shipping: $ ⊕   Navigation:

Eddie Bauer

www.eddiebauer.com

Click the Clearance link in the Shop EB area to find some great prices on Eddie Bauer apparel for men. You'll find shoes and bags, too.

Shipping: **$**   Navigation:

eOffPrice

www.eoffprice.com

Buy clothes by Ralph, Tommy, Donna, Calvin, and those wacky Brooks Brothers all at a discount. (Can you say 25 to 75 percent off?) Be sure to check out the Weekly Specials area for those special deals.

Shipping: **$ $ $**   Navigation:

Fashion Man Clothing

www.fashionman.com

Find men's suits, sport coats, dress slacks, and ties at a discount here.

Shipping: **$ $**   Navigation:

Gap

www.gap.com

Click the Sale link to find some good deals on your favorite clothes from the Gap.

Shipping: **$ $**   Navigation:

Guess

www.guess.com

Schwing! Click the Sale link for some good deals on Guess clothes (shoes, too!) for men. Claudia Schiffer, watch out!

Shipping: **$ $**   Navigation:

Hugestore.com

www.hugestore.com

Find dress shirts, suits, jeans, sport coats, ties, and more at Hugestore.com. They promise savings of about 40 percent!

Shipping: **$ $**   Navigation:

International Male

www.intmale.com

So who HASN'T drooled over this mail-order catalog? Now you can see those washboard abs on the WWW (sadly, though, they're not for sale). Okay, so yellow pants aren't for everyone, but you might find some good stuff if you look. Check the sales for some very good deals.

Shipping: $ $ $ Navigation:

Itali Fashions

www.itali.com

Find formal wear, suits, blazers, sport coats, dress slacks, dress shirts, and more — all at 40 to 60 percent off retail. Be sure to visit the Specials area.

Shipping: $ $ $ Navigation:

jcrew.com

www.jcrew.com

Click the Clearance link to find J. Crew goodies up to 60 percent off!

Shipping: $ $ Navigation:

JustShip.com

www.justship.com

Men's and boys' clothes at cheap prices. Register with the site to save even more.

Shipping: $ Navigation:

King Size

www.kingsizemen.com

If you're big and/or tall, this is the site for you. Be sure to check out the Clearance area for the very best prices.

Shipping: $ $ $ Navigation:

Lands End

www.landsend.com

Click the Overstocks link to save 20 to 68 percent on Lands End apparel for men! These garments are first quality, but must move to make room for new items in Lands End's stores.

Shipping: $ $ Navigation:

Levi's

http://store.us.levi.com

Click the Sale button at this site for some great prices on Levi's apparel for men.

Shipping: **$ $**   Navigation:

Macys

www.macys.com

Find loads of excellent apparel for men at Macys, some of it 15 percent off.

Shipping: **$ $**   Navigation:

Mata Factory Outlet

www.nauticom.net/users/mata

Find first-quality cashmere apparel for men at deep discount prices here. Be sure to check out the Bargain Basement and the auction for the best deals!

Shipping: **$ $**   Navigation:

Michael's Online

www.michaels-apparel.com

Click the Designer's Corner link for some killer deals on goods by Calvin Klein, DKNY, Polo, Versace, and more. Getting around is a bit tough, as is ordering, but, well, we must suffer to be beautiful.

Shipping: **$**   Navigation:

Northwest Express

www.northwestexpress.com

Find some great prices on comfy clothes, shoes, and bags for outdoorsy men. Also available: items for the home. Try your luck at the auction while you're there! Shipping's a bit steep, but the prices make up for it.

Shipping: **$ $ $**   Navigation:

Outlet Mall

www.outletmall.com

Find great clothes for men. DKNY, Prada, Ralph Lauren, Armani, and more at up to 85 percent off!

Shipping: **$ $**   Navigation:

Paul Fredrick Men Style
www.paulfredrick.com

Check out the Clearance Center area for the very best deals on menswear.

Shipping: **$ $**   Navigation: 👍

Raffaelo Leather Outlet
www.raffaelo.com

Leather goods at substantial savings. Check the Clearance area for the very best deals!

Shipping: **$ $** Navigation: 👍

San Diego Leather Jacket Factory
www.leather.com

Choose from 1,500 leather jackets, pants, gloves, vests, and more all at factory discount prices.

Shipping: **$ $** Navigation: ✋

SaviShopper.com
www.savishopper.com

This well-designed site deep-discounts first-quality, current season, brand-name clothes and accessories for men. The selection isn't huge, but you can still strike gold.

Shipping: **$**   Navigation: 👍

SellAndTrade.com
www.sellandtrade.com

Click the Clothing & Apparel link to see what goodies are on the auction block. Note that delivery charges will vary depending on the seller.

  Navigation: ✋

Shop4.com
www.shop4.com

You must become a member to save on this site, but once you do, you'll find goods for as much as 60 percent off retail. You'll find some nice apparel for men — not to mention sunglasses, luggage, and shoes. Click the Clearance link for the very best deals in every category.

Shipping: **$ $** Navigation: ✋

Spiegel

www.spiegel.com/spiegel/shopping/ulti-mate

Save 30 to 75 percent on Spiegel merchandise for men, women, and children.

Shipping: **$ $ $**   Navigation:

Style Shop Sales and Bargains

www.salesandbargains.com

You'll find apparel for men by Old Navy, Ralph Lauren, and more at some fair to very low prices. Selection isn't mind-bogglingly huge, but this site is definitely worth a visit.

Shipping: **$ $ $**   Navigation:

Suit Source USA

www.suitsource.com

Suits are 55 percent polyester, 45 percent worsted wool, and roughly 40 percent off!

Shipping: **$**   Navigation:

TiesOnSale

www.tiesonsale.com

TiesOnSale offers a wide selection of silk ties at discounted prices. Newbies will appreciate the "How to Knot a Tie" section. Free shipping!

Shipping: **$**   Navigation:

Trade Hall

www.tradehall.com

At this auction site, you'll find a variety of clothing for men. Note that shipping charges will vary by seller.

          Navigation:

Travel Smith

www.travelsmith.com

Check out the On Sale area for some nice deals on first-quality overstocks on men's travel apparel.

Shipping: **$ $**   Navigation:

Unclaimed Baggage Center
www.unclaimedbaggage.com

Oprah calls this site "One of the country's best shopping secrets"; far be it from me to contradict her. So maybe the prices aren't all rock-bottom, but if you're willing to look, you can find some serious deals on apparel for men.

Shipping: **$ $**   Navigation:

Up 4 Sale
www.up4sale.com

You'll find clothes up for auction in the General Merchandise area of this site. Note that shipping rates will vary by seller.

                    Navigation:

Value America
www.valueamerica.com

If you're looking to buy something, there's a good chance Value America's looking to sell it—including apparel, accessories, and footwear for men. Be sure to check out the hot buys! Become a member (it's free) and save even more.

Shipping: **$**   Navigation:

Yahoo! Auctions
http://auctions.yahoo.com

Click the Clothing & Accessories link to hunt down bargains among the items up for auction. You'll find accessories, athletic wear, leather and fur, and a variety of clothes for men. Note that shipping rates vary by seller.

                    Navigation:

Apparel for Women

A Denim Shop

www.denimshop.com

Find denim shirts, pants, jumpers, jackets, and more for women.

Shipping: **$ $**　　　　Navigation:

Alloy

www.alloy.com

Save up to 60 percent on your fave Gen X clothes in Alloy's Bargain Basement.

Shipping: **$ $ $**　　　　Navigation:

Amazon Auctions

www.amazon.com

Click the Auctions tab, and choose Clothing & Accessories. You'll find a variety of clothes for women plus maternity wear. Shoes and vintage clothes are also for sale! Shipping rates vary depending on who's selling the item you want to buy.

　　Navigation:

ApparelAve.com

www.apparelave.com

Find new, consignment, and vintage items for women here.

Shipping: **$ $**　　　　Navigation:

Auction Nation

www.auctionnation.com

Click the Clothing link to see what apparel items are up for sale. Note: Shipping costs vary depending on who's selling the item you want to buy.

　　Navigation:

Bargain News Auctions Online
www.bnauctions.com

Click the Jewelry & Fashion link to see what togs and trinkets are on the auction block. Delivery charges vary by seller.

 Navigation:

BargainClothing.com
www.bargainclothing.com

Buy brand-name clothing for women at 25 to 50 percent off retail prices. A plus-size collection is available!

Shipping: **$** Navigation:

Big Dogs
www.bigdogs.com

Internet shoppers receive special deals and free gifts at this site, which features casual clothing for women.

Shipping: **$ $** Navigation:

Bluefly
www.bluefly.com ☆

Save 25 to 75 percent on dresses, tops, skirts, pants, and more by designers like Anna Sui, Calvin Klein, BCBG, Ralph Lauren, and more. This site totally rules.

Shipping: **$ $** Navigation:

Boxlot
www.boxlot.com

You'll find a little of everything on the auction block here, including apparel for women (vintage, too!). Note that shipping rates vary by seller.

 Navigation:

Bugle Boy
www.bugleboy.com

Click the Clearance Sale link for great prices on Bugle Boy togs. Shipping's a little steep, but prices on goods may be low enough to make up for it.

Shipping: **$ $ $** Navigation:

Burlington Coat Factory Direct
www.coat.com/bcfdirect

Find some nice deals on clothes and (surprise!) coats for ladies. You'll also find luggage, and tons of other stuff here!

Shipping: **$ $ $**

Navigation:

Classifieds 2000
www.classifieds2000.com

Click the General Merchandise link and choose Clothing & Accessories to find thousands of auction and classified ads. Shipping charges vary by vendor.

Navigation:

Clearance World
www.clearanceworld.com

Find casual wear, shoes, accessories, and more at this site where (as its name would suggest) everything's on clearance.

Shipping: **$ $**

Navigation:

CyberShop
www.cybershop.com

Up to 80 percent of original prices! Click the Departments tab and select Apparel to find the deals. Click the CyberBargains link for the best prices on a variety of items.

Shipping: **$ $**

Navigation:

Delia's Discount Domain
www.discountdomain.com

All you alternative chicks out there should check out this site, where you'll find deals on retro-looking duds. One irritating caveat: You must be a member to get the deals, and membership is steep — $5 per month.

Shipping: **$ $**

Navigation:

DesignerOutlet.com

http://designeroutlet.com

Save 35 to 75 percent on clothes for everyone but the family pet. You'll find goods by (drool) Prada, Cynthia Rowley, DKNY, Versace, and Ralph Lauren, to name a few. Be sure to click the Specials button for the best deals.

Shipping: **$ $**   Navigation:

Dockers.com
www.dockers.com

Click the Hot Deals link for some bargains on Dockers (Note: you must register to view the bargains). Free shipping for orders over $60!

Shipping: **$**   Navigation:

The Dress Connection
www.dressconnection.com

The Dress Connection provides a variety of dresses priced at least 30 percent off retail.

Shipping: **$ $**   Navigation:

Eddie Bauer
www.eddiebauer.com

Click the Clearance link in the Shop EB area to find some great prices on Eddie Bauer apparel for women. You'll find shoes and bags, too.

Shipping: **$**   Navigation:

eOffPrice
www.eoffprice.com

Buy clothes by Ralph, Tommy, Donna, Calvin, and those wacky Brooks brothers — all at a discount. (Can you say 25 to 75 percent off?) Be sure to check out the Weekly Specials area for those special deals.

Shipping: **$ $ $**   Navigation:

Esprit
www.esprit.com

Just who out there DOESN'T love Esprit? Well, if you click the Web Deals link in the Shop Esprit area, you'll find items from past lines at 25 to 75 percent off the retail price!

Shipping: **$ $**   Navigation:

Gap

www.gap.com

Click the Sale link to find some good deals on your favorite clothes from the Gap.

Shipping: **$ $**   Navigation:

Guess

www.guess.com

Schwing! Click the Sale link for some good deals on Guess clothes (shoes, too!) for women. Claudia Schiffer, watch out!

Shipping: **$ $**   Navigation:

ILoveaDeal.com

www.iloveadeal.com

Find apparel featured in the Wireless, Seasons, and Signals catalogs, much of it 40 to 70 percent off! Be sure to click the Top 20 Bargains link for the best deals!

Shipping: **$ $**   Navigation:

J. Jill

www.jjill.com

I love the J. Jill catalog; now that it's on the Web, I'm one happy camper. Be sure to check out the sale items for some nice deals on comfy (yet elegant!) clothes.

Shipping: **$ $**   Navigation:

jcrew.com

www.jcrew.com   ☆

Click the Clearance link to find J. Crew goodies for up to 60 percent off!

Shipping: **$ $**   Navigation:

Lands End

www.landsend.com   ☆

Click the Overstocks link to save 20 to 68 percent on Lands End apparel for the whole family! These garments are first quality, but must move to make room for new items in Lands End's stores.

Shipping: **$ $**   Navigation:

Levi's

http://store.us.levi.com

Click the Sale button at this site for some great prices on Levi's apparel for women.

Shipping: **$ $**   Navigation:

Macys

www.macys.com

Find loads of excellent apparel for women at Macys, some of it 15 percent off.

Shipping: **$ $**   Navigation:

Marketplace Handwork of India

www.marketplaceindia.com

Buy apparel and accessories hand-crafted by women in India. Prices are very reasonable, especially on the sale items.

Shipping: **$ $ $**   Navigation:

Mata Factory Outlet

www.nauticom.net/users/mata

Find first-quality cashmere apparel for women at deep discount prices here. Be sure to check out the Bargain Basement and the auction for the best deals!

Shipping: **$ $**   Navigation:

Michael's Online

www.michaels-apparel.com

Click the Designer's Corner link for some killer deals on goods by Calvin Klein, DKNY, Polo, Versace, and more. Getting around is a bit tough, as is ordering, but, well, we must suffer to be beautiful.

Shipping: **$**   Navigation:

Northwest Express

www.northwestexpress.com

Find some great prices on comfy clothes, shoes, and bags for outdoorsy women. Also available: items for the home. Try your luck at the auction while you're there! Shipping's a bit steep, but the prices make up for it.

Shipping: **$ $ $**   Navigation:

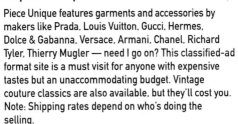

Outlet Mall

www.outletmall.com

Find a variety of clothes for women. DKNY, Prada, Ralph Lauren, Armani, and more at up to 85 percent off!

Shipping: **$ $**   Navigation:

Piece Unique

www.pieceunique.com

Piece Unique features garments and accessories by makers like Prada, Louis Vuitton, Gucci, Hermes, Dolce & Gabanna, Versace, Armani, Chanel, Richard Tyler, Thierry Mugler — need I go on? This classified-ad format site is a must visit for anyone with expensive tastes but an unaccommodating budget. Vintage couture classics are also available, but they'll cost you. Note: Shipping rates depend on who's doing the selling.

Navigation:

Raffaelo Leather Outlet

www.raffaelo.com

Leather goods at substantial savings. Check the Clearance area for the very best deals!

Shipping: **$ $**   Navigation:

San Diego Leather Jacket Factory

www.leather.com

Choose from 1,500 leather jackets, pants, gloves, halters, vests, skirts, and more — all at factory discount prices.

Shipping: **$ $**   Navigation:

SellAndTrade.com

www.sellandtrade.com

Click the Clothing & Apparel link to see what goodies are on the auction block. Note that delivery charges will vary depending on the seller.

Navigation:

Shop4.com
www.shop4.com

You must become a member to save on this site, but once you do, you'll find goods for as much as 60 percent off retail. You'll find apparel for women — not to mention sunglasses, luggage, and shoes. Click the Clearance link for the very best deals in every category.

Shipping: **$ $**   Navigation:

Spiegel
www.spiegel.com/spiegel/shopping/ultimate

Save 30 to 75 percent on Spiegel merchandise for women.

Shipping: **$ $ $**   Navigation:

Style Shop Sales and Bargains
www.salesandbargains.com

You'll find apparel for the whole family by Old Navy, Ralph Lauren, and more at some fair to very low prices. Selection isn't mind-bogglingly huge, but this site is definitely worth a visit.

Shipping: **$ $ $**   Navigation:

Trade Hall
www.tradehall.com

At this auction site, you'll find clothing (including bridal, last I checked) for women. Note that shipping charges will vary by seller.

     Navigation:

Travel Smith
www.travelsmith.com

Check out the On Sale area for some nice deals on first-quality overstocks on women's travel apparel.

Shipping: **$ $**   Navigation:

Tweeds
www.tweeds.com

Find great prices on clothes from the famous Tweeds catalog. Click the Special Sale link to find the best deals!

Shipping: **$ $**   Navigation:

Ulla Popken
www.ullapopken.com

This site offers some nice deals on clothes size 12 and up. Be sure to check out the Specials area.

Shipping: **$ $**   Navigation:

Unclaimed Baggage Center
www.unclaimedbaggage.com

Oprah calls this site "One of the country's best shopping secrets"; far be it from me to contradict her. So maybe the prices aren't all rock-bottom, but if you're willing to look, you can find some serious deals on luggage, apparel for women, and more.

Shipping: **$ $**   Navigation:

Up 4 Sale
www.up4sale.com

You'll find clothes up for auction in the General Merchandise area of this site. Note that shipping rates will vary by seller.

    Navigation:

Value America
www.valueamerica.com

If you're looking to buy something, there's a good chance Value America's looking to sell it—including apparel, accessories, and footwear for women. Be sure to check out the hot buys! Become a member (it's free) and save even more.

Shipping: **$**   Navigation:

Yahoo! Auctions
http://auctions.yahoo.com

Click the Clothing & Accessories link to hunt down bargains among the items up for auction. You'll find accessories, athletic wear, leather and fur, ladies' apparel, and more. Note that shipping rates vary by seller.

    Navigation:

Bags

1-800-Luggage
http://1-800-luggage.com

Save up to 60 percent on luggage from this site! Be sure to visit the Budget Store area for the best deals.

Shipping: **$ $**   Navigation:

Ashford.com
www.ashford.com

Ashford.com offers a nice assortment of distinctive hand-bags and other accessories, including the fabulous "Push-Up Bag" by Susan Briganti. Prices aren't dirt cheap, but they're close. Free shipping!

Shipping: **$**   Navigation:

Atlantic Luggage
www.atlanticluggage.com

Buy Atlantic Luggage bags at a handy discount!

Shipping: **$ $**   Navigation:

BagIt.com
www.bagsandall.com

Find luggage, business cases, and small leather goods at tidy discounts here. Free shipping!

Shipping: **$**   Navigation:

Bentley's
www.bentleys.com

Bentley's guarantees that its luggage, business cases, and fine leather accessories are at the lowest prices you'll find. If within 30 days you find the same item at a local authorized retailer for less, bring them proof and they will refund you the difference plus 10 percent. Be sure to check out the Monthly Specials area!

Shipping: **$ $**   Navigation:

Bluefly
www.bluefly.com

Save 25 to 75 percent on handbags by top designers (can you say Prada?). This site totally rules.

Shipping: **$ $**   Navigation:

Burlington Coat Factory Direct
www.coat.com/bcfdirect

Find some nice deals on luggage and (surprise!) coats for ladies, men, and kids.

Shipping: **$ $ $**   Navigation:

Classifieds 2000
www.classifieds2000.com

Click the General Merchandise link and choose Clothing & Accessories to find thousands of auction and classified ads. Shipping charges vary by vendor.

Navigation:

eBags
www.ebags.com

At eBags, you'll find great prices (up to 70 percent off!) on bags by brands like Samsonite, Timberland, Eagle Creek, and more.

Shipping: **$**   Navigation:

Eddie Bauer
www.eddiebauer.com

Click the Clearance link in the Shop EB area to find some great prices on Eddie Bauer bags for men and women.

Shipping: **$**   Navigation:

jcrew.com
www.jcrew.com

Click the Clearance link to find J. Crew goodies for up to 60 percent off!

Shipping: **$ $**   Navigation:

The Luggage Corner

www.luggagecorner.com

Find some good deals on luggage in the Hot Deals area.

Shipping: **$ $** Navigation:

The Luggage Factory

www.luggagefactoryoutlet.com

Find some pretty deep discounts on luggage and cases by a variety of manufacturers.

Shipping: **$ $** Navigation:

Northwest Express

www.northwestexpress.com

Find some great prices on bags for outdoorsy men and women. Try your luck at the auction while you're there! Shipping's a bit steep, but the prices make up for it.

Shipping: **$ $ $** Navigation:

Shop4.com

www.shop4.com

You must become a member to save on this site, but once you do, you'll find luggage for men and women for as much as 60 percent off retail. Click the Clearance link for the very best deals in every category.

Shipping: **$ $** Navigation:

Spiegel

www.spiegel.com/spiegel/shopping/ultimate ☆

Save 30 to 75 percent on Spiegel merchandise for men, women, and children.

Shipping: **$ $ $** Navigation:

Sumdex

www.sumdex.com

Briefcases galore, at some pretty OK prices (especially the specials).

Shipping: **$ $** Navigation:

Unclaimed Baggage Center
www.unclaimedbaggage.com

Oprah calls this site "One of the country's best shopping secrets"; far be it from me to contradict her. So maybe the prices aren't all rock-bottom, but if you're willing to look, you can find some serious deals on luggage.

Shipping: **$ $**   Navigation:

Value America
www.valueamerica.com

If you're looking to buy something, there's a good chance Value America's looking to sell it — including luggage. Be sure to check out the hot buys! Become a member (it's free) and save even more.

Shipping: **$**   Navigation:

Web Emporium
www.webporium.com

You'll find a bit of everything here at Web Emporium, including luggage at nice prices.

Shipping: **$ $**   Navigation:

World Traveler Luggage and Travel Goods
www.worldtraveler.com

Find discounted briefcases, computer cases, luggage, and travel accessories at World Traveler. Be sure to check out the Specials from the World Traveler area.

Shipping: **$ $**   Navigation:

Yahoo! Auctions
http://auctions.yahoo.com

Click the Clothing & Accessories link to hunt down bargains among the items (including bags) up for auction. Note that shipping rates vary by seller.

                    Navigation:

Bridal

Bridals Online
www.bridalsonline.com

Save 20 to 40 percent on wedding gowns from the current line by the best designers. You can't browse online, but if there's a gown you know you want, you can request a price and order it online.

Shipping: $ $ $ Navigation:

Bridesmaids.com
www.bridesmaids.com ☆

If you're always a bridesmaid but never a bride, check out the bridesmaid dresses by After Six, Bari Jay, Dessy, Jim Hjelm, Nicole Miller (yum), and more — all at some won't-blow-the-dowry prices.

Shipping: $ $ Navigation:

Carla's Vintage Wedding Gowns
http://hometown.aol.com/gowns4you

This site features some truly beautiful and one-of-a-kind vintage bridal gowns, and they're way less money than those new scratchy ones out there these days. The only downside: You can't order online.

Shipping: $ $ Navigation:

Classifieds 2000
www.classifieds2000.com

Click the General Merchandise link and choose Clothing & Accessories to find thousands of auction and classified ads. Shipping charges vary by vendor.

Navigation:

Discount Bridal Service
www.discountbridalservice.com

At this site, you can purchase first-quality wedding gowns, veils, attendant's dresses, and more at discounts of 20 to 40 percent off the suggested retail prices. You can't order online, but the savings may make it worth your while to call.

Shipping: **$$**   Navigation:

Gulden & Brown Antique Wedding Gowns

http://home.att.net/~design-house ☆

As Dame Edith at this Web site says, "Those that forget the fashions of the past are condemned to buy them again at retail." Take her words of wisdom to heart! Scrap those overpriced wedding gowns and go vintage! This site has a wide selection of BEAUTIFUL vintage wedding gowns at prices that will let you to go on a honeymoon.

Shipping: **$**   Navigation: 👍

NetBride.com

www.netbride.com

Save big on bridal gowns as well as apparel for brides-maids. The price quoted includes shipping if you live in the continental U.S.

Shipping: **$**   Navigation: 👍

The Next Step

www.bridalshoes.com

Brides! Buy your shoes and handbag for the happiest day of your life right here! Be sure to visit the Special Buys area. Shipping is free.

Shipping: **$**   Navigation: 👍

Savvy Bridal

www.savvybridal.com

At Savvy Bridal, you can save 20 to 40 percent off retail on wedding gowns, bridesmaid gowns, flower girl dresses, mother's gowns, headpieces and veils, wedding invitations, wedding accessories, and more. There's no online catalog; you must come armed with the manufacturer and style number of the item you want.

Shipping: **$$**   Navigation: ✋

Trade Hall

www.tradehall.com

At this auction site, you'll find a variety of bridal clothing for women. Note that shipping charges will vary by seller.

    Navigation: 👍

Maternity

Amazon Auctions

www.amazon.com

Click the Auctions tab, and choose Clothing & Accessories. You'll find clothes for maternity wear. Shoes and vintage clothes are also for sale! Shipping rates vary depending on who's selling the item you want to buy.

   Navigation:

Maternity for Less

http://maternity4less.com

It's such a drag to spend a fortune on maternity clothes, especially since you only wear them for a few months. Hence Maternity for Less; be sure to click the Seasonal Special link for the best deals!

Shipping: **$ $**   Navigation:

Shoes

Alloy
www.alloy.com

Save up to 60 percent on your fave Gen X shoes in Alloy's Bargain Basement.

Shipping: $ $ $ Navigation: 👍

Amazon Auctions
www.amazon.com

Click the Auctions tab, and choose Clothing & Accessories. You'll find shoes for men, women, and kids. Shipping rates vary depending on who's selling the item you want to buy.

 Navigation: 👍

Apparel Concepts for Men
www.apparelconcepts.com

Find men's shoes by makers you've actually heard of — such as Bass, Clarks, Rockport, Florsheim, and Johnston & Murphy — at below wholesale. Free shipping on orders over $100!

Shipping: $ Navigation: 👍

Birkenstock Express Online
https://secure.birkenstockexpress.com

Hey, who doesn't want comfy feet on the cheap? Click the Bargains link, enter your shoe size, and get out your wallet. Be sure to check the Sale Shelf for discontinued and "as-is" stuff.

Shipping: $ $ Navigation: ✋

Bluefly
www.bluefly.com

Save 25 to 75 percent on shoes by top designers. This site totally rules.

Shipping: $ Navigation: 👍

Cowtown Boots

www.cowtownboots.com

Omigod! You've been invited to go line dancing, and you haven't a thing to wear! Fear not. Visit Cowtown Boots for boots for the whole danged family (did you know they made boots out of ostrich?), not to mention western shirts. Be sure to check out the Monthly Specials area for the best deals.

Shipping: **$ $**   Navigation:

Dale's Shoes

www.dales-shoes.com

Save on shoes by Clarks, Ecco, Easy Spirit, New Balance, and more. Free shipping if you buy two or more pairs of shoes!

Shipping: **$**   Navigation:

DesignerShoes.com

www.designershoes.com

Choose from shoes by Bruno Magli, Evan Picone, Nickels, Steve Madden, Via Spiga (I LOVE those), and more — all for people with big feet (9 to 14). Be sure to visit the Clearance area for even better deals.

Shipping: **$ $**   Navigation:

Eddie Bauer

www.eddiebauer.com

Click the Clearance link in the Shop EB area to find some great prices on Eddie Bauer shoes for men and women.

Shipping: **$**   🌐   Navigation:

Efootwear

www.efootwear.com

Find great prices on athletic shoes by Reebok, Avia, New Balance, Converse, Fila, and more. Be sure to visit the Great Deals Under $40 area!

Shipping: **$ $**   Navigation:

Guess

www.guess.com

Schwing! Click the Sale link for some good deals on Guess shoes for men and women. Claudia Schiffer, watch out!

Shipping: **$ $**   Navigation: 👈

jcrew.com

www.jcrew.com

Click the Clearance link to find J. Crew goodies for up to 60 percent off!

Shipping: **$ $**   Navigation:

Just for Feet

www.feet.com

Find deals on shoes of all types: cheerleading, aerobics, cross-training, dress, cross-dressing (just kidding), and more. Be sure to visit the Combat Zone for savings of up to 70 percent! Shipping's a wee steep, but the savings make up for it.

Shipping: **$ $ $**   Navigation:

K-Swiss Outlet

www.kswiss-outlet.com

Find K-Swiss shoes at factory outlet prices. Be sure to visit the Bargains area for the best deals.

Shipping: **$ $**   Navigation:

Lands End

www.landsend.com ☆

Click the Overstocks link to save 20 to 68 percent on Lands End shoes and apparel! These items are first quality, but must move to make room for new items in Lands End's stores.

Shipping: **$ $**   ⊕   Navigation:

Northwest Express

www.northwestexpress.com

Find some great prices on comfy shoes for outdoorsy men and women. Also available: items for the home. Try your luck at the auction while you're there! Shipping's a bit steep, but the prices make up for it.

Shipping: **$ $ $**   Navigation:

OnlineShoes.com

www.onlineshoes.com

You'll find some serious deals on all types of shoes here, especially in the Best Buy Items and Clearance Items areas. Even better? Free shipping in the U.S.

Shipping: **$**   ⊕   Navigation:

Payless Shoe Store

www.payless.com

Admit it: You've got at least one pair of shoes from Payless. Okay, you've at least been in the store. Now you can find dirt-cheap shoes from Payless online!

Shipping: **$ $**   Navigation:

Sandal Factory Outlet

www.sandaloutlet.com

Find Birks at a slight discount here. Note that shipping is included in the price.

Shipping: **$**   Navigation:

Shoe Pavilion

www.shoepavilion.com   ☆

Save 30 to 70 percent on shoes by makers like Hush Puppies, Naturalizer, Fila, New Balance, Nike, and more for men, women, and teens (whoo hoo!).

Shipping: **$ $**   Navigation:

Shop4.com

www.shop4.com

You must become a member to save on this site, but once you do, you'll find goods for as much as 60 percent off retail. You'll find shoes for men, women, and children. Click the Clearance link for the very best deals in every category.

Shipping: **$ $**   Navigation:

SoftMoc

www.softmoc.com

Contrary to its name, this site sells more than soft mocs. No sir, I found some nice deals on Naots, Doc Martens, Tevas, and more. Prices aren't rock-bottom, but they're decent. Plus, shipping is free in North America.

Shipping: **$**   Navigation:

Spiegel

www.spiegel.com/spiegel/shopping/ultimate ☆

Save 30 to 75 percent on Spiegel merchandise for men, women, and children.

Shipping: **$ $ $**   Navigation:

The Urban Athlete
www.urban-athlete.com

Find tons of running shoes by makers like Asics, Brooks, and more, all at great prices. Free shipping!

Shipping: **$**   Navigation:

Value America
www.valueamerica.com

If you're looking to buy something, there's a good chance Value America's looking to sell it—including footwear (you'll find items for men, women, and children). Be sure to check out the hot buys! Become a member (it's free) and save even more.

Shipping: **$**   Navigation:

Underthings

Apparel Concepts for Men
www.apparelconcepts.com

Find men's socks and underwear at below wholesale prices. Free shipping on orders over $100!

Shipping: **$**   Navigation:

Bare Necessities
www.barenecessities.com

Find bras, panties, and sleepwear — most discounted 20 percent. Shipping is free on orders over $50.

Shipping: **$**   Navigation:

The Bargain Shopping Show Online Shopping Guide
http://inventoryliquidators.com/products/lingerie

Garments (or lack thereof) to satisfy the inner harlot, at prices to satisfy the inner cheapskate.

Shipping: **$ $ $**   Navigation:

Bluefly   ☆
www.bluefly.com

Save 25 to 75 percent on underthings by top designers. This site totally rules.

Shipping: **$ $**   Navigation:

Body Body
www.bodybody.com

Find discounts on teddies, robes, camis, tap pants, bras, bustiers, and loungewear. Also available: swim shorts, thongs, athletic tanks, and bikini separates.

Shipping: **$ $**   Navigation:

Caroline B

www.caroline-b.com

Find stockings and lingerie by some damn good brands at a discount. Be sure to click the Discount button to save big on some seriously expensive stuff (it's still expensive, but up to half off the regular price).

Shipping: **$ $**   Navigation:

Chock

www.chockcatalog.com

Save on underthings for men, women, children, and babies.

Shipping: **$ $**   Navigation:

DesignerOutlet.com

www.designeroutlet.com

Save 35 to 75 percent on underthings for everyone but the family pet. Be sure to click the Specials button for the best deals.

Shipping: **$ $**   Navigation:

Funky Boutique

www.funkyboutique.com

Find bustiers, bodystockings, panties, stockings and garters, edibles (!), and more. Be sure to visit the Clearance Rack for savings of up to 50 percent.

Shipping: **$ $**   Navigation:

L'eggs Online Store

www.pantyhose.com

Use the sizing system to figure out what size you need, select the hose you want, and pay 20 percent less than retail.

Shipping: **$ $**   Navigation:

Lingerie Gallery

www.lingeriegallery.com

This site includes a section of lingerie for $29.95 or less. Be sure to check out the Clearance area, where you'll find savings of up to 35 percent.

Shipping: **$ $**   Navigation:

One Hanes Place
www.onehanesplace.com

Save on Bali, Hanes, Champion, Wonderbra, Playtex, and more. Be sure to check the Closeouts area for the best deals.

Shipping: **$ $** Navigation:

SlickChicks Boutique
www.slickchicks.com

SlickChicks offers lingerie, leather, risque outerwear, and intimate underwear in regular and plus sizes not to mention exotic fetish items and costumes. Take 10 percent off all Internet orders.

Shipping: **$ $ $**   Navigation:

Spiegel
www.spiegel.com/spiegel/shopping/ultimate

Save 30 to 75 percent on Spiegel merchandise for men, women, and children.

Shipping: **$ $ $** Navigation:

Underneath.com
www.underneath.com

Buy your skivvies online on the cheap. Be sure to check the Clearance area for the best deals (all items marked down 35 percent or more). Free delivery on orders of $60 or more!

Shipping: **$**   Navigation:

Vintage

5 and Dime Vintage

www.510vintage.com

Buy vintage clothes for men and women. Used Levi's are a hit here! Prices aren't rock bottom, but you'll find some great pieces.

Shipping: $ $ Navigation:

Amazon Auctions

www.amazon.com

Click the Auctions tab and choose Clothing & Accessories. Shoes and vintage clothes are for sale here! Shipping rates vary depending on who's selling the item you want to buy.

 Navigation:

Antique Alley

http://bmark.com/aa

Click Search Antique Alley and select Vintage Clothing from the Category list to see what's up for grabs. Antique Alley is actually a network of individual vendors, so prices and shipping policies will vary depending on which vendor is selling the item you want.

Navigation:

ApparelAve.com

www.apparelave.com

Find new, consignment, and vintage items for women here.

Shipping: $ $ Navigation:

Ashford.com

www.ashford.com

Ashford.com offers an incredible assortment of distinctive men's and women's vintage timepieces. Free shipping!

Shipping: $ Navigation:

Ballyhoo Vintage Clothing

www.ballyhoovintage.com

Shop through the decades at Ballyhoo Vintage. Not everything is dirt cheap, but you'll find some incredible, one-of-
a-kind items!

Shipping: **$ $**   Navigation:

Bittersweet Boutique

www.bittersweetboutique.com

Find women's vintage clothing from as early as the 1800s
up through the 1970s — including (rejoice!) deadstock
Candies mules (much like the ones Ms. Olivia Newton-
John wore in "Grease").

Shipping: **$ $**   Navigation:

Black Cat Collectibles

www.blackcatcollectibles.com

Black Cat Collectibles specializes in vintage costume
jewelry and fashion accessories. Be sure to check out
the Bargain Gift Boutique area, where you'll find items
for $15 or less.

Shipping: **$**   Navigation:

Boxlot

www.boxlot.com

You'll find a little of everything on the auction block here
— including vintage apparel for men and women. Note
that shipping rates vary by seller.

     Navigation:

Carla's Vintage Wedding Gowns

http://hometown.aol.com/gowns4you

This site features some truly beautiful and one-of-a-kind
vintage bridal gowns, and they're way less money than
those new scratchy ones out there these days.

Shipping: **$ $**   Navigation:

The Cats Pajamas

www.catspajamas.com

This site has a fantastic collection of vintage clothing, including lingerie, menswear, kids stuff, and bridal wear (wistful sigh implied). There's a special section for those of us who, like Marilyn Monroe, wear a size 12 (and up). Be sure to check out the Bargain Basement area for the best deals!

Shipping: **$ $**   Navigation:

EnokiWorld

www.enokiworld.com

Move over, Elsa Klentsch. You'll develop a style all your own when you order from EnokiWorld. Prices aren't dirt cheap, but they're within reason, and the garments are one-of-a-kind.

Shipping: **$**   Navigation:

Eureka, I Found It!

www.eureka-i-found-it.com

Some great items (costume jewelry, Hawaiian shirts, and more) at very reasonable prices.

Shipping: **$ $**   Navigation:

Gulden & Brown Antique Wedding Gowns

http://home.att.net/~design-house ☆

As Dame Edith at this Web site says, "Those that forget the fashions of the past are condemned to buy them again — at retail." Take her words of wisdom to heart! Scrap those overpriced wedding gowns, and go vintage! This site has a wide selection of BEAUTIFUL vintage wedding gowns at prices that will enable you to afford a honeymoon.

Shipping: **$**   Navigation:

The Internet Antique Shop

www.tias.com

Select Vintage Clothing from the category list to see what's available. The Internet Antique Shop is actually a network of individual vendors, so prices and shipping policies will vary depending on which vendor is selling the item you want.

Navigation:

It's in the Past

www.itsinthepast.com

Find vintage shoes, purses, scarves, hats, lingerie, and clothing for men and women. Some beautiful garments are available, and at prices that won't break your heart.

Shipping: **$ $**   Navigation:

Jan's Jewels and More

www.jansjewels.com

Choose from a great selection of vintage jewelry, clothing, patterns, and purses. Jan's helpful descriptions help you figure out just what you're looking at.

Shipping: **$ $**   Navigation:

Kitty Girl Vintage

http://host.fptoday.com/kittygirl_vintage

Kitty Girl Vintage is an online clothing store offering antique and vintage women's clothing, platform shoes, and accessories; the store features plastic jewelry and fashions from the 20's to the 50's.

Shipping: **$ $**   Navigation:

Piece Unique

www.pieceunique.com   ☆

Piece Unique features vintage garments and accessories by makers like Louis Vuitton, Gucci, Hermes, and Chanel — need I go on? (They'll cost you.) This classified-ad format site is a must visit for anyone with expensive tastes but an unaccommodating budget. Note: Shipping rates depend on who's doing the selling.

Navigation:

Popula

www.popula.com

Click the Vintage/Designer link to see what swanky duds and baubles are up for auction. Note that shipping charges vary by seller.

Navigation:

Retro Active

www.designervintage.com

This site has some amazing finds, but if you're like me, you'll make a beeline for the Great Stuff Under $50 (gee, I just don't seem to be able to swing those Chanel Couture garments in the designer vintage area).

Shipping: **$**   Navigation:

The Retro Closet

www.eaglesnest.net/retrocloset

Find some great vintage bargains at this site, which tends to feature clothes from circa the Polyester Era. Prices are extremely reasonable, especially in the Bargain Basement.

Shipping: **$ $**   Navigation: 👍

RetroLives

www.angelfire.com/sk/retrolives

Selection at this site isn't huge, but you can find some real vintage gems at highly reasonable prices (last I visited, all shoes were $15 and all handbags were $10). Shipping's pretty reasonable, too!

Shipping: **$**   Navigation: 👍

The Rusty Zipper

www.rustyzipper.com

You'll find everything vintage here — Hawaiian stuff, bell-bottoms and flares, Levi's, bowling shirts, leisure suits, tuxedos, shoes, and more. Be sure to visit the Bargain Basement area!

Shipping: **$ $**   Navigation: 👍

Trashy Diva

www.trashy-diva.net

Hey, who DOESN'T want to be a trashy diva? You'll find some fabulously decadent dresses and other garments at this site. Prices aren't dirt cheap on everything (meaning I'd have to waitress more than one night to afford certain items), but there are some great finds here. Be sure to check out the sale items.

Shipping: **$ $ $**   Navigation: 👍

Vintage Blues
http://vintageblues.com

Tons o' vintage, including a whole section on 40s and 50s
stuff for you swing aficionados out there. Be sure to check
the Bargain Basement link to see what's being let go
cheap.

Shipping: **$ $ $**   Navigation:

Vintage USA
www.vintageusa.com

Browse this site for American vintage clothing and collectible sneakers; be sure to check out what's on the auction block, too.

Shipping: **$ $ $** Navigation:

Vintage Vixen
www.vintagevixen.com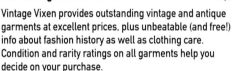

Vintage Vixen provides outstanding vintage and antique
garments at excellent prices, plus unbeatable (and free!)
info about fashion history as well as clothing care.
Condition and rarity ratings on all garments help you
decide on your purchase.

Shipping: **$ $** Navigation:

What Goes Around Comes Around
www.nyvintage.com

What Goes Around Comes Around sells all sorts of vintage, much for under $50 (visit the Under $50 virtual
store).

Shipping: **$** Navigation:

Leisure

Arts and Crafts

Art Xpress

www.artxpress.com

Prices on art supplies are reasonable here. Be sure to click the Specials link for the best deals.

Shipping: **$ $ $**   Navigation:

Crafts Etc.

www.craftsetc.com

Find goods for painting, candlemaking, needlework, and more at this excellent craft site.

Shipping: **$ $**   🌐   Navigation:

Cross Stitches

www.xstitches.com

Got a cross-stitch addiction? Feed your habit here. You'll find an online store as well as an auction. Free shipping on orders over $50 from the store; delivery charges for auction items vary by seller.

Shipping: **$**   Navigation: 🖐

Dick Blick Art Materials

www.craftsetc.com

Save on art supplies at Dick Blick (I just like saying that).

Shipping: **$ $**   Navigation: 👍

Discount Art Supplies

www.discountart.com

Save on everything you need to be the next Matisse. Be sure to check out the Specials area. Free shipping on orders over $100!

Shipping: **$**   Navigation:

DiscountNeedlework.com
http://discountneedlework.com

Save 20 percent on everything you need for cross-stitching, needlepoint, and crewel.

Shipping: **$ $**   Navigation:

Fabric by the Pound
www.fabricbythepound.com

Buy mill end strips, textile remnants, lace, craft patterns, and assorted trims from the curtain, drapery, and upholstery trade. Great for craft projects! Be sure to click the Sales link for the best deals.

Shipping: **$ $ $**   Navigation:

The Fabric Club
www.fabricclub.com

Find fantastic fabrics at great prices. Become a member and receive even better deals!

Shipping: **$ $**   Navigation:

Fabric Land
www.fabricland.com

Use this site's Fabric Finder to find beautiful fabrics, at nicely discounted prices.

Shipping: **$ $**   Navigation:

Fletch's Art Supply Store
www.artsupplystore.com

Save on everything you need to be the next Leonardo (or Leonardette, whichever the case may be).

Shipping: **$ $**   Navigation:

Mister Art
www.misterart.com

MisterArt.com calls itself the world's largest online discount art supply store. Prices are low across the board, but if you're a VIP member (it costs $15 per year), they're even better! Be sure to check out the Specials area for the best deals.

Shipping: **$ $**   Navigation:

Phoenix Textiles

www.phoenixtextiles.com

Find tons of dirt cheap fabrics that aren't hideous. Be sure to check out the Everything's $1.00 area for the dirtiest of the dirt cheap stuff.

Shipping: **$ $**   Navigation:

Seaway Artist Supplies

www.lukasamerica.com

Save on oil paints, watercolors, brushes, easels, and everything you need for your paint box.

Shipping: **$ $**   Navigation:

Sewing Machine Outlet

www.sewingmachineoutlet.com

This site is your source for new and used sewing machines, needles, parts, and more. One irritating caveat: You must contact them for information about their products, and you can't order online.

Shipping: **$ $ $**   Navigation:

Stained Glass Bargains

www.stainedglass-bargains.com

Stained Glass Bargains is your Internet source for some serious deals on stained glass supplies. Selection is very limited, but bargains can be found.

Shipping: **$ $ $**   Navigation:

Up 4 Sale

www.up4sale.com

You'll find craft and hobby items up for auction in the General Merchandise area of this site. Note that shipping rates will vary by seller.

                    Navigation:

WholesaleArt.com

www.wholesaleart.com

Artists, starve no longer! Visit WholesaleArt.com for art supplies galore, some at 40 to 60 percent off. The more you buy, the less it costs. Sadly, shipping is a bit steep.

Shipping: **$ $ $**   Navigation:

Wood-n-Crafts Inc.
www.wood-n-crafts.com

Buy your craft, hobby, and woodworking supplies whole-sale here. Free shipping on orders over $70!

Shipping: **$**   Navigation:

Yahoo! Auctions
http://auctions.yahoo.com

Click the Sports & Recreation link and choose Hobbies and Crafts to find deals on supplies for basketry, beading, birding, crafts, sewing and needlecrafts, and more. Shipping rates vary by seller.

                    Navigation:

Books

1000's of Discount Books
www.ptdiscountbooks.com

Books on this site are discounted 20 to 90 (that's not a typo) percent.

Shipping: **$ $**   Navigation:

1bookstreet.com
www.1bookstreet.com

Buy New York Times hardcover fiction for 40 percent off. Also, be sure to click the 1 Bargain Book Street link for even greater savings.

Shipping: **$**   Navigation:

A1 Books
www.a1books.com

Find, among other things, discounted textbooks here (think of the extra Ramen noodles you'll be able to buy!).

Shipping: **$ $** Navigation:

Absolute Magazines
www.absolutemagazines.com

By ordering your favorite magazines from Absolute Magazines, you'll save as much as 80 percent off the cover price!

Shipping: **$** Navigation:

Academy Bookstore
www.academy-bookstore.com

Academy Bookstore sells used and other discounted books on a wide range of scholarly subjects, with particular strengths in art, architecture, photography, history, and philosophy.

Shipping: **$ $** Navigation:

Add All Book Searching and Price Comparison

www.bookarea.com

How great is THIS? Enter in your shipping destination; the currency you use; and the title, author, ISBN, or keyword of the book you want to find, and this site compares the pricing and services at 39 stores (at present) to find the cheapest offering. Stop here before you buy to make sure you get the best deal!

Navigation:

AlphaCraze.com

www.alphacraze.com

At AlphaCraze.com, you'll find over 3.1 million titles available at up to 50 percent off.

Shipping: **$ $**   Navigation:

Amazon Auctions

www.amazon.com

Click the Auctions tab, and choose Books, Movies & Video to see what's available. Shipping rates vary depending on who's selling the item you want to buy.

    Navigation:

Amazon.com

www.amazon.com ☆

Amazon's not kidding when it says it has Earth's Biggest Selection. They sell books, videos, music, toys, and more. If you live in the UK, check out amazon.co.uk for great deals and cheaper shipping.

Shipping: **$ $**   ⊕   Navigation:

Auction Nation

www.auctionnation.com

Click the Books/Mags link to see what items are up for sale. Note: Shipping costs vary depending on who's selling the item you want to buy.

    Navigation:

Auction Universe

www.auctionuniverse.com

Click the Books, Autographs & Paper link to see what's up for grabs. Delivery charges vary by vendor.

  Navigation:

AuctionAddict.com

www.auctionaddict.com

Click the Books & Magazines link to see what's available. Shipping rates vary by seller.

  Navigation:

Auctionscape

www.auctionscape.com

Click the Books, Music, Entertainment link to search for items on the auction block. Shipping costs vary by seller.

  Navigation:

Audio Books Online

www.audiobooksonline.com

Save 40 percent on just about every audio book you can dream up.

Shipping: **$ $**   Navigation:

Bargain News Auctions Online

www.bnauctions.com

Click the Books, Autographs & Paper link to see what's on the auction block. Delivery charges vary by seller.

  Navigation:

Barnes&Noble.com

www.barnesandnoble.com ☆

New York Times bestsellers are 50 percent off at this site. You'll also find one helluva selection of music, software, and magazines. Click the Bargains tab for even hotter deals.

Shipping: **$ $** Navigation:

Bear Mountain Books & Music

www.bargainbooks.com

Books and videos are up to 70 percent off; classical CDs sell for $4.99. Pinch me (gently, of course)!

Shipping: **$ $**  Navigation:

Big Words

www.bigwords.com

Rent or buy new or used college textbooks here. Free shipping!

Shipping: **$** Navigation:

Blake's Books

www.blakesbooks.com

Blake's Books is an online used and antiquarian book-store that carries a wide array of books for scholars and readers in all subjects including art, philosophy, religion, math, science, history, literature and the humanities.

Shipping: **$ $** Navigation:

Book World

www.bookworld.com

Save 20 percent across the board on books you order at Book World.

Shipping: **$ $** Navigation:

Book Zone

www.bookzone.com

Use the Book Zone's Super Catalog to find thousands of books and audio books at discounted prices.

Shipping: **$ $** Navigation:

Book-of-the-Month Club

www.englishbooks.com

You don't have to be a member to browse this site, but joining does have its advantages. You'll find some great deals on new books.

Shipping: **$ $** Navigation:

BookBuyers Outlet
www.bookbuyer.com

Save 20 to 40 percent on more than 500,000 in-stock titles.

Shipping: **$ $**　　　　　　　　　Navigation:

BookCloseOuts.com
www.bookexpress.com

Like the site says, BookCloseOuts.com has five million books at blowout prices (I found one for 91 percent off). You probably won't find the most recent releases, but you're sure to find something you'll want.

Shipping: **$**　　　　　　　　　Navigation:

Bookpool.com
www.bookpool.com

Discount technical books on topics like certification, computer applications, databases, desktop and server apps, the Internet, and more. Save almost 50 percent!

Shipping: **$ $**　　　　Navigation:

Books & Bytes
www.bytes.com

Computer books at a discount. Be sure to visit the Specials area for the best deals.

Shipping: **$ $**　　　　　　　　　Navigation:

Books Now
www.booksnow.com

Books Now claims to offer all books currently in print, most with discounts of 10 to 30 percent. Be sure to check out the Bargain Basement for even better deals.

Shipping: **$ $**　　　　Navigation:

Books Unlimited
www.booksunlimited.com

Visit this Denver used bookstore's online shop for some great prices on a huge selection of used books.

Shipping: **$ $**　　　　Navigation:

Books.com

www.books.com

You can find good prices (20 to 40 percent off) on all sorts
of titles, from bestsellers to technical tomes.

Shipping: **$ $**   Navigation:

BooksAmerica

www.booksamerica.com

This site helpfully suggests books you might want to buy.
When I visited, "The Silent Plague: Constipation" (!) was a
featured title.

Shipping: **$**   Navigation:

BooksAMillion.com

www.booksamillion.com ☆

You'll find tons of current and popular books at deep discount (some as much as 55 percent). Click the Bargain
Books link for even greater savings.

Shipping: **$ $**   Navigation:

Borders.com

www.borders.com ☆

Borders.com boasts 10 million books, CDs, and videos,
many of which are 50 percent off.

Shipping: **$ $**   Navigation:

Business & Computer Bookstore

www.bcb.com

At the Business & Computer Bookstore, you'll find, uh,
business and computer books—all at a discount. Be sure
to visit the Bargain Book Listings area.

Shipping: **$ $**   Navigation:

Buy.com

www.buy.com

Click the Books tab for serious savings (one bestseller
was 55 percent off).

Shipping: **$ $**   Navigation:

Children's Books

www.childsbooks.com

Buy children's books at a discount here. Click the Products link to see what's on sale.

Shipping: **$ $**   Navigation:

Classifieds 2000

www.classifieds2000.com

Click the General Merchandise link and choose Books, Music & Movies to find thousands of auction and classified ads.

Shipping: **$ $**   Navigation:

ConsciousMedia.com

http://consciousmedia.com

This site sells books, music, videos, and spoken audio tapes dedicated to body, mind, and spirit—at or below the price the mega online bookstores charge.

Shipping: **$ $**   Navigation:

DigitalGuru.com

www.digitalguru.com

Shopping at DigitalGuru.com can save you big if you're in the market for computer books—and you don't have to settle for last year's titles, either.

Shipping: **$ $**   Navigation:

Discount-PCBooks.com

www.discount-pcbooks.com

At Discount-PCBooks.com, new books are priced at least 30 percent off the publishers' list prices, while remaindered books are priced 50 to 90 percent off—with an average discount of 63 percent! Be sure to check the Clearance area.

Shipping: **$ $**   Navigation:

DiscountMedBooks.com

http://discountmedbooks.com

At this site, you can buy medical textbooks, software, and equipment—discounted 10 to 30 percent, all the time.

Shipping: **$ $** Navigation:

ebay

www.ebay.com

When you see how many items are for sale here, you'll understand why eBay's considered the big daddy of the auction sites. Last I checked, 340,202 items were for auction in the Books, Movies, Music area. Note that shipping rates vary depending on who's selling the item you want to buy.

  Navigation:

ecampus.com

www.ecampus.com

Buy new and used textbooks here, and save up to 50 percent. You'll also find some groovy college merchandise. Free shipping!

Shipping: **$** Navigation:

edeal

www.edeal.com

Visit the Books, Movies & Music area of this auction site to see what's up for grabs. Note: shipping and handling charges may vary by seller.

  Navigation:

efollett

www.shabang.com

Buy new and used college textbooks here.

Shipping: **$ $** Navigation:

The Electronic Library

www.books.com/scripts/lib.exe

Books.com supplies this electronic library as a free public service. Thousands of free, downloadable titles are available on a variety of subject areas.

Navigation:

The Electronic Text Center
http://etext.lib.virginia.edu/

Thousands of free, electronic texts—in English, French, German, Japanese, and Latin—including fiction, science fiction, poetry, theology, essays, and histories.

Navigation:

enews.com
www.enews.com

All your favorite magazines, up to 80 percent off. Also, many featured magazines let you have a free trial issue so you can check things out before you buy.

Shipping: **$**   Navigation:

eswap
www.eswap.com

Click the Books link to see what's up for grabs. Note that shipping varies depending on who's selling the item you want to buy.

Navigation:

fatbrain.com
www.fatbrain.com   ☆

Are you an IT professional or other type of geek? If you said yes, then you should check out fatbrain.com, where you'll find the newest and best technical books (many 20 to 40 percent off). Note: if you find a lower price on any item they carry from Amazon.com or barnesandnoble.com, they'll match that price and chip off an extra five percent to boot.

Shipping: **$ $**   Navigation:

HamiltonBook.com
www.hamiltonbook.com

Thousands of books at HamiltonBook.com can be had at up to 80 percent off list prices! Shipping's cheap, too.

Shipping: **$**   Navigation:

Harvard Book Store

www.harvard.com

Just because you didn't go to Harvard doesn't mean you can't visit the Harvard Book Store (and if you did go to Harvard, what do you need a book on bargain shopping for anyhow?). Be sure to check out the Bargains areas for some wicked good deals (note the Boston anachronism) on remainders, used books, and bestsellers alike.

Shipping: **$ $**   Navigation:

Just Good Books

www.justgoodbooks.com

Just Good Books has one of the largest inventories of new and used sporting books (site categories include Fly Fishing, Hunting, Guns, and Dogs). Shipping's a bit steep, but if you're looking for these hard-to-find books, it may still be worth it.

Shipping: **$ $ $**   Navigation:

KingBooks.com

www.kingbooks.com

Book prices at this site aren't always as low as at other sites, but the shipping is cheaper, which makes up for a lot.

Shipping: **$**   Navigation:

Laissez Faire Books

www.lfb.org/

Laissez Faire offers the world's largest selection of books and tapes about liberty and libertarian thought and interest. Many of the bargain books on this site are discounted up to 70 percent off the publisher's price.

Shipping: **$ $**   Navigation:

Magazine Source

www.magazinesource.com

Save up to 50 percent off the cover price when you subscribe to your favorite magazines through Magazine Source. Be sure to visit the Sweet Deals area to see what specials are available.

Shipping: **$**   Navigation:

Magazines.com

www.magazines.com

Browse, search, and order from Magazine.com's 1,200 titles at the lowest publisher authorized prices.

Shipping: **$**   Navigation:

Manager's Bookwatch

www.bookwatch.com

This site has a large selection of books on management, as well as children's books (which, frankly, ought to be read by management as well, if you ask me). Books are 20 to 35 percent off.

Shipping: **$ $**   Navigation:

Mystery Books

www.mysterybooksonline.com

All Mystery, All the Time. Find your favorite books (new and used) by Robert B. Parker, Patricia Cornwell, and Michael Connelly—not to mention Agatha Christie and Arthur Conan-Doyle—here.

Shipping: **$ $**   Navigation:

NC Buy

www.ncbuy.com

Save on books and magazines at this site.

Shipping: **$ $**   Navigation:

One Web Place

www.onewebplace.com

Click the Art & Entertainment link to get your fill of books, movies, and music—all on the auction block. Delivery rates vary by seller.

   Navigation:

The Online Books Page

www.cs.cmu.edu/books.html

You can't get much cheaper than free. The Online Books Page contains more than 9,000 books online, which you can print directly from your computer. Great for students!

Navigation:

Online Smart Shopper
www.booneconsulting.com/general.htm

Select Books from the drop-down list and click Search to find books below wholesale prices.

Shipping: **$** Navigation:

Opamp Technical Books
www.opampbooks.com

Find technical books at a discount here.

Shipping: **$ $**   Navigation:

Papyrus Books
www.papyrusbooks.com

This site sells reference books on archaeology, ancient numismatics, and antiquities. Check out the Book Specials area for savings of 50 percent (sometimes more!).

Shipping: **$ $**   Navigation:

Popula
www.popula.com

Check out the Hollywood, Books, and Music areas to find some interesting items on the auction block (including vinyl). Note: shipping rates vary by seller.

  Navigation:

Powell's Books
www.powells.com

Find loads of new and used books here—at some great prices (up to 75 percent off). Be sure to visit the Endcap Features and Great Deals areas!

Shipping: **$ $**   Navigation:

Project Gutenburg
www.promo.net/pg/

Use this site to download books (mostly classics) free of charge.

Navigation:

Reader's Digest Shop at Home
http://shopping.readersdigest.com

Find some nice deals on books and magazines at the Reader's Digest Shop at Home site. Shipping's a bit steep, but the prices may make up for it. Be sure to check out the Great Buys area.

Shipping: **$ $ $**   Navigation:

Readme.doc
www.readmedoc.com

At this discount computer book site, the more books you buy, the higher your discount.

Shipping: **$ $ $**   Navigation:

Science Fiction Book Club
www.sfbc.com

Like science fiction? Consider joining the Science Fiction Book Club, and save big.

Shipping: **$ $**   Navigation:

SellAndTrade.com
www.sellandtrade.com

Click the Art & Literature link to find books on the auction block. Note that shipping charges will vary depending on the seller.

Shipping: **$ $**   Navigation:

Shop4.com
www.shop4.com

You must become a member to save on this site, but once you do, you'll find goods for as much as 60 percent off retail on books (among other things). Click the Clearance link for the very best deals.

Shipping: **$ $**   Navigation:

Shopping.com
www.shopping.com

Not everything here is dirt cheap, but bargains can be found.

Shipping: **$ $**   Navigation:

SoldUSA.com
www.soldusa.com

You'll find lots of books at this auction site. Note that delivery charges may vary by seller.

 Navigation:

Textbooks.com
http://textbooks.com

Save up to 50 percent on textbooks. New and used available.

Shipping: **$** Navigation:

Thriftybooks
www.thriftybooks.com

All titles 50 percent off retail. Selection is varied and limited. If you see something you like, snatch it! It might be gone the next time you check!

Shipping: **$ $ $** Navigation:

Up 4 Sale
www.up4sale.com

You'll find books up for auction in the General Merchandise area of this site. Note that shipping rates will vary by seller.

 Navigation:

USAuctions.com
www.usauctions.com

Click the Media/Film link to see what types of movies, magazines, music, and books are for sale. Note that shipping rates will vary depending on who is selling the item you want to buy.

 Navigation:

Value America
www.valueamerica.com

If you're looking to buy something, there's a good chance Value America's looking to sell it—including books (save up to 50 percent on bestsellers!). Be sure to check out the hot buys! Become a member (it's free) and save even more.

Shipping: **$** Navigation:

varsitybooks.com
www.varsitybooks.com

Save up to 40 percent on textbooks, fiction, and more.

Shipping: **$ $**   Navigation:

Wal Mart Online
www.wal-mart.com

So there's no greeter, but that doesn't mean the online version of Wal Mart is a total bust. Click the Books and Music & Video links for great prices on all your entertainment needs. Free shipping on some items (you'll know it when you see it).

Shipping: **$**   Navigation:

WordsWorth
www.wordsworth.com

WordsWorth is a book lover's dream, offering a wonderful selection of books at a discounted price.

Shipping: **$ $**   Navigation:

Yahoo! Auctions
http://auctions.yahoo.com

Click the Arts & Entertainment links to find books, music, magazines, musical instruments, movies, and more up for auction. Note that shipping rates vary by seller.

    Navigation:

Your Computer Book Store
www.computerlibrary.com

Every computer book at this site is discounted, and on orders over $20, freight within the continental U.S. is free.

Shipping: **$**   Navigation:

Movies

Abby Road
http://abbyroad.com

Abby Road specializes in discount CD, video, and DVD sales.

Shipping: **$ $**   Navigation:

Amazon Auctions
www.amazon.com

Click the Auctions tab, and choose Books, Movies & Video to see what's available. Shipping rates vary depending on who's selling the item you want to buy.

                    Navigation:

Amazon.com
www.amazon.com

Amazon's not kidding when it says it has Earth's Biggest Selection. They sell books, videos, music, toys, and more. If you live in the UK, check out amazon.co.uk for great deals and cheaper shipping.

Shipping: **$ $**   Navigation:

Auction Universe
www.auctionuniverse.com

Click the TV & Entertainment links to see what's up for grabs. Delivery charges may vary by vendor.

                    Navigation:

AuctionAddict.com
www.auctionaddict.com

Click the Movies & Music link to see what's on the block. Shipping rates vary by seller.

                    Navigation:

Auctionscape

www.auctionscape.com

Click the Books, Music, Entertainment link to search for items on the auction block. Shipping costs vary by seller.

 Navigation:

Bargain News Auctions Online

www.bnauctions.com

Click the Music, TV & Entertainment links to see what's on the auction block. Delivery charges vary by seller.

 Navigation:

Barnes&Noble.com

www.barnesandnoble.com ☆

You'll find one helluva selection of movies here. Click the Bargains tab for even hotter deals.

Shipping: **$ $** Navigation:

Bear Mountain Books & Music

www.bargainbooks.com ☆

Books and videos are up to 70 percent off; classical CDs sell for $4.99. Pinch me (gently, of course)!

Shipping: **$ $** Navigation:

Bigstar.com

www.bigstar.com

100,000 movie titles (DVDs and VHS tapes). Click the Videos Under $10 link for the best deals.

Shipping: **$ $** Navigation:

Blockbuster.com

www.blockbuster.com

It shouldn't surprise you that you'll find a Goliath selection of DVDs and VHS tapes at this site, and the prices are pretty decent. One downside: You can't buy previously viewed movies online.

Shipping: **$ $** Navigation:

Borders.com

www.borders.com

Borders.com boasts 10 million books, CDs, and videos, many of which are 50 percent off.

Shipping: **$ $** 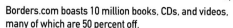 Navigation:

Buy.com

www.buy.com

Click the Videos tab for serious savings.

Shipping: **$ $** Navigation:

CD Connection

www.cdconnection.com

Prices on DVDs and VHS tapes at this site are reasonable (though not the cheapest of the cheap). However, shipping is only $3.50 no matter how many discs you order—or free if your order is for more than $100.

Shipping: **$** Navigation:

CD World

www.cdworld.com

CD World calls itself "The World's Largest Discount Entertainment Store." You'll find some nice prices on movies here.

Shipping: **$ $** Navigation:

Classifieds 2000

www.classifieds2000.com

Click the General Merchandise link and choose Books, Music & Movies to find thousands of auction and classified ads. Shipping charges vary by vendor.

Navigation:

Columbia House

www.columbiahouse.com

Columbia House offers as many clubs as you'll find in a golf bag—one for music, one for videos, one for DVDs, and one for CD-ROMs. Shipping and handling's a bit steep, but being a member does have its advantages.

Shipping: **$ $ $** Navigation:

ConsciousMedia.com

http://consciousmedia.com

This site sells videos dedicated to body, mind, and spirit—at or below the price the mega online stores charge.

Shipping: $ $ Navigation: 👍

Digital Eyes

www.digitaleyes.net/

Save up to 25 percent on all DVDs (check the Used, Clearance, and Punchout sections for even better deals). Shipping is free if you order four or more items.

Shipping: $ Navigation: 👍

DVD Express

www.dvdexpress.com

Choose from a gargantuan selection of DVDs, all at pretty nice prices. Check out the Bargain Basement for savings of 40 to 50 percent on titles you've actually heard of. Shipping's pretty danged cheap, too.

Shipping: $ Navigation: 👍

eBay

www.ebay.com

When you see how many items are for sale here, you'll understand why eBay's considered the big daddy of the auction sites. Last I checked, 340,202 items were for auction in the Books, Movies, Music area. Note that shipping rates vary depending on who's selling the item you want to buy.

            Navigation: 👍

edeal

www.edeal.com

Visit the Books, Movies & Music area of this auction site to see what's up for grabs. Note: shipping and handling charges may vary by seller.

            Navigation: 👍

FirstAuction

www.firstauction.com

The Music & Entertainment category features loads of books, games, memorabilia, music, and videos up for auction. Note: shipping costs will vary depending on the seller.

  Navigation:

FLIX

www.dvdflix.com

Prices on DVDs are good; check the Weekly Super Sale for deeper discounts. Shipping is free if you order $100 of merchandise or more. VHS tapes and laser discs also available.

Shipping: **$ $** Navigation:

J&R

www.jandr.com

Find deals on videos here. Prices aren't spectacular, but it's worth a look.

Shipping: **$ $** Navigation:

Mass Music

http://massmusic.com

Be sure to check out the Hot DVD Deals area to find some great prices on some great movies. Shipping within the U.S. is pretty reasonable, too.

Shipping: **$** ⊕ Navigation:

Movies 2 Go

www.movies2go.com

Buy movies at 15 to 30 percent below retail.

Shipping: **$ $** Navigation:

One Web Place

www.onewebplace.com

Click the Art & Entertainment link to get your fill of books, movies, and music—all on the auction block. Delivery rates vary by seller.

  Navigation:

Popula
www.popula.com

Check out the Hollywood area to find some interesting items on the auction block. Note: shipping rates vary by seller.

 Navigation:

Reader's Digest Shop at Home
http://shopping.readersdigest.com

Find some nice deals on videos at the Reader's Digest Shop at Home site. Note that most of these videos are not movies per se; you'll find lots of travel videos, and compendiums such as "Legends of Comedy." Shipping's a bit steep, but the prices may make up for it. Be sure to check out the Great Buys area.

Shipping: $ $ $ Navigation:

Reel.com
www.reel.com

This is the big mama of sites that sell movies—in DVD and VHS format. Be sure to click the On Sale, Used Movies, and Studio Specials links for the best deals!

Shipping: $ $ Navigation:

SecondSpin.com
www.secondspin.com

Buy and sell used DVDs and VHS tapes here.

Shipping: $ Navigation:

Shop4.com
www.shop4.com

You must become a member to save on this site, but once you do, you'll find movies for as much as 60 percent off retail. Click the Clearance link for the very best deals.

Shipping: $ $ Navigation:

Shopping.com
www.shopping.com

Not everything here is dirt cheap, but bargains can be found.

Shipping: $ $ Navigation:

SoldUSA.com

www.soldusa.com

You'll find lots of movies at this auction site. Note that delivery charges may vary by seller.

 Navigation:

LEISURE

Total E

www.totale.com

You'll find some great prices on movies you've actually heard of—both in DVD and VHS form.

Shipping: **$ $** Navigation:

Tower Records

www.towerrecords.com

The Tower Records site has a nice selection of movies—VHS and DVD—at some pretty nice prices. Be sure to check out the videos under $10 area!

Shipping: **$ $** Navigation:

USAuctions.com

www.usauctions.com

Click the Media/Film link to see what types of movies are for sale. Note that shipping rates will vary depending on who is selling the item you want to buy.

 Navigation:

Video Universe

www.videouniverse.com

Prices aren't exactly deep discount, but they are cheaper than retail and the selection is great, offering both VHS tapes and DVDs.

Shipping: **$ $** Navigation:

Wal Mart Online

www.wal-mart.com

So there's no greeter, but that doesn't mean the online version of Wal Mart is a total bust. Click the Books and Music & Video links for great prices on all your entertainment needs. Free shipping on some items (you'll know it when you see it).

Shipping: **$** Navigation:

Yahoo! Auctions
http://auctions.yahoo.com

Click the Arts & Entertainment links to find movies and
more up for auction. Note that shipping rates vary by
seller.

 Navigation:

Music

4Tunes.com

www.4tunes.com

Bid for your favorite CDs—often at prices much lower than you'd find elsewhere! Shipping rates vary depending on who's selling the item you want to buy.

 Navigation:

800.com

www.800.com

Find gazillions of CDs, some of them under $10, and with free shipping!

Shipping: **$** Navigation:

Abby Road

http://abbyroad.com

Abby Road specializes in discount CD, video, and DVD sales.

Shipping: **$ $** Navigation:

AllDirect.com

www.alldirect.com

Find music at discounts of 30 to 40 percent.

Shipping: **$ $** Navigation:

Allegro

www.allegro-music.com

Allegro is one of the largest independent music distributors in North America; their catalog includes a broad range of music, including classical, opera, jazz, blues, world, new age, and more. Members receive price breaks (membership is free). Free shipping in the U.S. if you order four or more CDs!

Shipping: **$ $** Navigation:

Amazon Auctions

www.amazon.com

Click the Auctions tab, and choose Music to see what's available. Shipping rates vary depending on who's selling the item you want to buy.

 Navigation:

Amazon.com

www.amazon.com

Amazon's not kidding when it says it has Earth's Biggest Selection. They sell books, videos, music, toys, and more. If you live in the UK, check out amazon.co.uk for great deals and cheaper shipping.

Shipping: $ $ Navigation:

Auction Nation

www.auctionnation.com

Click the Music link to see what items are up for sale. Note: Shipping costs may vary depending on who's selling the item you want to buy.

 Navigation:

Auction Universe

www.auctionuniverse.com

Click the Music, TV & Entertainment link to see what's up for grabs. Delivery charges may vary by vendor.

 Navigation:

AuctionAddict.com

www.auctionaddict.com

Click the Movies & Music link to see what's up for grabs. Shipping rates vary by seller.

 Navigation:

Auctionscape

www.auctionscape.com

Click the Books, Music, Entertainment link to search for items on the auction block. Shipping costs vary by seller.

 Navigation:

Audio House CD Club

http://amsquare.com/ahcd/

Join Audio House CD Club (membership is free) to take advantage of some great prices on pre-owned (that's "used" to laypeople like you and me) compact discs. They're guaranteed to play like new! Over 8,000 titles in stock.

Shipping: **$ $**   Navigation:

AudioHighway.com

www.audiohighway.com

For you MP3ophiles out there, this site offers loads of FREE audio, plus the kind you have to buy. You'll also find various MP3-related software applications, as well as some nicely priced computer goods (including, not surprisingly, MP3 players).

Shipping: **$**   Navigation:

Bargain News Auctions Online

www.bnauctions.com

Click the Music, TV & Entertainment link to see what's on the auction block. Delivery charges vary by seller.

    Navigation:

Barnes&Noble.com   ☆

www.barnesandnoble.com

You'll find one helluva selection of music here. Click the Bargains tab for even hotter deals.

Shipping: **$ $**   Navigation:

Bear Mountain Books & Music

www.bargainbooks.com   ☆

Classical CDs sell for $4.99. Pinch me (gently, of course)!

Shipping: **$ $**   Navigation:

Best Used CDs

www.bestusedcds.com

It's not like CDs go bad or anything, so why not buy them used? Visit this site to see what used CDs are up for grabs.

Shipping: **$ $**   Navigation:

BMG Music Service

www.bmgmusicservice.com

Get 12 CDs for the price of one, with nothing more to buy ever. Of all the music clubs out there, this one's probably the best deal! Shipping's a bit steep, though.

Shipping: **$ $ $**   Navigation:

Borders.com

www.borders.com

Borders.com boasts 10 million books, CDs, and videos, many of which are 50 percent off.

Shipping: **$ $**   Navigation:

Buy.com

www.buy.com

Click the Music tab for serious savings (one bestseller was 55 percent off).

Shipping: **$ $**   Navigation:

CD Connection

www.cdconnection.com

Prices here are reasonable (though not the cheapest of the cheap). However, shipping is only $3.50 no matter how many discs you order—or free if your order is for more than $100. DVDs and VHS tapes also available.

Shipping: **$**   Navigation:

CD Source

www.cdsource.com

CD Source features a music magazine, plus nice prices on a vast selection of CDs. If you're up to speed on MP3, check this site out for 27,000,000 free MP3 downloads!

Shipping: **$ $**   Navigation:

CD Universe

www.cduniverse.com

You won't find rock-bottom prices here, but prices are reasonable and selection is good.

Shipping: **$ $**   Navigation:

CD USA

www.cdusa.com

Find more than 200,000 CDs, cassettes, videos, and DVDs from over 75 categories. Pay a flat $4.95 for shipping for as many as 29 items.

Shipping: **$**   Navigation:

CD World

www.cdworld.com

CD World calls itself "The World's Largest Discount Entertainment Store." You'll find some nice prices on music.

Shipping: **$ $**   Navigation:

CDBargains.com

www.cdbargains.com

Used CDs at great prices, including a selection of 2,000 CDs that are $5.99 or less.

Shipping: **$ $**   Navigation:

CDNOW

www.cdnow.com

CDNOW has teamed up with MusicBoulevard to provide about a gazillion CDs at up to 30 percent off. Be sure to click the Sales and Specials link for the best deals.

Shipping: **$ $**   Navigation:

Classifieds 2000

www.classifieds2000.com

Click the General Merchandise link and choose Books, Music & Movies to find thousands of auction and classified ads. Note: If you're looking for musical instruments, check under Just for Fun. Shipping charges may vary by vendor.

Shipping: **$ $**   Navigation:

Columbia House

www.columbiahouse.com

Columbia House offers as many clubs as you'll find in a golf bag—one for music, one for videos, one for DVDs, and one for CD-ROMs. Shipping and handling's a bit steep, but being a member does have its advantages.

Shipping: **$ $ $**   Navigation:

Compact Discount
www.compactdiscsforsale.com

All CDs at Compact Discount are previously owned, but the site promises that everything is like new. You'll find some major bargains here.

Shipping: **$ $** Navigation:

ConsciousMedia.com
http://consciousmedia.com

This site sells books, music, videos, and spoken audio tapes dedicated to body, mind, and spirit—at or below the price the mega online bookstores charge.

Shipping: **$ $** Navigation:

Customdisc.com
www.customdisc.com

Why pay for a whole CD when you only want one song from it? With Customdisc.com, you can make CD mixes that contain only the songs you like, from a variety of albums. The cost of your CD depends on what tracks you select (many are free). This is hands-down one of the coolest sites on the Web.

Shipping: **$** Navigation:

Disc Trader
www.disctrader.com

Join Disc Trader and save big on used CDs (their guarantee: All CDs will play like new, or your money back). Shipping's cheap, too.

Shipping: **$** Navigation:

Disc Vault
www.discvault.com

Disc Vault is Asia's largest online music store, with discs at some very nice prices. Amazingly, shipping isn't terribly expensive—although it takes a bit longer for goods to reach the U.S.

Shipping: **$ $** Navigation:

DVD Express
www.dvdexpress.com

You wouldn't think that a site called DVD Express would have music, but it does. The twist? Selection is heavy on movie soundtracks. Prices are decent, and shipping's pretty danged cheap, too.

Shipping: **$**   Navigation:

eBay
www.ebay.com

When you see how many items are for sale here, you'll understand why eBay's considered the big daddy of the auction sites. Last I checked, 340,202 items were for auction in the Books, Movies, Music area. Note that shipping rates vary depending on who's selling the item you want to buy.

  Navigation:

edeal
www.edeal.com

Visit the Books, Movies & Music area of this auction site to see what's up for grabs. Note: shipping and handling charges may vary by seller.

  Navigation:

emusic.com
www.emusic.com

Got an MP3 player? Check out emusic.com for loads of downloadable music titles. Free tracks are available.

Navigation:

FirstAuction
www.firstauction.com

The Music & Entertainment category features loads of music up for auction. Note: shipping costs will vary depending on the seller.

  Navigation:

FLIX
www.dvdflix.com

Click the CD link for a decent selection of CDs at reasonable prices. Not everything's dirt cheap, but you never know—the disc you're looking for might be!

Shipping: **$ $**   Navigation:

GetMusic.com
www.getmusic.com

Choose from a vast selection of music, in categories like Adult, Alternative, Classical, Country, Jazz, Latin, Pop, R&B/Rap, Rock, and more.

Shipping: **$ $**   Navigation:

J&R
www.jandr.com

Find deals on CDs here. Prices aren't spectacular, but it's worth a look.

Shipping: **$ $**   Navigation:

K-TEL
www.ktel.com

Find music at the K-TEL site, including those compilations you always see ads for at 2 a.m. on TV. Click the Custom CD link to make your own CD. Be sure to check out the Auctions area!

Shipping: **$ $**   Navigation:

Mass Music
http://massmusic.com

This site features imported and hard-to-find music on the cheap (featured CDs were $9.95 last I checked). Shipping within the U.S. is pretty reasonable, too.

Shipping: **$**   Navigation:

Music Favorites
www.musicfavorites.com

This site, presented by Kmart, offers some nice deals on more than 100,000 titles.

Shipping: **$ $**   Navigation:

Music Spot
www.musicspot.com

Search Music Spot's database for the CDs you want; they're reasonably priced, and shipping won't break the bank.

Shipping: **$**   Navigation:

Music World CD
www.musicworldcd.com

This site promises the lowest prices the lowest prices on the Web, or shipping is free.

Shipping: **$ $**   Navigation:

LEISURE

Music.Recycler.com
http://music.recycler.com

This site does more than sell music on the cheap—it's a great resource for aspiring musicians. View classified ads for instruments, check the Musician Connection for bands seeking musicians and vice versa, and more.

Shipping: **$ $**   Navigation:

Musicstrip.com
www.musicstrip.com

Click the $5 CD link for, you guessed it, CDs that are $5 (the downside: You have to email customer service to reserve your selections instead of being able to click to purchase them on the spot).

Shipping: **$**   Navigation:

Muzic Depot
www.muzicdepot.com

Save up to 30 percent on all types of music—rock, pop, jazz, blues, country, folk, R&B, hip hop, world, new age, classical, Christian/gospel, and more. You'll find track lists, samples, and reviews of loads of albums, plus a nifty "Muzic Advizor" to help you find tunes you'll like.

Shipping: **$ $**   Navigation:

One Web Place
www.onewebplace.com

Click the Art & Entertainment link to get your fill of music—all on the auction block. Delivery rates vary by seller.

   Navigation:

Pentagon CDs and Tapes
www.pentagonmusic.com

At Pentagon, all full-length CDs are $11.99 or less. Great selection!

Shipping: **$ $**   Navigation:

Popula

www.popula.com

Check out the Hollywood, Books, and Music areas to find some interesting items on the auction block (including vinyl). Note: shipping rates vary by seller.

 Navigation:

Reader's Digest Shop at Home

http://shopping.readersdigest.com

Find some nice deals on music at the Reader's Digest Shop at Home site (note that most of the offerings are compendium CDs, like "The World's Best-Loved Waltzes"). If prices look high, look further: Most of these are multi-disc packages. Shipping's a bit steep, but the prices may make up for it. Be sure to check out the Great Buys area.

Shipping: **$ $ $** Navigation:

SecondSpin.com

www.secondspin.com

Buy and sell your used CDs, DVDs, and VHS tapes! The Cool Deals of the Week section has some major blowouts.

Shipping: **$** Navigation:

Shop4.com

www.shop4.com

You must become a member to save on this site, but once you do, you'll find goods for as much as 60 percent off retail on music. Click the Clearance link for the very best deals.

Shipping: **$ $** Navigation:

Shopping.com

www.shopping.com

Not everything here is dirt cheap, but bargains can be found.

Shipping: **$ $** Navigation:

SoldUSA.com

www.soldusa.com

You'll find lots of music at this auction site. Note that delivery charges may vary by seller.

 Navigation:

Total E
www.totale.com

All new releases are 30 percent off! Choose from over 150,000 titles.

Shipping: **$ $**

Navigation:

Tower Records
www.towerrecords.com

☆

This online version of the famed Tower Records chain has a superb selection and some nice prices. Be sure to check out the CDs under $7 area!

Shipping: **$ $**

Navigation:

Up 4 Sale
www.up4sale.com

You'll find music up for auction in the General Merchandise area of this site. Note that shipping rates will vary by seller.

 Navigation:

USAuctions.com
www.usauctions.com

Click the Media/Film link to see what music is up for sale. Note that shipping rates will vary depending on who is selling the item you want to buy.

 Navigation:

Wal Mart Online
www.wal-mart.com

So there's no greeter, but that doesn't mean the online version of Wal Mart is a total bust. Click the Books and Music & Video links for great prices on all your entertainment needs. Free shipping on some items (you'll know it when you see it).

Shipping: **$**

Navigation:

Yahoo! Auctions
http://auctions.yahoo.com

Click the Arts & Entertainment links to find music and more up for auction. Note that shipping rates vary by seller.

 Navigation:

Musical Instruments

American Drum Shop
www.americandrumshop.com

Find new and used drums and accessories here. One downside: You can't order online.

Shipping: **$**   Navigation:

AuctioNet.com
www.auctionet.com

Click the Music Studio link to find guitars, keyboards, amps, and more—all for auction. Note that shipping rates vary depending on who's selling the item you want to buy.

    Navigation:

Classifieds 2000
www.classifieds2000.com

Click the Just for Fun link if you're looking for musical instruments. Shipping charges may vary by vendor.

Navigation:

Discount Music Center
www.discountmusic.com

Discount Music Center has brought its 10,000 square foot showroom to the Web. You'll find some great prices on guitars, drums, keyboards, PA systems, and DJ and lighting supplies. Be sure to check out the blowout section!

Shipping: **$ $**   Navigation:

eBay
www.ebay.com   ☆

When you see how many items are for sale here, you'll understand why eBay's considered the big daddy of the auction sites. If you're looking for musical instruments, you'll find them under Miscellaneous. Note that shipping rates vary depending on who's selling the item you want to buy.

    Navigation:

Guitar Auction
www.guitarauction.com

Guitar Auction is your source for used, new, and vintage guitars by Martin, Gibson, Fender, Taylor, and others. Find great deals on guitars and other musical merchandise. Note: shipping and handling charges will vary from seller to seller.

 Navigation:

Music.Recycler.com
http://music.recycler.com

This site does more than sell music on the cheap—it's a great resource for aspiring musicians. View classified ads for instruments, check the Musician Connection for bands seeking musicians and vice versa, and more.

Shipping: **$ $** Navigation:

Rock Auction
www.rockauction.com

Find amps, drums, guitars, keyboards, PA equipment, and more up for auction at this site. Note that shipping and handling charges may vary by seller.

 Navigation:

SamAsh.com
www.samash.com

Find musical instruments, sound and lighting gear, DJ equipment, recording equipment, sheet music, and more. Be sure to visit the SamAsh.com Specials area for some seriously low prices.

Shipping: **$ $**   Navigation:

The SpiderGear Connection
www.spidergear.com

Click the Musical Inst. link to find music products at a discount. Site members get first stab at new products, and better prices.

Shipping: **$ $ $** Navigation:

Zigmart's Online Auctions
www.ziggiesmusic.com

Need a used mandolin? Find musical instruments galore up for auction here. Note that shipping rates vary by seller.

Shipping: **$ $** Navigation:

BARGAIN SHOPPING Online

Home and Garden

Appliances

ABC Vacuum Warehouse

www.abcvacuum.com

Prices for vacuums are dirt cheap (har, har) at this site. Be sure to check out the ABC Bargains Page for the best deals.

Shipping: **$ $** Navigation:

Andy's Garage Sale

www.andysgarage.com

As Andy says, this is where you'll find "Good Stuff, Dirt Cheap." Getting around this site is kind of tough, but if you can find your way, you'll find some good deals. Be sure to check out Andy's auction area.

Shipping: **$ $** Navigation:

Appliances.com

www.appliances.com

Buy tons of kitchen appliances here, at some pretty hard-to-beat prices.

Shipping: **$ $** Navigation:

Auction Universe

www.auctionuniverse.com

Click any of a number of links for items for your home. Shipping rates may vary by vendor.

  Navigation:

Auction World

www.a-world.com

Click the Home/Office link to check out the goods up for auction. Be sure to check the Pick of the Week, Dollar Mania, Steals & Deals, and Out of This World areas for the best bargains! Shipping rates vary by seller.

  Navigation:

Bargain News Auctions Online

www.bnauctions.com

Click the Home, Garden & Pet Supplies link to see what's on the auction block. Delivery charges vary by seller.

Navigation:

Bid.com

www.bid.com

Click For The Home at this auction site for rock-bottom prices on small appliances, tools, and so on—bids start at $1 for many items! Note: Charges for delivery vary by seller.

Navigation:

Classifieds 2000

www.classifieds2000.com

Click the General Merchandise link and choose Home Living to find thousands of auction and classified ads for items for your home. Shipping charges may vary by vendor.

Navigation:

Costco Online

www.costco.com

You've probably heard of Costco, which is one of those warehouse clubs. Now Costco's online, offering members some great deals on some great merchandise (it costs a minimum of $40 to join, but if you shop there enough, prices will make up for it). Among other items, you'll find appliances, goods for your lawn and garden, and other home essentials at Costco.

Shipping: **$ $**

Navigation:

CyberShop

http://cybershop.com

Up to 80 percent off original prices! Click the Departments tab and select Kitchen and Home to find deals on appliances.

Shipping: **$ $**

Navigation:

deals.com
www.deals.com

Click the Home & Office link to find appliances.

Shipping: **$**   Navigation:

edeal
www.edeal.com

Click the Home & Garden link to see what items are on the block. Subcategories include Kitchen Items/Appliances. Note: Delivery charges will vary by seller.

                    Navigation:

Electronics.net
www.electronics.net/

Click the links under Appliances and Housewares for deals on refrigerators, washers, dryers, dishwashers, ranges, air conditioners, kitchen appliances, microwaves, and more.

Shipping: **$ $**   Navigation:

EZbid.com
www.ezbid.com

Click the Home & Leisure link to find small appliances — all up for auction. Click the Rebate button to see which items on the site have rebates! Note: shipping and handling costs will differ depending on the seller.

                    Navigation:

EZshop.com
www.ezshop.com   ☆

Find small appliances —all for prices that won't keep you from sending your kids to college. Be sure to click the Special Offers link for the very best deals!

Shipping: **$**   Navigation:

The Internet Kitchen
www.your-kitchen.com

Find small appliances for your kitchen from manufacturers like Krups, Cuisinart, and more at discounted prices. Free shipping on orders over $300.

Shipping: **$ $**   Navigation:

Recycler.com
www.recycler.com

Click the Home & Home Improvement link to browse the available items.

Shipping: **$ $**   Navigation:

RedTag.com
www.redtagoutlet.com

Find a variety of kitchen appliances.

Shipping: **$ $**   Navigation:

Shop4.com
www.shop4.com

You must become a member to save on this site, but once you do, you'll find goods for as much as 60 percent off retail. You'll find ovens and other appliances. Click the Clearance link for the very best deals.

Shipping: **$ $**   Navigation:

Shoppers Advantage
www.shoppersadvantage.com

Click the Home, Kitchen & Garden link for great savings on appliances. Note: you must register to become a member in order to cash in on the great savings on this site.

Shipping: **$ $**   Navigation:

Toastmaster
www.toastmaster.com

Toastmaster makes small appliances for the kitchen (think toaster ovens, coffee makers, and the like). Click the Factory Outlet link to find the deals.

Shipping: **$ $ $**   Navigation:

Vacuum Depot
www.vacdepot.com

Shop at Vacuum Depot and save on vacuums by Hoover, Eureka, Sharp, and more.

Shipping: **$ $**   Navigation:

Value America

www.valueamerica.com

If you're looking to buy something, there's a good chance Value America's looking to sell it—including major home appliances. Be sure to check out the hot buys! Become a member (it's free) and save even more.

Shipping: **$**   Navigation:

Web Emporium

www.webporium.com

You'll find a bit of everything here at Web Emporium—including appliances—all at nice prices.

Shipping: **$ $**   Navigation:

Your Home Center

www.yourhomecenter.com

Your Home Center, which offers low prices on appliances, is part of Buy It Now (see the chapter on agents and other shopping services for more information). Become a member of Buy It Now for special deals at Your Home Center. Certain products ship free of charge (you'll see a Free Shipping tag on those items).

Shipping: **$ $**   Navigation:

Yahoo! Auctions

http://auctions.yahoo.com

Click the Home & Garden link to find goodies for your home up for auction. Note that shipping rates vary by seller.

          Navigation:

Bed and Bath

Andy's Garage Sale

www.andysgarage.com

As Andy says, this is where you'll find "Good Stuff, Dirt Cheap." Getting around this site is kind of tough, but if you can find your way, you'll find some good deals. Be sure to check out Andy's auction area.

Shipping: **$ $**   Navigation:

Auction Universe

www.auctionuniverse.com

Click any of a number of links for items for your bath. Shipping rates may vary by vendor.

                    Navigation:

Bargain Bungalow

www.galaxymall.com/product/bargain/index.html

Find items for the bedroom. Be sure to visit the Bargain Basement area! Shipping's a bit steep, but prices might be low enough to make up for it.

Shipping: **$ $ $**   Navigation:

Bargain News Auctions Online

www.bnauctions.com

Click the Home, Garden & Pet Supplies link to see what bed and bath products are on the auction block. Delivery charges vary by seller.

                    Navigation:

BedAndBath.com

www.bedandbath.com

This site guarantees that you will not find the same products online for a lower price; if you do, they'll refund the difference plus 5 percent. Check the Clearance Corner for the best deals. Also, shipping is free if you spend more than $250.

Shipping: **$ $**   Navigation:

Burlington Coat Factory Direct
www.coat.com/bcfdirect

Find accessories for bed and bath — all at nice prices

Shipping: $ $ $ Navigation:

Catalog Closeouts
http://catalogcloseouts.com

Buy the goods that catalogs couldn't sell—at a discount!
Be sure to click the Specials link for the best deals!

Shipping: $ Navigation:

Clearance World
www.clearanceworld.com

Find items for the bedroom, bathroom and more at this
site, where, as the name would suggest, everything's on
clearance.

Shipping: $ $ Navigation:

Cuddledown of Maine Online Outlet
www.cuddledown.com

Find down comforters, bed linens and other sewn items,
furniture, and accessories. Click the Sale Merchandise
link for special discounts.

Shipping: $ $ Navigation:

Domestications
www.domestications.com

Find items for the bed, bath, and more. Be sure to check
out the What's On Sale, Web Specials, and Clearance
areas. To save an extra 10 percent, join the Buyer's Club (it
costs $19.95). Shipping's a bit steep, but the prices may
make up for it.

Shipping: $ $ $ Navigation:

EZshop.com
www.ezshop.com ☆

Find a variety of bed and bath products — all for prices
that won't keep you from sending your kids to college. Be
sure to click the Special Offers link for the very best deals!

Shipping: $ Navigation:

FirstAuction
www.firstauction.com

Visit the Home & Leisure and Furniture areas to find items for the bed and bath — all up for auction.

Shipping: **$ $** Navigation:

Pacific Coast Feather Company
www.pacificcoast.com

Click the Outlet Store link for deals on Pacific Coast comforters, pillows, feather beds, and more.

Shipping: **$ $** Navigation:

RedTag.com
www.redtagoutlet.com

Find a variety of bed and bath products here.

Shipping: **$ $** Navigation:

Shop4.com
www.shop4.com

You must become a member to save on this site, but once you do, you'll find goods for as much as 60 percent off retail. You'll find bed and bath items, among other things. Click the Clearance link for the very best deals.

Shipping: **$ $** Navigation:

Shoppers Advantage
www.shoppersadvantage.com

Click the Home, Kitchen & Garden link for great savings. Note: you must register to become a member in order to cash in on the great savings on this site.

Shipping: **$ $** Navigation:

Spiegel
www.spiegel.com/spiegel/shopping/ultimate/

Save 30 to 75 percent on Spiegel merchandise for your home, including goodies for bed and bath.

Shipping: **$ $ $** Navigation:

Furniture

Abracadabra Furniture Online
www.a-furniture.com

Find great prices on all types of furniture. Shipping's steep (a flat rate of 15 percent), but the prices make up for it.

Shipping: **$ $ $**   Navigation:

AffordableFurniture.com
www.affordablefurniture.com

Find some very nice prices on furniture at this site. An added plus: prices include shipping and handling costs, so there'll be no surprises money-wise.

Shipping: **$**   Navigation:

Amazon Auctions
http://auctions.amazon.com

Choose Home & Garden to see what's available in the way of home furnishings. Shipping rates vary depending on who's selling the item you want to buy.

                    Navigation:

The Atrium Furniture Mall
www.theatrium.com

The Atrium, a collection of 36 furniture stores, promises discounts of 40 to 50 percent (sale, clearance and market sample prices can even be lower). The irritating part: you can't simply order online; you have to submit a request for information about the item you're interested in. Shipping rates vary, depending on which store you order from.

Navigation:

Auction Universe
www.auctionuniverse.com

Click any of a number of links for items for your home. Shipping rates may vary by vendor.

                    Navigation:

Auction World
www.a-world.com

Click the Home/Office link to check out the goods up for auction. Be sure to check the Pick of the Week, Dollar Mania, Steals & Deals, and Out of This World areas for the best bargains! Shipping rates vary by seller.

 Navigation:

AuctionAddict.com
www.auctionaddict.com

Click the Home Furnishings link to see what items are up for auction. Shipping rates vary by seller.

 Navigation:

Classifieds 2000
www.classifieds2000.com

Click the General Merchandise link and choose Home Living to find thousands of auction and classified ads for items for your home. Shipping charges may vary by vendor.

Navigation:

DealDeal.com
www.dealdeal.com

Find home furnishings and kitchen items, all up for auction. Note: delivery charges may vary depending on the seller.

 Navigation:

Domestications
www.domestications.com

Find furniture items, like lamps, tableware, you name it. Be sure to check out the What's On Sale, Web Specials, and Clearance areas. To save an extra 10 percent, join the Buyer's Club (it costs $19.95). Shipping's a bit steep, but the prices may make up for it.

Shipping: **$ $ $** Navigation:

ebay
www.ebay.com ☆

Click the Miscellaneous link to find items for the home, including furnishings. Note that shipping rates vary depending on who's selling the item you want to buy.

 Navigation:

edeal

www.edeal.com

Click the Home & Garden link to see what items are on the
block. Subcategories include Furniture. Note: Delivery
charges will vary by seller.

 Navigation:

EZshop.com

www.ezshop.com

Furniture for prices that won't keep you from sending
your kids to college. Be sure to click the Special Offers
link for the very best deals!

Shipping: **$** Navigation:

Factory Direct Furniture

www.furnituredirect2u.com

Furniture for your home office or business, at closeout
prices (click the Specials link for the best deals).

Shipping: **$ $** Navigation:

FirstAuction

www.firstauction.com

Visit the Home & Leisure and Furniture areas to find
home furnishing items up for auction.

Shipping: **$ $** Navigation:

Furniture.com

www.furniture.com

This site rules. Easily find great furniture (their selection
really is good!) for every room in your house, at fantastic
prices (with listings at up to 40 percent off, you'll save
hundreds of dollars).

Shipping: **$** Navigation:

FurnitureFind.com

www.furniturefind.com

FurnitureFind.com sells name-brand furniture at 30 to 50
percent off retail, and delivered to your door free at charge.

Shipping: **$** Navigation:

HomePoint.com
www.homepoint.com

Find a variety of furniture. All of these items represent
excess inventory or customer returns. This is a great site!

Shipping: **$**   Navigation:

Recycler.com
www.recycler.com

HOME AND GARDEN

Click the Home & Home Improvement link to browse the
available items.

Shipping: **$ $**   Navigation:

The Retail/Wholesale Futon Outlet Page
www.eskimo.com/~futon

Order frames, mattresses, slipcovers, and accessories—
at discount prices.

Shipping: **$ $**   Navigation:

Shop4.com
www.shop4.com

You must become a member to save on this site, but once
you do, you'll find goods for as much as 60 percent off
retail. You'll find a variety of furnishings. Click the
Clearance link for the very best deals.

Shipping: **$ $**   Navigation:

Shoppers Advantage
www.shoppersadvantage.com

Click the Home, Kitchen & Garden link for great savings
on furniture. Note: you must register to become a member in order to cash in on the great savings on this site.

Shipping: **$ $**   Navigation:

Tek Discount Warehouse
http://tekgallery.com

Click the Furnishings link for some deals on furniture. An
irritating caveat: some items require you to email for price
information.

Shipping: **$ $**   Navigation:

uBid Online Auction

www.ubid.com

Bid for furniture at this auction site. Click More Categories, and you'll find entries for furniture, appliances, antiques, and other cool stuff. Note: Delivery charges may vary by seller.

 Navigation:

Value America

www.valueamerica.com

If you're looking to buy something, there's a good chance Value America's looking to sell it—including home furniture. Be sure to check out the hot buys! Become a member (it's free) and save even more.

Shipping: **$** Navigation:

Yahoo! Auctions

http://auctions.yahoo.com

Click the Home & Garden link to find goodies for your home up for auction. Note that shipping rates vary by seller.

 Navigation:

Home Décor

Absolutely Unique Lamps on the Web
www.LampsOnTheWeb.com

Find great prices on a wide selection of lamps. Some of these are really cool, and seriously cheap! Shipping's steep (a flat rate of 15 percent), but the prices make up for it.

Shipping: **$ $ $**   Navigation:

Amazon Auctions
http://auctions.amazon.com

Choose Home & Garden to see what goodies are available. Shipping rates vary depending on who's selling the item you want to buy.

    Navigation:

Andy's Garage Sale
www.andysgarage.com

As Andy says, this is where you'll find "Good Stuff, Dirt Cheap." Getting around this site is kind of tough, but if you can find your way, you'll find some good deals. Be sure to check out Andy's auction area.

Shipping: **$ $**   Navigation:

Auction Nation
www.auctionnation.com

Click the links to see what home décor items are up for sale. Note: Shipping costs may vary depending on who's selling the item you want to buy.

    Navigation:

Auction Universe
www.auctionuniverse.com

Click any of a number of links for decorative items for your home. Shipping rates may vary by vendor.

    Navigation:

AuctionAddict.com
www.auctionaddict.com

Click the Home Furnishings link to see what home décor items are up for auction. Shipping rates vary by seller.

Navigation:

BlindsGalore.com
www.blindsgalore.com

Blindsgalore.com guarantees its low prices; if you find a lower price on any blind they sell, they will refund you the difference plus 10 percent! Makers include Hunter Douglas, Graber, Levolor, Louverdrape, Kirsch, Del Mar, Vista, Mark Woods, Nanik, and Castec. Free shipping in the continental US!

Shipping: **$**   Navigation:

Bluefly
www.bluefly.com

Click House to save 25 to 75 percent on frames, sheets, towels, and more by designers like Ralph Lauren and Nancy Koltes.

Shipping: **$ $**   Navigation:

Candles Plus
www.candlesplus.com

You'll find a wide variety of candles and candle accessories, including pillars, votives, floating, translucent, tapers, beeswax, holiday/seasonal, and specialty candles—all at below retail. Be sure to check out the monthly specials.

Shipping: **$ $ $**   Navigation:

Catalog Closeouts
http://catalogcloseouts.com

Buy the goods that catalogs couldn't sell—at a discount! Be sure the click the Specials link for the best deals!

Shipping: **$**   Navigation:

Costco Online

www.costco.com

You've probably heard of Costco, which is one of those warehouse clubs. Now Costco's online, offering members some great deals on some great merchandise (it costs a minimum of $40 to join, but if you shop there enough, prices will make up for it). Among other items, you'll find home décor and other home essentials at Costco.

Shipping: **$ $**   Navigation:

HOME AND GARDEN

deals.com

www.deals.com

Click the Home & Office link to find goods like lamps, appliances, and more.

Shipping: **$**   Navigation:

Domestications

www.domestications.com

Find items for your home décor. Be sure to check out the What's On Sale, Web Specials, and Clearance areas. To save an extra 10 percent, join the Buyer's Club (it costs $19.95). Shipping's a bit steep, but the prices may make up for it.

Shipping: **$ $ $**   Navigation:

ebay

www.ebay.com   ☆

Click the Miscellaneous link to find some delightful home décor items. Note that shipping rates vary depending on who's selling the item you want to buy.

    Navigation:

edeal

www.edeal.com

Click the Home & Garden link to see what items are on the block. Subcategories include Home Décor. Note: Delivery charges will vary by seller.

    Navigation:

EZshop.com

www.ezshop.com

Decorations for your home at prices that won't keep you from sending your kids to college. Be sure to click the Special Offers link for the very best deals!

Shipping: **$**   Navigation:

FirstAuction

www.firstauction.com

Visit the Home & Leisure and Furniture areas to find great decorative items — all up for auction.

Shipping: **$ $**   Navigation:

HomePoint.com

www.homepoint.com

Find furniture, decorative items, lighting, and wall art here. All of these items represent excess inventory or customer returns. This is a great site!

Shipping: **$**   Navigation:

House Décor

www.housedecor.com

House Décor, which offers low prices on all sorts of home items, is part of Buy It Now (see the chapter on agents and other shopping services for more information). Become a member of Buy It Now for special deals at House Décor. Certain products ship free of charge (you'll see a Free Shipping tag on those items).

Shipping: **$ $**   Navigation:

ILoveaDeal.com

www.iloveadeal.com

Find prints and housewares featured in Wireless, Seasons, and Signals catalogs, many at 40 to 70 percent off! Be sure to click the Top 20 Bargains link for the best deals.

Shipping: **$ $**   Navigation:

Lighting Outlet

www.lightoutlet.com

Find some great lamps, chandeliers, wall sconces, ceiling fans, dome lights, billiard lights, and more at some seriously nice prices. Shipping is way steep, but the prices might make up for it, especially if you buy more than one item.

Shipping: **$ $ $**   Navigation:

Macys

www.macys.com

Find furnishings and more for the home at Macys, some at 15 percent off.

Shipping: **$ $**   Navigation:

Northwest Express

www.northwestexpress.com

Find some great prices on items for the home. Try your luck at the auction while you're there! Shipping's a bit steep, but the prices make up for it.

Shipping: **$ $ $**   Navigation:

Popula

www.popula.com

For the modernist in you, this site offers swanky home items for auction. Note that charges for shipping and handling will vary by seller.

                    Navigation:

Recycler.com

www.recycler.com

Click the Home & Home Improvement link to browse the available home décor items.

Shipping: **$ $**   Navigation:

Ross-Simons

www.ross-simons.com

As the site puts it, "Life's Luxuries for a Lot Less." This site offers home décor items, and more at up to 70 percent off. Click the Shop the Outlet link for the best deals.

Shipping: **$ $ $**   Navigation:

Shop4.com
www.shop4.com

You must become a member to save on this site, but once you do, you'll find goods for as much as 60 percent off retail. You'll find a variety of home decorations. Click the Clearance link for the very best deals.

Shipping: **$ $**   Navigation:

Shoppers Advantage
www.shoppersadvantage.com

Click the Home, Kitchen & Garden link for great savings. Note: you must register to become a member in order to cash in on the great savings on this site.

Shipping: **$ $**   Navigation:

The Shopping Moon
http://shoppingmoon.com

The Shopping Moon sells a wide variety of unique items for your house and home—all at discounted prices. You'll find lamps, furnishings, and more. Be sure to see what's up for grabs among the closeout items!

Shipping: **$ $**   Navigation:

Spiegel
www.spiegel.com/spiegel/shopping/ultimate/

Save 30 to 75 percent on Spiegel merchandise for your home, including décor and draperies.

Shipping: **$ $ $**   Navigation:

Teks Discount Warehouse
http://tekgallery.com

Click the Furnishings link for deals on decorative objects. An irritating caveat: some items require you to email for price information.

Shipping: **$ $**   Navigation:

Value America
www.valueamerica.com

If you're looking to buy something, there's a good chance Value America's looking to sell it—including home decoratives. Be sure to check out the hot buys! Become a member (it's free) and save even more.

Shipping: **$**   Navigation:

Yahoo! Auctions
http://auctions.yahoo.com

Click the Home & Garden link to find goodies for your home up for auction. Note that shipping rates vary by seller.

  Navigation: 👍

Your Home Center
www.yourhomecenter.com

Your Home Center, which offers low prices on home décor items is part of Buy It Now (see the chapter on agents and other shopping services for more information). Become a member of Buy It Now for special deals at Your Home Center. Certain products ship free of charge (you'll see a Free Shipping tag on those items).

Shipping: **$ $**   Navigation: 👍

Home Improvement/ Hardware

Amazon Auctions
http://auctions.amazon.com

Choose Home & Garden to see what's available. Shipping rates vary depending on who's selling the item you want to buy.

 Navigation:

Andy's Garage Sale
www.andysgarage.com

As Andy says, this is where you'll find "Good Stuff, Dirt Cheap." Getting around this site is kind of tough, but if you can find your way, you'll find some good deals. Be sure to check out Andy's auction area.

Shipping: $ $ Navigation:

Auction Universe
www.auctionuniverse.com

Click any of a number of links for items for your home. Shipping rates may vary by vendor.

 Navigation:

Bargain News Auctions Online
www.bnauctions.com

Click the Home, Garden & Pet Supplies link to see what home improvement items are on the auction block. Delivery charges vary by seller.

 Navigation:

Bid.com
www.bid.com

Click For The Home at this auction site for rock-bottom prices on tools—bids start at $1 for many items! Note: Charges for delivery vary by seller.

 Navigation:

Catalog Closeouts

http://catalogcloseouts.com

Buy the goods that catalogs couldn't sell—at a discount! Be sure the click the Specials link for the best deals!

Shipping: **$**   Navigation:

Classifieds 2000

www.classifieds2000.com

Click the General Merchandise link and choose Home Living to find thousands of auction and classified ads for items for your home. Shipping charges may vary by vendor.

Navigation:

Coastal Tool

www.coastaltool.com

Can you say "discount power tools"? You'll find drills, saws, routers, sanders, polishers, grinders, compressors, planers and more by brands like Bosch, Black & Decker, Dewalt, Delta, Makita, Milwaukee, Porter-Cable, Skil, Senco, and Hitachi—all at some very nice prices. Shipping's reasonable, too!

Shipping: **$**   Navigation:

deals.com

www.deals.com

Click the Home & Office link to find goods like tools.

Shipping: **$**   Navigation:

DoItBest.com

www.doitbest.com

This online hardware store has everything you need and none of the hassle of having to go out and find it. You'll find supplies for plumbing, electrical work, lawn and garden, painting, building, and heating, not to mention tools, small appliances, hardware and fasteners, and more.

Shipping: **$**   Navigation:

ebay

www.ebay.com

Click the Miscellaneous link to find items for the home and garden, including tools. Note that shipping rates vary depending on who's selling the item you want to buy.

 Navigation:

EZbid.com

www.ezbid.com

Click the Home & Leisure link to find home improvement goodies and more—all up for auction. Click the Rebate button to see which items on the site have rebates! Note: shipping and handling costs will differ depending on the seller.

 Navigation:

Recycler.com

www.recycler.com

Click the Home & Home Improvement link to browse the available items.

Shipping: **$ $**   Navigation:

RedTag.com

www.redtagoutlet.com

Find home improvement items and more.

Shipping: **$ $**   Navigation:

Shop4.com

www.shop4.com

You must become a member to save on this site, but once you do, you'll find goods for as much as 60 percent off retail. You'll find hardware and items for your yard and garden. Click the Clearance link for the very best deals.

Shipping: **$ $**   Navigation:

Shoppers Advantage

www.shoppersadvantage.com

Click the Home, Kitchen & Garden link for great savings. Note: you must register to become a member in order to cash in on the great savings on this site.

Shipping: **$ $**   Navigation:

Shopping.com

www.shopping.com

Click the Home Improvement tab for bargains on all the tools you need to make your abode shine.

Shipping: $ $ Navigation:

SuperBuild.com

www.superbuild.com

Okay, this site rules. In addition to offering cheap shipping and low prices on 40,000 items, it also offers tons of do-it-yourself projects. Pinch me.

Shipping: $ Navigation:

Tooling Around

www.toolingaround.com

Tooling Around, which offers low prices on all sorts of tools (including power tools—whoo hoo!), is part of Buy It Now (see the chapter on agents and other shopping services for more information). Become a member of Buy It Now for special deals at Tooling Around. Certain products ship free of charge (you'll see a Free Shipping tag on those items).

Shipping: $ $ Navigation:

Value America

www.valueamerica.com

If you're looking to buy something, there's a good chance Value America's looking to sell it—including home improvement goodies. Be sure to check out the hot buys! Become a member (it's free) and save even more.

Shipping: $ Navigation:

Web Emporium

www.webporium.com

You'll find a bit of everything here at Web Emporium, including tools, all at nice prices.

Shipping: $ $ Navigation:

Your Home Center

www.yourhomecenter.com

Your Home Center, which offers low prices on lighting, appliances, items for home improvement, and more, is part of Buy It Now (see the chapter on agents and other shopping services for more information). Become a member of Buy It Now for special deals at Your Home Center. Certain products ship free of charge (you'll see a Free Shipping tag on those items).

Shipping: **$ $** Navigation:

Yahoo! Auctions

http://auctions.yahoo.com

Click the Home & Garden link to find goodies for your home up for auction. Note that shipping rates vary by seller.

 Navigation:

Kitchen

A Cook's Wares

www.cookswares.com

Click the Specials link for extra savings; join the e-club to be eligible for even better deals.

Shipping: **$ $ $**

Navigation:

Andy's Garage Sale

www.andysgarage.com

As Andy says, this is where you'll find "Good Stuff, Dirt Cheap." Getting around this site is kind of tough, but if you can find your way, you'll find some good deals. Be sure to check out Andy's auction area.

Shipping: **$ $**

Navigation:

Appliances.com

www.appliances.com

Buy tons of kitchen appliances here, at some pretty hard-to-beat prices.

Shipping: **$ $**

Navigation:

Auction Nation

www.auctionnation.com

Click the links to see what home items are up for sale. Note: Shipping costs may vary depending on who's selling the item you want to buy.

Navigation:

Auction Universe

www.auctionuniverse.com

Click any of a number of links for items for your kitchen. Shipping rates may vary by vendor.

Navigation:

Bargain Bungalow

www.galaxymall.com/product/bargain/index.html

Find items for the kitchen. Be sure to visit the Bargain Basement area! Shipping's a bit steep, but prices might be low enough to make up for it.

Shipping: **$ $ $**   Navigation:

Bargain News Auctions Online

www.bnauctions.com

Click the Home, Garden & Pet Supplies link to see what's on the auction block. Delivery charges vary by seller.

  Navigation:

Catalog Closeouts

http://catalogcloseouts.com

Buy the goods that catalogs couldn't sell—at a discount! Be sure the click the Specials link for the best deals!

Shipping: **$** Navigation:

ChefStore.com

www.chefstore.com

Find deals on kitchenware by Le Creuset, All Clad, and more. If you find a lower price somewhere else, ChefStore.com will gladly match it.

Shipping: **$ $ $**   Navigation:

Clearance World

www.clearanceworld.com

Find items for the kitchen and more at this site, where, as the name would suggest, everything's on clearance.

Shipping: **$ $** Navigation:

Cookware & More

www.outletsonline.com/cgibin/SoftCart.exe /shop/cook/catalog.html?L+cook+zpcp771 8+934488762

Save 35 to 48 percent on cookware by All-Clad, Scanpan, Kuhn Rikon, and Wusthof Trident. One irritating caveat: some prices are not listed, requiring you to call or email for information.

Shipping: **$ $** Navigation:

CookwareOnSale.com
www.cookwareonsale.com

CookwareOnSale.com sells first-quality, brand-new cookware items with full factory warranties. Selection is limited, but check back often, as the specials change regularly.

Shipping: **$**   Navigation:

CyberShop
http://cybershop.com

Up to 80 percent of original prices! Click the Departments tab and select Kitchen and Home to find deals on cookware, crystal and glassware, appliances, and more.

Shipping: **$ $**   Navigation:

DealDeal.com
www.dealdeal.com

Find must-have kitchen items, all up for auction. Note: delivery charges may vary depending on the seller.

                    Navigation:

Domestications
www.domestications.com

Find items for the kitchen. Be sure to check out the What's On Sale, Web Specials, and Clearance areas. To save an extra 10 percent, join the Buyer's Club (it costs $19.95). Shipping's a bit steep, but the prices may make up for it.

Shipping: **$ $ $**   Navigation:

edeal
www.edeal.com

Click the Home & Garden link to see what items are on the block. Subcategories include Kitchen Items/Appliances. Note: Delivery charges will vary by seller.

                    Navigation:

EZbid.com

www.ezbid.com

Click the Home & Leisure link to find kitchen items up for auction. Click the Rebate button to see which items on the site have rebates! Note: shipping and handling costs will differ depending on the seller.

 Navigation:

EZshop.com

www.ezshop.com

Items for the kitchen —all for prices that won't keep you from sending your kids to college. Be sure to click the Special Offers link for the very best deals!

Shipping: **$** Navigation:

FirstAuction

www.firstauction.com

Visit the Home & Leisure and Furniture areas to find items for the kitchen up for auction.

Shipping: **$ $** Navigation:

For the Kitchen

www.forthekitchen.com

For the Kitchen, which offers low prices on all sorts of kitchen items, is part of Buy It Now (see the chapter on agents and other shopping services for more information). Become a member of Buy It Now for special deals at For the Kitchen. Certain products ship free of charge (you'll see a Free Shipping tag on those items).

Shipping: **$ $** Navigation:

Kitchen Collection

www.kitcol.com

Kitchen Collection represents many of the nation's leading manufacturers as their exclusive authorized factory outlet.

Shipping: **$ $** Navigation:

KitchenCorner

http://kitchencorner.com

Save on kitchen gadgets, bakeware, coffee accessories, and cutlery at this site. Be sure to visit the Specials page for the best deals!

Shipping: **$ $ $**   Navigation:

HOME AND GARDEN

ProKitchen

www.prokitchen.com

Find low prices on items for the kitchen and bar, including cutlery, cookware, equipment, and more! Be sure to click the Specials button to find the best deals.

Shipping: **$ $**   Navigation:

RedTag.com

www.redtagoutlet.com

Find kitchen appliances, cookware, domestics, and more.

Shipping: **$ $**   Navigation:

Shoppers Advantage

www.shoppersadvantage.com

Click the Home, Kitchen & Garden link for great savings on kitchen items. Note: you must register to become a member in order to cash in on the great savings on this site.

Shipping: **$ $**   Navigation:

Spiegel   ☆

www.spiegel.com/spiegel/shopping/ultimate/

Save 30 to 75 percent on Spiegel merchandise for your home, including kitchen items.

Shipping: **$ $ $**   Navigation:

Toastmaster

www.toastmaster.com

Toastmaster makes small appliances for the kitchen (think toaster ovens, coffee makers, and the like). Click the Factory Outlet link to find the deals.

Shipping: **$ $ $**   Navigation:

uBid Online Auction
www.ubid.com

Bid for kitchen items at this auction site. Click More Categories, and you'll find entries for furniture, appliances, antiques, and other cool stuff. Note: Delivery charges may vary by seller.

 Navigation:

Web Emporium
www.webporium.com

You'll find a bit of everything here at Web Emporium, including kitchen items, at nice prices.

Shipping: **$ $** Navigation:

Yahoo! Auctions
http://auctions.yahoo.com

Click the Home & Garden link to find goodies for your kitchen up for auction. Note that shipping rates vary by seller.

Navigation:

Lawn, Garden, Patio, and Pool

Amazon Auctions

http://auctions.amazon.com

Choose Home & Garden to see what's available. Shipping rates vary depending on who's selling the item you want to buy.

    Navigation:

Andy's Garage Sale

www.andysgarage.com

As Andy says, this is where you'll find "Good Stuff, Dirt Cheap." Getting around this site is kind of tough, but if you can find your way, you'll find some good deals. Be sure to check out Andy's auction area.

Shipping: **$ $**   Navigation:

Auction Universe

www.auctionuniverse.com

Click any of a number of links for items for your garden. Shipping rates may vary by vendor.

    Navigation:

Bargain Bungalow

www.galaxymall.com/product/bargain/index.html

Find items for the patio. Be sure to visit the Bargain Basement area! Shipping's a bit steep, but prices might be low enough to make up for it.

Shipping: **$ $ $**   Navigation:

Bargain News Auctions Online

www.bnauctions.com

Click the Home, Garden & Pet Supplies link to see what garden items are on the auction block. Delivery charges vary by seller.

    Navigation:

Catalog Closeouts

http://catalogcloseouts.com

Buy the goods that catalogs couldn't sell—at a discount! Be sure the click the Specials link for the best deals!

Shipping: **$**   Navigation:

Classifieds 2000

www.classifieds2000.com

Click the General Merchandise link and choose Home Living to find thousands of auction and classified ads for items for your garden. Shipping charges may vary by vendor.

Navigation:

Clearance World

www.clearanceworld.com

Find items for the garden at this site, where, as the name would suggest, everything's on clearance.

Shipping: **$ $**   Navigation:

Costco Online

www.costco.com

You've probably heard of Costco, which is one of those warehouse clubs. Now Costco's online, offering members some great deals on some great merchandise (it costs a minimum of $40 to join, but if you shop there enough, prices will make up for it). Among other items, you'll find goods for your lawn and garden, and other home essentials at Costco.

Shipping: **$ $**   Navigation:

Discount Pool Mart

www.discountpoolmart.com

Find low prices on pool supplies galore, including test kits and refills, skimmers and leaf rakes, vacuum heads, brushes, thermometers, fountains, hoses and fittings, leaf baggers, and, amazingly, entire above-ground pools. The downside: Shipping's a bit high.

Shipping: **$ $ $**   Navigation:

DoItBest.com
http://doitbest.com

This online hardware store has everything you need and none of the hassle of having to go out and find it. You'll find supplies for lawn and garden.

Shipping: **$**   Navigation:

ebay
www.ebay.com

Click the Miscellaneous link to find items for the lawn and garden. Note that shipping rates vary depending on who's selling the item you want to buy.

                    Navigation:

edeal
www.edeal.com

Click the Home & Garden link to see what items are on the block. Subcategories include Garden Items. Note: Delivery charges will vary by seller.

                    Navigation:

EZshop.com
www.ezshop.com

Buy garden items for prices that won't keep you from sending your kids to college. Be sure to click the Special Offers link for the very best deals!

Shipping: **$**   Navigation:

Garden.com
www.garden.com

Find plants, trees, shrubs, bulbs, tools, outdoor furniture, seeds, and more at reasonable prices. Click the What's on Sale link for the best deals.

Shipping: **$ $ $**   Navigation:

Gardener's Supply Company
www.gardeners.com

Find some nice prices on everything you need for the garden, from gardening tools to fertilizers. Be sure to check out the Clearance area for the best deals.

Shipping: **$ $ $**   Navigation:

Outside Living
www.outsideliving.com

Outside Living, which offers low prices on outdoor grills, patio items, gardening supplies, and more, is part of Buy It Now (see the chapter on agents and other shopping services for more information). Become a member of Buy It Now for special deals at Outside Living. Certain products ship free of charge (you'll see a Free Shipping tag on those items).

Shipping: **$ $**   Navigation:

Shop4.com
www.shop4.com

You must become a member to save on this site, but once you do, you'll find goods for as much as 60 percent off retail. You'll find items for your yard and garden. Click the Clearance link for the very best deals.

Shipping: **$ $** Navigation:

Shoppers Advantage
www.shoppersadvantage.com

Click the Home, Kitchen & Garden link for great savings. Note: you must register to become a member in order to cash in on the great savings on this site.

Shipping: **$ $** Navigation:

Shopping.com
www.shopping.com

Click the Home Improvement tab to find everything you need to keep your abode spruced up, including items for lawn and garden.

Shipping: **$ $** Navigation:

Value America
www.valueamerica.com

If you're looking to buy something, there's a good chance Value America's looking to sell it—including items for your garden and patio. Be sure to check out the hot buys! Become a member (it's free) and save even more.

Shipping: **$** Navigation:

Virtual Seeds Company
www.virtualseeds.com

Buy seeds for herbs, vegetables, flowers, and more.
Check out the Red Check Sale area for the best prices.
Free shipping on orders over $30.

Shipping: **$**   Navigation:

Yahoo! Auctions
http://auctions.yahoo.com

Click the Home & Garden link to find goodies for your
home up for auction. Note that shipping rates vary by
seller.

                    Navigation:

Pet Supplies

Amazon Auctions
http://auctions.amazon.com

Choose Home & Garden to see what pet supplies are available. Shipping rates vary depending on who's selling the item you want to buy.

 Navigation:

Auction Universe
www.auctionuniverse.com

Click any of a number of links for items for your pet. Shipping rates may vary by vendor.

 Navigation:

Bargain News Auctions Online
www.bnauctions.com

Click the Home, Garden & Pet Supplies link to see what's on the auction block. Delivery charges vary by seller.

 Navigation:

Catalog Closeouts
http://catalogcloseouts.com

Buy the goods that catalogs couldn't sell—at a discount! Be sure the click the Specials link for the best deals!

Shipping: **$** Navigation:

Creative Aquatics and Pets
www.pohina.com/creative/

Creative Aquatics and Pets features thousands of products for reptiles, dogs, cats, birds, fish, and more, at discount prices. You'll find name-brand goods by manufacturers like Aquatrol, Aspen, Booda, Coralife, ESU Reptile, Fish Vet Inc., Flex Watt, Hova-Bator, Multi-Pet, O'Dell, T-Rex, Zoo Med, and many more. Free shipping on orders over $75!

Shipping: **$ $** Navigation:

ebay

www.ebay.com

Click the Miscellaneous link to find items for pet supplies. Note that shipping rates vary depending on who's selling the item you want to buy.

       Navigation:

edeal

www.edeal.com

Click the Home & Garden link to see what items are on the block. Subcategories include Pet Supplies/Services. Note: Delivery charges will vary by seller.

       Navigation:

FirstAuction

www.firstauction.com

Visit the Home & Leisure and Furniture areas to find items for your pet up for auction.

Shipping: **$ $**   Navigation:

P.S. Affordable

www.psaffordable.com

Dog lovers, unite! P.S. Affordable has a nice selection of discount dog products including toys, snacks, grooming supplies, show leads, collars, harnesses, and obedience training equipment (which, presumably, dogs can use to keep their owners in line) at 25 to 50 percent off.

Shipping: **$**   Navigation:

Pet Expo

www.pet-expo.com

Pet Expo has a massive selection of pet-related products—over 25,000 items—many of which are discounted or sold at wholesale prices.

Shipping: **$ $**   Navigation:

Pet Express

www.petxpress.com

Save on pet food with 3-, 6-, and 12-month plans (save even more if you pre-pay). Food is delivered to you on a monthly basis (saving you money AND time).

Shipping: **$ $**   Navigation:

Pet Ranch

www.petranchdiscount.com

Find everything you need for your special critter, whether it's a fish, dog, cat, bird, reptile, ferret, gerbil, or other small furry member of the genus rodent. Be sure to check out the specials!

Shipping: **$ $ $**   Navigation:

PetMarket.com

www.petmarket.com

Find discount pet supplies. Click the Clearance link for the best deals.

Shipping: **$ $**   Navigation:

PetQuarters

www.petquarters.com

Whether you're parent to a puppy or a python, PetQuarters has the pet supplies you need—all at a discount.

Shipping: **$ $**   Navigation:

Pets Deluxe

www.petsdeluxe.com

Pets Deluxe, which offers low prices on pet supplies, is part of Buy It Now (see the chapter on agents and other shopping services for more information). Become a member of Buy It Now for special deals at Pets Deluxe. Certain products ship free of charge (you'll see a Free Shipping tag on those items).

Shipping: **$ $**   ⊕   Navigation: ⮡

Pets.com

www.pets.com   ☆

Schedule deliveries of pet food on a monthly basis, and save 50 percent! You'll find great prices on everything for Fido and Fluffy (not to mention Polly, Guppy, and whatever ferrett's and reptiles are traditionally called), from toys to treats to apparel (that's right, apparel). This is a truly fabulous site.

Shipping: **$ $**   Navigation:

Shopping.com

www.shopping.com

Click the Home Improvement tab to find everything you
need in the way of pet supplies.

Shipping: **$ $**   Navigation: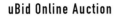

uBid Online Auction

www.ubid.com

Bid for pet supplies at this auction site. Note: Delivery
charges may vary by seller.

                    Navigation:

Yahoo! Auctions

http://auctions.yahoo.com

Click the Home & Garden link to find goodies for your pet
up for auction. Note that shipping rates vary by seller.

                    Navigation:

Tableware

CyberShop
http://cybershop.com

Up to 80 percent of original prices! Click the Departments tab and select Kitchen and Home to find deals on cookware, crystal and glassware, and more.

Shipping: $ $ Navigation:

Domestications
www.domestications.com

Find tablewear items. Be sure to check out the What's On Sale, Web Specials, and Clearance areas. To save an extra 10 percent, join the Buyer's Club (it costs $19.95). Shipping's a bit steep, but the prices may make up for it.

Shipping: $ $ $ Navigation:

Popula
www.popula.com

For the modernist in you, this site offers swanky home items, including tableware for auction. Note that charges for shipping and handling will vary by seller.

                    Navigation:

Ross-Simons
www.ross-simons.com   ☆

As the site puts it, "Life's Luxuries for a Lot Less." This site offers china, crystal, flatware, and more—at up to 70 percent off. Click the Shop the Outlet link for the best deals.

Shipping: $ $ $ Navigation: 👍

Shoppers Advantage
www.shoppersadvantage.com

Click the Home, Kitchen & Garden link for great savings

on tableware. Note: you must register to become a member in order to cash in on the great savings on this site.

Shipping: **$ $** Navigation:

Silver Superstore

www.silversuperstore.com

Save up to 75 percent off suggested retail on sterling silverware here! You'll also find bowls, trays, baby silver, and ornaments. Be sure to visit the On Sale area. One downside: You can't order online; you have to call the toll-free number to order.

Shipping: **$ $** Navigation:

uBid Online Auction

www.ubid.com

Bid for tableware items at this auction site. Click More Categories, and you'll find entries for furniture, appliances, antiques, and other cool stuff. Note: Delivery charges may vary by seller.

  Navigation:

Your World at Home

www.ywh.com

Quality tableware from brands like Spode (my favorite), Lenox, Mikasa, Waterford, and more—all at a discount.

Shipping: **$ $** Navigation:

Wall Art

Art Expression
www.artexpression.com

Choose from more than 2,000 fine art prints and posters by the world's greatest artists, all at near wholesale prices. Be sure to click the Specials link for the best deals.

Shipping: **$** Navigation:

Art 4 Less Liquidators
www.art-4-less.com

Art 4 Less guarantees that every item on the site is at 50 percent off retail. Search by artist or subject, or click the Gallery link. Click the Artist's Clearing House link for the best deals.

Shipping: **$ $ $** Navigation:

Art.com
www.art.com

Find good deals on framed and unframed prints and posters. Tons to choose from! Free shipping on orders more than $100. Be sure to check out their auction area.

Shipping: **$ $ $** Navigation:

ArtFrames
www.artframes.com

Find quality, wooden frames for your works of art—many at wholesale prices.

Shipping: **$ $ $** Navigation:

Artprint Collection
www.artprintcollection.com

This site features tons of posters at very reasonable prices, including, I might add, an entire collection of posters by my favorite artist on this planet: Tamara DeLempicka. Check out the Vintage Posters area to see some swinging prints.

Shipping: **$ $** Navigation:

ArtSelect

www.artselect.com

Save 40 to 50 percent on custom framing and prints.
Shipping is included.

Shipping: **$**　　　　　　　　Navigation:

AuctionAddict.com

www.auctionaddict.com

Click the Home Furnishings link to see what art items are
up for auction. Shipping rates vary by seller.

　　　Navigation:

Barewalls.com

www.barewalls.com

Barewalls.com calls itself the Internet's largest art print
and poster store, offering savings on tens of thousands of
prints in stock.

Shipping: **$ $**　　　　　　　Navigation:

Catalog Closeouts

http://catalogcloseouts.com

Buy the goods that catalogs couldn't sell—at a discount!
Be sure the click the Specials link for the best deals!

Shipping: **$**　　　　　　　　Navigation:

Domestications

www.domestications.com

Find items for wall décor. Be sure to check out the
What's On Sale, Web Specials, and Clearance areas. To
save an extra 10 percent, join the Buyer's Club (it costs
$19.95). Shipping's a bit steep, but the prices may make
up for it.

Shipping: **$ $ $**　　　　　　Navigation:

HomePoint.com

www.homepoint.com

Find wall art here. These items represent excess inventory or customer returns. This is a great site!

Shipping: **$**　　　　　　　　Navigation:

ILoveaDeal.com

www.iloveadeal.com

Find prints featured in Wireless, Seasons, and Signals
catalogs, many at 40 to 70 percent off! Be sure to click the
Top 20 Bargains link for the best deals.

Shipping: **$ $**   Navigation:

Internet Fine Art Marketplace

www.art4sale.com

You'll find classified ads as well as an auction at this site!
Note that shipping costs may vary depending on who's
selling the item you want to buy.

                    Navigation:

BARGAIN SHOPPING Online

Jewelry and Gifts

Cigars, Pipes, and Cigarettes

Cheaphumidors.com

www.cheaphumidors.com

This site, "The Home of the Affordable Humidor," offers humidors at wholesale prices—and sometimes below. Check out their Super Duper Sale Specials for even better prices.

Shipping: $ $ $ Navigation:

CigarBargains.com

www.cigarbargains.com

This site should be the starting point for anyone looking for cheap cigars and accessories. Vendors the Net over list cigar products for sale on the cheap. Shipping rates vary from listing to listing, depending on the vendor.

Navigation:

Cigar Express

www.cigarexpress.com

You'll find an extensive list of cigars for sale here, as well as cigar accessories and the like. Subscribe to their Bargain Cigars listserv to be in the know. Special discounts for military, law-enforcement, and fire-department personnel.

Shipping: $ $ Navigation:

Cigar Specialist

www.infohwy.com/cyberia/cigar/

You'll find an extensive selection of the finest brands available here. Free shipping!

Shipping: $ Navigation:

Cigaroma

www.cigaroma.com

Selection is limited, but there are some serious deals here on cigars and humidors.

Shipping: **$ $**   Navigation:

Cigars Plus

www.cigarsplus.com

This isn't exactly the slickest site ever, but you will find some nice specials on cigars and accessories. Free shipping on orders over $100.

Shipping: **$**   Navigation:

Cigars-R-Us

www.cigars-r-us.com

Sometimes a cigar is just a cigar—unless it's a DISCOUNTED cigar! Find cigars and cigar accessories for lower-than-retail prices here.

Shipping: **$ $ $**   Navigation:

Discount Cigarettes

www.discountcigarettes.net/

Support your habit here. Buy cartons of cigarettes, chewing tobacco, cigarette papers, lighters, and more. Free shipping if you order five cartons or more.

Shipping: **$ $**   Navigation:

Discount Zippo Lighters

http://integracom.net/smoker/

Find loads of Zippo lighters (they rule) at discount prices. Shipping's more than reasonable—even internationally.

Shipping: **$**   Navigation:

Don Tuto Cigars

www.dontuto.com

Check the Specials area at Don Tuto for some nice prices on cigars. Free shipping!

Shipping: **$**   Navigation:

Edward's Pipe and Tobacco

www.edwardstampa.com

Find pipes, cigars, lighters, pipe tobacco, cigar accessories, pipe accessories, and more—at pretty reasonable prices. Be sure to check out the monthly specials.

Shipping: **$ $**   Navigation:

Lighters Galore Plus

www.pipeshop.com

Find some nice prices on lighters and other tobacco accessories here. Free shipping!

Shipping: **$**   Navigation:

The Digital Humidor

www.digitalhumidor.com

Buy cigars, humidors, cigar accessories, and more at this online tobacconist. Be sure to check out the Specials.

Shipping: **$ $**   Navigation:

TheSmokeShop.com

www.thesmokeshop.com

Find discounted cigars by brand or by rating. Be sure to check the Specials area for the best deals.

Shipping: **$ $**   Navigation:

Virtual Cigar Shop

www.vcigar.com

Be sure to check out the Today's Sale area to see what cigars and accessories are up for grabs. Shipping's a bit steep (a flat $7, no matter what you buy) unless you buy in bulk.

Shipping: **$ $ $**   Navigation:

Coffee and Tea

Coffee Wholesale USA

www.cw-usa.com

Save up to 50 percent off retail on a large selection of gourmet coffee, tea, and espresso, not to mention coffee makers and the like.

Shipping: **$ $**   Navigation:

Jason's Coffee

http://jasonscoffee.com

Buy wholesale coffee here. The downside: You have to order by phone.

Shipping: **$ $**   Navigation:

Flowers

1-800 Flowers
www.1800flowers.com

Not everything's dirt cheap here, but prices on flowers are
reasonable (even if delivery sometimes seems a bit steep).

Shipping: $ $ $ Navigation:

BestFlowers.com
www.bestflowers.com ☆

Check out the special area for bargain hunters at this site
to find bouquets under $30.

Shipping: $ $ $ Navigation:

Costco Online
www.costco.com

You've probably heard of Costco, which is one of those
warehouse clubs. Now Costco's online, offering members
some great deals on some great merchandise (it costs a
minimum of $40 to join, but if you shop there enough,
prices will make up for it). Among other items, you'll find
some nice prices on floral delivery services.

Shipping: $ $ Navigation:

Florist.com
www.florist.com

Find all sorts of flower arrangements. Prices aren't exactly rock bottom, but delivery is reasonable—and if you call
before 2:30 p.m., they can deliver on the same day.

Shipping: $ $ Navigation:

GivingNature.com
www.givingnature.com ☆

Buy these grower-direct flowers at reasonable prices
(sample deal: two dozen roses for $39.95).

Shipping: $ $ Navigation:

GreatFlowers.com
www.greatflowers.com

Buy flowers grower direct, and save as much as 50 percent (I found two dozen roses for $39.95). If you never remember those important days (birthdays, anniversaries, holidays, and such) that merit flowers, sign up for the reminder service.

Shipping: **$ $ $**   Navigation:

ProFlowers.com
www.proflowers.com

ProFlowers buys direct from the grower, and provides a fast, easy, and reliable way to buy the freshest quality cut flowers at a competitive price.

Shipping: **$ $**   Navigation:

Jewelry and Watches

Alle Fine Jewelry
www.allejewelry.com

Find superior quality jewelry at up to 50 percent off! Be sure to check out their Sale area for the best deals.

Shipping: **$ $**   Navigation:

Amazon Auctions
www.amazon.com

Click the Auctions tab, and choose Gemstones & Jewelry to see what's available. Shipping rates vary depending on who's selling the item you want to buy.

                    Navigation:

Ashford.com
www.ashford.com

Ashford.com offers an incredible assortment of distinctive men's and women's sport, casual, and dress watches—over 70 brands and 7,000 models. Prices aren't dirt cheap, but they're close. If you're looking for a hard-to-find make and model, this may be the place to go. Vintage watches also available. Another perk: free shipping!

Shipping: **$**   Navigation:

AuctionAddict.com
www.auctionaddict.com

Click the Jewelry & Gems link to find pieces up for auction. Shipping rates vary by seller.

                    Navigation:

Auction Nation
www.auctionnation.com

Click the Jewelry/Gems link to see what baubles are up for sale. Note: Shipping costs vary depending on who's selling the item you want to buy.

                    Navigation:

AuctioNet.com

www.auctionet.com

Click the Jewelry link to find bracelets, earrings, rings, and more —all for auction. Note that shipping rates vary depending on who's selling the item you want to buy.

 Navigation:

AuctionFloor.com

www.auctionfloor.com

Click the Jewelry tab to see what's up for auction (choose from Diamonds, Loose Gems, Gold, Miscellaneous, and Silver). Note that shipping prices may vary depending on who's selling the item you want to buy.

 Navigation:

Auctionscape

www.auctionscape.com

Click the Jewelry & Fashion link to see what groovy duds are on the auction block. Note that shipping rates vary by seller.

 Navigation:

Auction Universe

www.auctionuniverse.com

Click the Jewelry & Fashion link to find watches, gem-stones, and more. Delivery charges vary by vendor.

 Navigation:

Bid.com

www.bid.com

Click the Jewelry link at this auction site for rock-bottom prices on rings, earrings, bracelets, necklaces, watches —you name it. Bids start at $1 for many items! Note: Charges for delivery vary by seller.

 Navigation:

Boxlot

www.boxlot.com

You'll find a little of everything on the auction block here— including some incredible jewelry. Bid on beads, costume jewelry, vintage jewelry, southwestern jewelry, loose gem-stones, and more. Note that shipping rates vary by seller.

 Navigation:

Burlington Coat Factory Direct

www.coat.com/bcfdirect

So the name's a little misleading—but you can find jewelry here amidst the coats.

Shipping: **$ $ $** Navigation:

Certified Diamonds and Rolex Watches

www.diarolex.com

Searching for a loose diamond? Browse this site's Diamond List, where you'll find diamonds listed at prices below the U.S. wholesale market. Gently used Rolex watches also available—check out the Rolex Exchange. Free shipping!

Shipping: **$** Navigation:

Costco Online

www.costco.com

Costco's online, offering members some great deals on some great merchandise (it costs a minimum of $40 to join, but if you shop there enough, prices will make up for it). Among other items, you'll find some great jewelry, including bracelets, rings, earrings, and necklaces with diamonds, gold, pearls, gems, and more. Watches are also available.

Shipping: **$ $** Navigation:

CyberShop

http://cybershop.com

Find watches (Tag Heuer, Seiko, Movado, and more) at up to 80 percent off! Click the Departments tab and choose Watches and Clocks for the deals.

Shipping: **$ $** Navigation:

Deals.com

www.deals.com

Click the Apparel & Jewelry link for deals on jewelry. They had Cartier watches for about 40 percent off last time I visited!

Shipping: **$** Navigation:

Deep Discounted Jewelry
www.gold-silver-jewelry.com

As their name might suggest, this site offers deep-discounted gold and silver jewelry. Free shipping on orders over $50!

Shipping: **$**   Navigation:

DiamondDepot.com
www.diamonddepot.com

Buy loose diamonds, jewelry (including estate jewelry), watches, and gifts here. All at bargain prices!

Shipping: **$ $**   Navigation:

eBay
www.ebay.com   ☆

There's a reason this site's the big daddy of the auctions—it's HUGE. Click the Jewelry, Gemstones link to see what's available (last time I visited, 100,665 items were up for auction in this category). Note that shipping rates vary depending on who's selling the item you want to buy.

                    Navigation:

edeal
www.edeal.com

Visit the Jewelry & Gemstones area of this auction site to see what baubles are up for grabs. Note: shipping and handling charges may vary by seller.

                    Navigation:

Egghead Surplus Auctions
www.surplusauction.com

If you can figure out how to navigate this auction site, you can find some seriously good deals on jewelry and watches. Check the Surplus area for items that aren't up for auction, but are up for sale cheap.

Shipping: **$ $**   🌐   Navigation:

eJeweler
www.ejeweler.net

Expect to save 25 to 50 percent at eJeweler. You'll find tons of deals on rings, watches, and the like—not to mention crystal, leather goods (can you say "Coach"?), and more.

Shipping: **$ $**   Navigation:

eswap

www.eswap.com/

Click the Jewelry link to see what's available. Note that shipping rates may vary depending on who's selling the item you want to buy.

 Navigation:

FirstAuction

www.firstauction.com

The items up for auction in the Gold & Silver Jewelry, Jewelry with Gemstones, and Accessories & Watches categories should satisfy even the most picky shoppers. Note: Shipping costs vary depending on the seller.

 Navigation:

Gems Direct

www.gemsdirect.com

Buy bracelets, earrings, necklaces, pendants, rings, and gemstones tax-free and direct from the manufacturer here. Free shipping!

Shipping: **$**   Navigation:

Gems for Less

www.gemsforless.com

Find some very beautiful antique and estate reproduction jewelry here, at some very nice prices. Selection is limited, but heavy on pendants.

Shipping: **$**   Navigation:

Goldhaus Wholesale Jewelry

www.goldhaus.com

14K gold at rock-bottom prices. It's not Tiffany's, but it is gold.

Shipping: **$**   Navigation:

ILoveaDeal.com

www.iloveadeal.com

Find apparel featured in the Wireless, Seasons, and Signals catalogs, much of it 40 to 70 percent off! Be sure to click the Top 20 Bargains link for the best deals!

Shipping: **$ $**   Navigation:

Jewelry for Less

www.jewelry4less.com

You'll find some interesting pieces of jewelry here—including gold, silver, platinum, diamonds, precious gems, pearls, health crystals, and more—at very reasonable prices.

Shipping: **$ $**   Navigation:

Jewelry Gift

www.jewelrygift.com

Find earrings, rings, bracelets, pendants, pins, necklaces, watches, and chains at discount prices. Be sure to click the Blowout Items link to see what's available!

Shipping: **$ $ $**   Navigation:

Jewelry Mall

www.jewelrymall.com

Jewelry Mall is a collection of jewelry-related links that are sorted and categorized for ease of use. You can search the stores featured on this site by price or by item. Be sure to see what jewelry specials are available to Jewelry Mall customers when you visit! Note that shipping varies by seller.

Navigation:

JewelryWeb.com

www.jewelryweb.com

Save 40 to 60 percent over retail at JewelryWeb.com.

Shipping: **$ $**   Navigation:

Macys

www.macys.com

Find loads of jewelry at Macys, including watches and more—some of it 15 percent off.

Shipping: **$ $**   Navigation:

Merlite Jewelry

www.merlite.com

Find loads of costume jewelry at discount prices here. Be sure to check out the closeouts and the items under $16.

Shipping: **$ $ $**   Navigation:

Nu Concepts Online Catalog
www.sell-free.com/NuConcepts

Find a little of everything—including jewelry—at this site.

Shipping: **$ $**   Navigation:

Princeton Watches
www.princetonwatches.com

Save hundreds on watches made by Citizen, Chase-Durer, and Seiko, including that groovy kinetic watch. Free shipping!

Shipping: **$**   Navigation:

One Web Place
www.onewebplace.com/

Click the Jewelry link to get your fill of baubles—all on the auction block. Delivery rates vary by seller.

          Navigation:

Rings-Online.com
www.rings-online.com

With the free matching wedding band you get with each diamond ring you buy at this site —not to mention the free shipping— two-months salary will go a lot farther here.

Shipping: **$**   Navigation:

SellAndTrade.com
www.sellandtrade.com

Click the Jewelry link to see what goodies are on the auction block. Note that delivery charges will vary depending on the seller.

          Navigation:

Shop4.com
www.shop4.com

You must become a member to save on this site, but once you do, you'll find goods for as much as 60 percent off retail. You'll find some nice deals on jewelry. Click the Clearance link for the very best deals in every category.

Shipping: **$ $**   Navigation:

The Shopping Moon
shoppingmoon.com

The ShoppingMoon sells some great, unique watches—all at discounted prices. Be sure to see what's up for grabs among the closeout items!

Shipping: **$ $**   Navigation:

The SpiderGear Connection
www.spidergear.com

Click the Jewelry link to find jewelry and watches at a discount. Site members get first stab at new products and better prices.

Shipping: **$ $ $**   Navigation:

SoldUSA.com
www.soldusa.com

You'll find lots of jewelry at this auction site, including rings, bracelets, earrings, necklaces, watches, and more. Note that delivery charges may vary by seller.

                  Navigation:

Spiegel
www.spiegel.com/spiegel/shopping/ultimate

Save 30 to 75 percent on Spiegel jewelry.

Shipping: **$ $ $**   Navigation:

Swiss Army Depot
www.swissarmydepot.com

The company that makes Swiss Army brand watches and knives demands that all retailers sell those items at the retail price, which is why they're not discounted here. However, you will find discounted Victorinox and Wenger watches. This site sometimes runs free shipping specials, but not every day. Don't forget to check the Specials area for the best deals (up to 50 percent off).

Shipping: **$ $**   ⊕   Navigation:

ThinkBid.com
www.thinkbid.com

At this auction site, you'll find gold, silver, and costume jewelry, plus watches and jewelry boxes. Note that delivery charges will vary by seller.

                  Navigation:

Trade Hall
www.tradehall.com

At this auction site, you'll find jewelry for men and women. Note that shipping charges will vary by seller.

 Navigation:

uBid Online Auction
www.ubid.com

Bid on bracelets, necklaces, earrings, watches, rings, and more at this auction site. Note: Delivery charges may vary by seller.

 Navigation:

Unclaimed Baggage Center
www.unclaimedbaggage.com

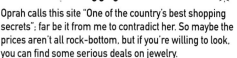

Oprah calls this site "One of the country's best shopping secrets"; far be it from me to contradict her. So maybe the prices aren't all rock-bottom, but if you're willing to look, you can find some serious deals on jewelry.

Shipping: **$ $** Navigation:

Up 4 Sale
www.up4sale.com

You'll find jewelry up for auction in the General Merchandise area of this site. Note that shipping rates will vary by seller.

Shipping: **$ $** Navigation:

USAuctions.com
www.usauctions.com

Click the Jewelry & Watches link to see what's available. Note that shipping prices will vary depending on who is selling the item you want to buy.

 Navigation:

Value America
www.valueamerica.com

If you're looking to buy something, there's a good chance Value America's looking to sell it—including watches and jewelry (you'll find diamonds, gemstones, pearls, silver, gold, and more). Be sure to check out the hot buys! Become a member (it's free) and save even more.

Shipping: **$** Navigation:

Watch Shoppe

www.watchshoppe.com

Find high-quality (if not exactly name brand) watches at 50 to 80 percent off retail.

Shipping: **$ $** Navigation:

Watchzone

www.watchzone.com

Check out Watchzone for deals on watches by a zillion different manufacturers, including Bulova, Citizen, Movado, Nike, Swatch, Swiss Army, and more.

Shipping: **$**   Navigation:

Web Emporium

www.webporium.com

You'll find a bit of everything here at Web Emporium—including jewelry and watches—at some nice prices.

Shipping: **$ $** Navigation:

Wholesale Jewelry

www.wholesalejewelry.net

Buy costume jewelry here, sold in bulk.

Shipping: **$ $ $** Navigation:

World of Watches

www.worldofwatches.com

Find great watches from makers like Tag Heuer, Seiko, Bulova, Swiss Army, Citizen, Movado, and more—at some seriously nice prices. You'll save hundreds here.

Shipping: **$ $** Navigation:

Wristwatch.com

www.wristwatch.com

Save hundreds on fantastic watches from makers like Tag Heuer, Swiss Army, Seiko, Movado, and more. This is a great site.

Shipping: **$ $**   Navigation:

Yahoo! Auctions
http://auctions.yahoo.com

Click the Clothing & Accessories link to find the jewelry up
for auction. You'll find ancient and ethnographic jewelry,
beaded jewelry, carved and cameo jewelry, contemporary
jewelry, costume jewelry, antique pieces, fine jewelry,
gemstones, diamonds, gold, silver—need I go on? Note
that shipping rates vary by seller.

   Navigation:

Perfume and Cologne

1-800-98-Perfume

www.98perfume.com

Save up to 70 percent on genuine fragrances by authentic name brands such as Bijan, Halston, Giorgio, Chanel, Ralph Lauren, Calvin Klein, Giorgio Armani, and many more. Shipping is free!

Shipping: **$**   Navigation:

Ashford.com

www.ashford.com

Ashford.com offers a tremendous assortment of fragrances for men and women, including scents by Calvin Klein, Chanel, Paloma Picasso, Tiffany, and more. Prices aren't dirt cheap, but if you're looking for an obscure perfume or cologne, this may be the best place to find it. Free shipping!

Shipping: **$**   Navigation:

Costco Online

www.costco.com

You've probably heard of Costco, which is one of those warehouse clubs. Now Costco's online, offering members some great deals on some great merchandise (it costs a minimum of $40 to join, but if you shop there enough, prices will make up for it). Among other items, you'll find some nice prices on fragrances for men and women.

Shipping: **$ $**   Navigation:

CyberShop

http://cybershop.com

Getting to the part of this site that sells perfume is a bit of a chore (click the Departments tab, choose Gifts, and select Fragrances), but you'll be glad you made the effort.

Shipping: **$ $**   Navigation:

Fragrance Discounter

www.fragrancediscounter.com

Get perfume and cologne on the cheap—especially when you buy Fragrance Discounter's versions of popular scents.

Shipping: **$ $ $** Navigation:

FragranceNet

www.fragrancenet.com/html/

This site helps you out by showing the suggested retail price alongside FragranceNet's price. Prices here are noticeably low (up to 70 percent off!), and shipping is free within the continental U.S.

Shipping: **$** Navigation:

Fragrances Plus

www.fragrancesplus.com

A variety of fragrances at reasonable prices. Be sure to click the Fragrance Specials link for the best deals.

Shipping: **$ $ $** Navigation:

La Parfumerie

www.laparfumerie.com

Save 25 to 75 percent on perfumes by famous makers like Elizabeth Arden, Estee Lauder, Guerlain, Calvin Klein, Chanel, and more.

Shipping: **$ $** Navigation:

Paris Fragrance

www.paris-fr.com

Just because you don't want to pay top dollar for designer prices doesn't mean you don't want to smell like them. Check out this site, where you'll find some pretty good prices on a decent selection. Shipping's cheap, too.

Shipping: **$** Navigation:

Perfumania

www.perfumania.com

Perfumania sells designer fragrances, bath and body products, cosmetics, and more, all at a discount. Be sure to visit the Red Tag area for savings of up to 70 percent.

Shipping: **$** Navigation:

Perfume Center
www.perfumecenter.com/main.htm

More than 1,200 original brand-name fragrances for men and women. Prices are mucho reasonable!

Shipping: **$ $** Navigation:

JEWELRY AND GIFTS

Perfume for Less
www.perfumeforless.com

Save up to 70 percent on original, brand-name perfumes. Specials sometimes include free shipping!

Shipping: **$ $** Navigation:

The Perfume Mart
www.perfumemart.com

This online perfume store has nearly every fragrance product (for men and women) on the market for sale. Savings aren't always huge, but you get free samples and gift-wrapping along with your order.

Shipping: **$** Navigation:

Perfume$mart
www.perfumesmart.com

Prices for the 1,000+ designer and hard to find fragrances are guaranteed less than the retail department store prices (in many cases with savings of up to 70 percent). Be sure to click the Testers link for great prices on unboxed bottles.

Shipping: **$** Navigation:

Perfumes Direct
www.perfumesdirect.com

An extensive selection of original, brand-name, designer men's and women's perfumes at discount prices. Shipping is free for orders over $100.

Shipping: **$** Navigation:

Quality King Distributors
www.qualityking.com

Click the Designer Fragrances link to find your favorite scents on the cheap (some products are discounted 50 percent or more).

Shipping: **$ $** Navigation:

Scent Warehouse

www.scentwarehouse.com

Find great prices on scents for men and women by
famous makers like Donna Karan, Gucci, Gaultier, and
more.

Shipping: **$**   Navigation:

Shoppers Advantage

www.shoppersadvantage.com

Click the Fragrances & Jewelry link for great savings.
Note: you must register to become a member in order to
cash in on the great savings on this site.

Shipping: **$ $**   Navigation:

Web Emporium

www.webporium.com

You'll find a bit of everything here at Web Emporium —
especially fragrances— at nice prices.

Shipping: **$ $**   Navigation:

Sweets

BulkCandy.com

www.bulkcandy.com

Buy candy in bulk! Click the Closeouts link in the catalog for the best deals for your sweet tooth.

Shipping: **$ $ $**   Navigation:

BulkFoods.com

www.bulkfoods.com

Buy bulk candies, nuts, spices, and dried fruits.

Shipping: **$**   Navigation:

Candy Direct

www.candydirect.com

Buy candy in bulk to save your money (if not your teeth). Hard-to-find candies are available a-plenty at this site!

Shipping: **$ $ $**   Navigation:

First Discount Popcorn

www.firstpopcorn.com

Save 20 to 30 percent on fresh popcorn from First Discount Popcorn. You'll find a nice selection of cool canisters! Makes for a nice gift.

Shipping: **$ $ $**   Navigation:

Sweety's Candies

www.sweetys.com

Sweety's sells bulk candy, novelty candy, and gifts.

Shipping: **$ $**   Navigation:

Wine and Spirits

AuctionVine
www.auctionvine.com

Bid on fine and rare wines here. Prices won't necessarily be rock-bottom, but if you're a true connoisseur, you can probably take the hit. Note that delivery charges vary by seller.

   Navigation:

Brentwood Wine Company
www.brentwoodwine.com

Click the Wine Auctions link to find some good deals on wines. Note that delivery charges may vary depending on who's selling.

   Navigation:

City Wine
www.citywine.com

Featured wines on this site are discounted 15 percent (20 percent if you buy by the case). Check the double-discounted case for the best deals!

Shipping: $ $ Navigation:

Libation
www.libation.com

Click the Values and Specials links to find some nice prices on beer and wine. Note: Unless you live in California, Oregon, or Washington, you'll have to give up your first-born for shipping.

Shipping: $ $ $ Navigation:

Wine Country
www.winecountryonline.com

Whoo hoo! A site for cheapskate wine lovers! Every bottle at this site is priced between $8 and $15; buy a case, and save 10 percent. Each wine entry includes the "Wine Spectator" rating. Shipping's a bit steep, but not as bad as at some sites. My overall opinion? This site rules.

Shipping: **$ $ $**   Navigation: 👍

JEWELRY AND GIFTS

Writing Instruments

Ashford.com

www.ashford.com

Ashford.com offers a nice assortment of distinctive writing instruments, including pens by my personal favorite, Mont Blanc. Prices aren't dirt cheap, but they're plenty reasonable. Free shipping!

Shipping: **$**   Navigation:

Bentley's

www.bentleys.com

In amidst the luggage at this site, you'll find deals on Mont Blanc, Waterman, and other pens.

Shipping: **$ $**   Navigation:

Costco Online

www.costco.com

You've probably heard of Costco, which is one of those warehouse clubs. Now Costco's online, offering members some great deals on some great merchandise (it costs a minimum of $40 to join, but if you shop there enough, prices will make up for it). Among other items, you'll find some nice prices on Mont Blanc pens.

Shipping: **$ $**   Navigation:

PenExpress.com

www.penexpress.com

PenExpress sells fountain pens and other fine writing instruments—including Parker, MontBlanc, Cross, Pelikan, and more—discounted 20 percent and shipped free of charge. You'll also find a pen auction on this site—check it out for even better deals!

Shipping: **$**   Navigation:

Health and Beauty

Beauty

Beauty Buys

www.beautybuys.com

Find hair products, cosmetics (including—pinch me—Chanel) and fragrances at discount prices. Shipping is free on orders of $60 or more!

Shipping: **$ $**   Navigation:

BeautyMax.com

http://beautymax.com

BeautyMax.com strives to provide all the best name brands in cosmetics and hair care products, at discount prices.

Shipping: **$ $**   Navigation:

Buy It on the Web

www.buyitontheweb.com

All types of beauty products, hawked by TV stars of old. Have skin like Judith Light, have teeth like Kim Alexis, defy age like Connie Sellecca —all at bargain prices!

Shipping: **$ $** Navigation:

Costco Online

www.costco.com

You've probably heard of Costco, which is one of those warehouse clubs. Now Costco's online, offering members some great deals on some great merchandise (it costs a minimum of $40 to join, but if you shop there enough, prices will make up for it). Among other items, you'll find some nice prices on cosmetics and skin-care products by Estee Lauder.

Shipping: **$ $** Navigation:

CheaperByTheDozen.com
www.cheaperbythedozen.com

At CheaperByTheDozen.com, you'll see up to three prices listed for each item: their regular low price, a discounted price that applies to all orders in quantities of 7 to 12, and a further discounted price for quantities over 12. You'll find products like Braun shavers, Oral B plaque removers, Teledyne Water Piks, PUR drinking water filter systems, and more.

Shipping: **$ $**   Navigation:

Drugstore.com
www.drugstore.com

While the prices aren't rock bottom, you'll find that you manage to save a bit on most of the products you buy at this site. Shipping is reasonable (it's free for prescription orders!).

Shipping: **$** Navigation:

FirstAuction
www.firstauction.com

Check out the Beauty category for cosmetics, skin care, fragrances, and bath and body products. Note: Shipping costs will vary by seller.

  Navigation:

Jeffrey Bruce Cosmetics
www.jeffreybrucecosmetics.com

Internet shoppers receive special discounts on cosmetics by Jeffrey Bruce, who's given countless makeovers on TV talk shows.

Shipping: **$ $**   Navigation:

Macys
www.macys.com

Find loads of cosmetics and skin-care accoutrements at Macys, including products by Lancome, Elizabeth Arden, Shiseido, Borghese, Clarins, Christian Dior, Biotherm, Fashion Fair and more—some of it 15 percent off.

Shipping: **$ $** Navigation:

More.com
www.more.com

This site is extremely easy to navigate, and has some great deals on all your health and beauty needs. Shipping's cheap, too!

Shipping: $ Navigation:

MyHairCare.com
www.mynailcare.com

Click the MyHairCare.com link to find deals on products by Paul Mitchell, Sebastian, Joico, and Back to Basics.

Shipping: $ $ Navigation:

mynailcare.com
www.mynailcare.com

Find manicure supplies at eminently reasonable prices here. Make sure to visit the Free Offers and Best Bets areas to see what's up for grabs!

Shipping: $ $ Navigation:

Quality King Distributors
www.qualityking.com

Click the Salon Hair and Nail link to find hair and nail care products at wholesale prices; click the Health and Beauty Aids link to find wholesale deals on all your tools for toilette. Be sure to check the Specials area for even bigger savings.

Shipping: $ $ Navigation:

Value America
www.valueamerica.com

If you're looking to buy something, there's a good chance Value America's looking to sell it—including cosmetics, hair and skin care products, bath and body goodies, and more. Be sure to check out the hot buys! Become a member (it's free) and save even more.

Shipping: $ Navigation:

Wal Mart Online
www.wal-mart.com

So there's no greeter, but that doesn't mean the online version of Wal Mart is a total bust. Click the Health and Medical link for great prices on vitamins, suncare, medical supplies, and more. Free shipping on some items (you'll know it when you see it).

Shipping: $ Navigation:

Nutritional Aids

Advanced Nutrition
www.n2health.com

Check out this one-stop source for high-quality vitamins, minerals, herbs, homeopathics, and sports nutrition products, all at competitive prices. Check the Specials area for deeper discounts.

Shipping: **$ $** Navigation:

Discount Sport Nutrition
www.sportsupplements.com

Find some great prices on vitamins and sports supplements here!

Shipping: **$ $** Navigation:

eNutrition
www.eNutrition.com

This site's filled with info about various aspects of nutrition; after you've read up on the latest news, skip over to the Vitamins and Supplements area to stock up on discounted goodies. Free shipping for orders over $15.

Shipping: **$** Navigation:

Fit-1.com
www.fit-1.com

In addition to selling exercise equipment—including cardio equipment, free weights, and accessories—at some nice prices, this site also discounts supplements.

Shipping: **$ $** Navigation:

Green Tree
www.greentree.com

Vitamins, supplements, and other nutritional aids on the cheap. Be sure to check the weekly specials for the best deals.

Shipping: **$** Navigation:

HealthShop.com
www.healthshop.com

Find nutrients and supplements from vitamin A to the mineral Zinc. Choose from hundreds of herbs, homeopathic remedies, body care items, and more. Click the Specials link for the best deals.

Shipping: **$ $**   Navigation:

HealthZone.com
www.healthzone.com

HealthZone.com sells more than 16,000 health-related products at 15 to 60 percent below suggested retail.

Shipping: **$ $**   Navigation:

J&J Health Foods and Sports Nutrition
www.getbigger.com

Find some great prices on vitamins, supplements, and the like, by brands like Met-RX, Nature's Best.

Shipping: **$**   Navigation:

Kmart.com
www.kmart.com

Click the Family and Fitness link to find vitamins, minerals, antioxidants, herbs, supplements, and personal hygiene items at low prices. Click the Hot Deals link for the best prices on all sorts of items!

Shipping: **$ $**   Navigation:

More.com
www.more.com

This site is extremely easy to navigate, and has some great deals on all your health needs. Shipping's cheap, too!

Shipping: **$**   Navigation:

MotherNature.com
www.mothernature.com

Save up to 50 percent on vitamins, supplements, and more. Free shipping on orders over $50! This is a great site.

Shipping: **$**   Navigation:

PeakHealth.net
www.peakhealth.net

Shipping's a bit steep, but you'll find some deals on lots of different vitamins, supplements, and more.

Shipping: **$ $ $** Navigation:

Royco
http://royco.net/

Find sports supplements at discounted prices. Be sure to click the On Sale link to see what's being blown out.

Shipping: **$ $**   Navigation:

Sports Nutrition and Vitamins 4 You
www.frontdoordistributors.com

Save up to 40 percent on sports nutrition products. Be sure to check out the Monthly Specials.

Shipping: **$ $**   Navigation:

The Vitamin Discount Connection
http://gem.lightlink.com/vitamin/

14,000 vitamins, herbs, and supplements at 25 to 45 percent off. Be sure to click the Bargain Basement link for some even better deals!

Shipping: **$ $** Navigation:

Vitamins Network
www.vitamins.net/

In addition to offering some nice prices on vitamins, minerals, and other nutritional aids, this site offers lots of information about health and fitness.

Shipping: **$ $** Navigation:

Warehouse Sport Sales
www.warehousesportsales.com

Find wholesale prices on sports supplements, vitamins, herbs, health and beauty aids, and homeopathy.

Shipping: **$ $** Navigation:

Whole Health Discount Center

www.health-pages.com

Buy vitamins, herbs, supplements, and other natural health products at 25 to 40 percent off.

Shipping: **$**   Navigation:

Optical Care

Aardvark Sunglasses Company
www.discountshades.com

Aardvark Sunglasses offers many models from the top designers (I.e. Furore, Gargoyles, Killer Loop, Hobie, Serengeti, Suncloud, H2Optix, Swiss Army Brand, [X]oor, Vuarnet, and Ray-Ban) at prices that are up to 30 percent off retail.

Shipping: **$ $ $**   Navigation:

ACLens.com
www.aclsoptical.com

Buy contact lenses, designer eyeglass frames (up to 70 percent off), and sunglasses (up to 60 percent off makers like Ray-Ban, Serengeti, Gargoyles, and more) at this site.

Shipping: **$ $**   Navigation:

Andy's Shade Shack
www.andysgarage.com

Click the Andy's Shade Shack link for humongous savings (I'm talking as much as 90 percent, here) on sunglasses by makers like Ray Ban and Revo.

Shipping: **$ $**   Navigation:

Ashford.com
www.ashford.com

Ashford.com offers a nice assortment of sunglasses for men and women, including shades by Ray-Ban, Revo, Serengeti, Versace, and Vuarnet. Prices aren't dirt cheap, but on the plus side, shipping is free in the USA.

Shipping: **$**   Navigation:

Contact Lens Connection
www.contactlensconnection.com

First-quality contact lenses at a fraction of the price. Brands include Acuvue, Bausch & Lomb, CIBA Vision, CooperVision, and more. Free shipping!

Shipping: **$**   Navigation:

HEALTH AND BEAUTY

Costco Online

www.costco.com

You've probably heard of Costco, which is one of those warehouse clubs. Now Costco's online, offering members some great deals on some great merchandise (it costs a minimum of $40 to join, but if you shop there enough, prices will make up for it). Among other items, you'll find some nice prices on sunglasses by makers like Revo and Gucci.

Shipping: **$ $**   Navigation:

Deals.com

www.deals.com

Click the Apparel & Jewelry link for deals on, well, apparel and jewelry. You'll find sunglasses here, too!

Shipping: **$**   Navigation:

Eyeglass Factory Outlet

www.eyeglassfactoryoutlet.com

Buy eyeglasses for the price of dirt. Eyeglass Factory Outlet sells single vision lenses with frames for $29.50, bifocal lenses with frames for $44.50, and progressive no-line bifocal lenses with frames for $69.50. Frame styles aren't what you'd call "up-to-the-minute" fashion-wise, and they don't put them all online, but the price is right...

Shipping: **$ $**   Navigation:

EYE-Mate

www.eyemate.com

Buy contact lenses online at great savings.

Shipping: **$ $**   Navigation:

EyeSite.com

www.eyesite.com

Buy sunglasses, prescription glasses, and contact lenses at a discount here. You can't shop and order online; instead, you must come to this site prepared with the exact make and model of the glasses you want to purchase, submit a request for price information, and call the toll-free number to order.

Shipping: **$ $**   Navigation:

jcrew.com

www.jcrew.com

Click the Clearance link to find J. Crew sunglasses and other goodies for up to 60 percent off!

Shipping: **$ $**　　　　　　　　Navigation:

Lens Express

www.lensexpress.com

Quick, cheap, and convenient! Buy your contacts over the Web at this site.

Shipping: **$ $**　　　　Navigation:

Lens1st

www.lensfirst.com

Lens1st boasts over 500,000 contacts in stock, ready to ship. They carry tons of brands of all types of lenses (no generics!), including disposables, tints, opaques, vials, torics, and gas permeables. Purchase four or more boxes or vials online and receive free shipping!

Shipping: **$**　　　　　　　　Navigation:

Opti Land

www.optiland.com

At Opti Land, you get factory-direct pricing (that's savings of 40 to 60 percent) on contact lenses, plus the latest frames and lenses. You'll find brands like Gant, Joan Collins, Stetson , Perry Ellis, Elizabeth Arden, Pierre Cardin, Calvin Klein, Giorgio Armani, Nautica, Tommy Hilfiger, Autoflex, and more. The downside: There's no catalog online; you have to know which glasses you want beforehand.

Shipping: **$ $**　　　　　　　　Navigation:

Quik Lens

www.quiklens.com

Find disposable, torics, specialty contact lenses, and more on the cheap here. Free shipping!

Shipping: **$**　　　　　　　　Navigation:

Shades.com

www.shades.com

Shades.com offers great prices on sunglasses by Revo, Ray Ban, Gucci, Serengeti, Gargoyles, and more.

Shipping: **$**   Navigation:

Shop4.com

www.shop4.com

You must become a member to save on this site, but once you do, you'll find goods for as much as 60 percent off retail. You'll find a variety of sunglasses, among other things. Click the Clearance link for the very best deals in every category.

Shipping: **$ $**   Navigation:

Site4Sight.com

www.site4sight.com

Save big (up to 70 percent) on sunglasses and prescription eyeglasses at Site4Sight. Frames are designer, and lenses aren't no-name either (Silor, Sola, Gentex, and Hoya).

Shipping: **$ $ $**   Navigation:

SunglassSite

www.sunglasssite.com

Save big on sunglasses by Bolle, Vuarnet, Ray Ban, Revo, and more. They'll beat any price!

Shipping: **$ $**   Navigation:

Value America

www.valueamerica.com   ☆

If you're looking to buy something, there's a good chance Value America's looking to sell it—including sunglasses. Be sure to check out the hot buys! Become a member (it's free) and save even more.

Shipping: **$**   Navigation:

Personal Hygiene

CheaperByTheDozen.com
www.cheaperbythedozen.com

At CheaperByTheDozen.com, you'll see up to three prices listed for each item: their regular low price, a discounted price that applies to all orders in quantities of 7 to 12, and a further discounted price for quantities over 12. You'll find products like Braun shavers, Oral B plaque removers, Teledyne Water Piks, PUR drinking water filter systems, and more.

Shipping: **$ $**   Navigation:

Drugstore.com
www.drugstore.com

While the prices aren't rock bottom, you'll find that you manage to save a bit on most of the products you buy at this site. Shipping is reasonable (it's free for prescription orders!).

Shipping: **$**   Navigation:

Harmon Discount
www.harmondiscount.com

This site's not much to look at, but you'll save 20 to 65 off the suggested retail prices.

Shipping: **$ $**   Navigation:

Kmart.com
www.kmart.com

Click the Family and Fitness link to find personal hygiene items at low prices. Click the Hot Deals link for the best prices on all sorts of items!

Shipping: **$ $**   Navigation:

More.com

www.more.com

This site is extremely easy to navigate, and has some great deals on all your health and beauty needs. Shipping's cheap, too!

Shipping: **$**   Navigation:

Planet RX

www.planetrx.com

Not everything at this cyber drugstore is dirt cheap, but some nice deals can be had. Be sure to check the specials in each category to see what's up for grabs; last time I checked, there were some "Buy This Item, Get This Other Item Free" deals. Free delivery in the continental USA when you buy a prescription item!

Shipping: **$**   Navigation:

Quality King Distributors

www.qualityking.com

Click the Health and Beauty Aids link to find wholesale deals on all your tools for toilette.

Shipping: **$ $**   Navigation:

Value America

www.valueamerica.com

If you're looking to buy something, there's a good chance Value America's looking to sell it—including personal hygiene items. Be sure to check out the hot buys! Become a member (it's free) and save even more.

Shipping: **$**   Navigation:

Wal Mart Online

www.wal-mart.com

So there's no greeter, but that doesn't mean the online version of Wal Mart is a total bust. Click the Health and Medical link for great prices on everything you need to avoid being smelly and dirty. Free shipping on some items (you'll know it when you see it).

Shipping: **$**   Navigation:

Pharmaceuticals

Drugstore.com

www.drugstore.com

While the prices aren't rock bottom, you'll find that you manage to save a bit on most of the products you buy at this site. Shipping is reasonable (it's free for prescription orders!).

Shipping: **$**   Navigation:

HEALTH AND BEAUTY

More.com

www.more.com ☆

This site is extremely easy to navigate, and has some great deals on all your health and beauty needs. Shipping's cheap, too!

Shipping: **$**   Navigation:

Planet RX

www.planetrx.com ☆

Not everything at this cyber drugstore is dirt cheap, but some nice deals can be had. Be sure to check the specials in each category to see what's up for grabs; last time I checked, there were some "Buy This Item, Get This Other Item Free" deals. Free delivery in the continental USA when you buy a prescription item!

Shipping: **$**   Navigation:

Value America

www.valueamerica.com ☆

If you're looking to buy something, there's a good chance Value America's looking to sell it—including prescription medicines. Be sure to check out the hot buys! Become a member (it's free) and save even more.

Shipping: **$**   Navigation:

Wal Mart Online

www.wal-mart.com

So there's no greeter, but that doesn't mean the online version of Wal Mart is a total bust. Click the Health and Medical link for great prices on vitamins, suncare, medical supplies, and more. Free shipping on some items (you'll know it when you see it).

Shipping: **$**   Navigation: 👍

BARGAIN SHOPPING Online

Babies and Kids

Apparel

A Denim Shop
www.denimshop.com

Find denim shirts, pants, jumpers, jackets, and more for the little wee ones.

Shipping: **$ $**   Navigation:

Amazon Auctions
www.amazon.com

Click the Auctions tab, and choose Clothing & Accessories. You'll find clothes for infants, and kids—plus maternity wear. Shoes and vintage clothes are also for sale! Shipping rates vary depending on who's selling the item you want to buy.

   Navigation:

BabyAnt.com
www.babyant.com

Find baby toys, clothes, furniture, and more at BabyAnt.com. Prices are more than reasonable!

Shipping: **$ $**   Navigation:

BabyCenter
www.babycenter.com

Visit BabyCenter's baby store for some good deals on baby accessories, apparel, and more. Check out the Clearance Center area for the best deals (the ducky rompers were my favorite).

Shipping: **$ $**   Navigation:

Big Dogs
www.bigdogs.com

Internet shoppers receive special deals and free gifts at this site, which features casual clothing for children.

Shipping: **$ $**   Navigation:

Bluefly

http://www.bluefly.com

Click the Kids link to save 25 to 75 percent on clothes for newborns, infants, toddlers, and big kids by brands like Beatrix Potter, Levi's, Converse, and more.

Shipping: **$ $** ⊕ Navigation:

Bugle Boy

www.bugleboy.com

Click the Clearance Sale link for great prices on Bugle Boy togs. Shipping's a little steep, but prices on goods may be low enough to make up for it.

Shipping: **$ $ $** Navigation:

Burlington Coat Factory Direct

www.coat.com/bcfdirect

Find some nice deals on clothes and (surprise!) coats for kids and babies. You'll also find luggage and tons of other stuff here!

Shipping: **$ $ $** Navigation:

Chock

www.chockcatalog.com

Save on underthings for children and babies here.

Shipping: **$ $** ⊕ Navigation:

Cute as a Bug

http://cuteasabug.com

Great clothes for wee ones (infants to 7-year-olds). Be sure to check out the weekly specials and the items on clearance.

Shipping: **$ $** ⊕ Navigation:

CyberShop

http://cybershop.com

Up to 80 percent off original prices! Click the Departments tab and select Apparel to find the deals. Click the CyberBargains link for the best prices on a variety of items.

Shipping: **$ $** Navigation:

DesignerOutlet.com
http://designeroutlet.com

Save 35 to 75 percent on clothes for everyone but the family pet (including the wee ones). Be sure to click the Specials button for the best deals.

Shipping: **$ $**　　　　　　　Navigation: 👍

eOffPrice
www.eoffprice.com

Buy kids clothes by big names—all at a discount. (Can you say 25 to 75 percent off?) Be sure to check out the Weekly Specials area for those special deals.

Shipping: **$ $ $**　　🌐　　　Navigation: 👍

iBaby.com
www.ibaby.com

iBaby.com has it all: toys, clothes, furniture, carriers, and more. Not everything's on sale, but good deals can be had.

Shipping: **$**　　　　　　　　Navigation: ✋

Kmart.com
www.kmart.com

Click the Baby of Mine link to find all sorts of baby goods—for sleepy time, feeding time, bath time, play time, learning time, and travel time—at low prices.

Shipping: **$ $**　　　　　　　Navigation: 👍

Lands End
www.landsend.com

Click the Overstocks link to save 20 to 68 percent on Lands End apparel for the whole family, including the kiddos! These garments are first quality, but must move to make room for new items in Lands End's stores.

Shipping: **$ $**　　🌐　　　Navigation: 👍

Macys
www.macys.com

Find loads of excellent apparel for babies and kids at Macys, some of it 15 percent off.

Shipping: **$ $**　　　　　　　Navigation: 👍

Outlet Mall

www.outletmall.com

Find great clothes for kids here! DKNY, Prada, Ralph Lauren, Armani, and more—at up to 85 percent off!

Shipping: **$ $**

Navigation:

PipKicks Clubhouse and Specialty Store

www.pipkicks.com

Save 20 to 30 percent on high-quality children's apparel and accessories. Be sure to check the Sales and Close-out Specials area.

Shipping: **$ $**

Navigation:

Shop4.com

www.shop4.com

You must become a member to save on this site, but once you do, you'll find goods for as much as 60 percent off retail. You'll find a nice selection of apparel for children—not to mention sunglasses, luggage, and shoes. Click the Clearance link for the very best deals in every category.

Shipping: **$ $**

Navigation:

Spiegel

www.spiegel.com/spiegel/shopping/ultimate

☆

Save 30 to 75 percent on Spiegel merchandise for children — plus mommies and daddies too!

Shipping: **$ $ $**

Navigation:

Timeke Funktional Kids Wear

www.timeke.com

☆

Timea Hynes, mother of two year old Ben and president and designer of Timeke Funktional Kids Wear, offers "designer" garments for parents on a budget. Be sure to visit the Clearance area for the best deals. Shipping's a bit steep, but it's a flat rate, so the more you order the better.

Shipping: **$ $ $**   ⊕   Navigation:

BABIES AND KIDS

Value America

www.valueamerica.com

If you're looking to buy something, there's a good chance Value America's looking to sell it—including items for babies, toys, apparel, and more. Be sure to check out the hot buys! Become a member (it's free) and save even more.

Shipping: **$**   Navigation:

WebClothes

www.webclothes.com

Save on clothing for infants, toddlers, and big boys and girls. Check the Bargain Bin area for the best deals.

Shipping: **$ $**   Navigation:

Yahoo! Auctions

http://auctions.yahoo.com

Click the Clothing & Accessories link to hunt down bargains among the items up for auction. You'll find a variety of accessories, athletic wear, and clothes for kids. Note that shipping rates vary by seller.

                    Navigation:

Baby Gear

BabyAnt.com

www.babyant.com

Find baby toys, clothes, furniture, and more at
BabyAnt.com. Prices are more than reasonable!

Shipping: **$ $**　　　　　　　　Navigation:

Baby Best Buy

www.babybestbuy.com

Save on everything for baby—bathing accoutrements,
bedding, cribs, diapers, feeding tools, high chairs,
strollers (need I go on?). Be sure to visit the Red Hot Deals
and Supersale areas for savings of up to 70 percent.

Shipping: **$ $**　　　　　　Navigation:

Baby Catalog of America

www.babycatalog.com

Shop Baby Catalog of America's Web site and save 10 to
50 percent on pregnancy, baby, and toddler products. Be
sure to shop the Specials and Closeouts areas for the best
deals. Buy a Baby Club membership and save even more.

Shipping: **$ $**　　　　　　　　Navigation:

BabyCenter

www.babycenter.com

Visit BabyCenter's baby store for some good deals on
baby accessories and more. Check out the Clearance
Center area for the best deals.

Shipping: **$ $**　　　　　　　　Navigation:

BabyFurniture.com

www.babyfurniture.com

Suit up your critter with all the best in baby gear, including
strollers, high chairs, cribs, car seats, and more.

Shipping: **$**　　　　　　　　Navigation:

BabyProductsOnline.com
www.babyproductsonline.com

Lowest prices on baby goods are guaranteed. Be sure to click the Specials link to find the best deals.

Shipping: **$**   Navigation:

Burlington Coat Factory Direct
www.coat.com/bcfdirect

Find some nice deals on baby furniture and accessories, not to mention toys and apparel.

Shipping: **$ $ $**   Navigation:

For a Kid
www.forakid.com

For a Kid, which offers low prices on all sorts of toys, furniture, and baby accessories, is part of Buy It Now (see the chapter on agents and other shopping services for more information). Become a member of Buy It Now for special deals at For a Kid. Certain products ship free of charge (you'll see a Free Shipping tag on those items).

Shipping: **$ $**   Navigation:

iBaby.com
www.ibaby.com

iBaby.com has it all: toys, clothes, furniture, carriers, and more. Not everything's on sale, but good deals can be had.

Shipping: **$**   Navigation:

Kmart.com
www.kmart.com

Click the Baby of Mine link to find all sorts of baby goods—for sleepy time, feeding time, bath time, play time, learning time, and travel time—at low prices.

Shipping: **$ $**   Navigation:

Shoppers Advantage
www.shoppersadvantage.com/

Click the Babies, Kids & Toys link for great savings. Note: you must register to become a member in order to cash in on the great savings on this site.

Shipping: **$ $**   Navigation:

Wal Mart Online
www.wal-mart.com

So there's no greeter, but that doesn't mean the online version of Wal Mart is a total bust. Click the Baby Shop link for great prices on stuff for baby. Free shipping on some items (you'll know it when you see it).

Shipping: **$**   Navigation: 👍

Value America
www.valueamerica.com

If you're looking to buy something, there's a good chance Value America's looking to sell it—including items for babies, toys, apparel, and more. Be sure to check out the hot buys! Become a member (it's free) and save even more.

Shipping: **$**   Navigation: 👍

Toys

3D Auction

www.3dauction.com

Find all sorts of goods at this auction site, including toys
and games. Shipping rates vary depending on who's selling the item you want to buy.

     Navigation:

A2Z Toys

www.a2ztoys.com

Find some nice prices on a decent selection of toys,
including Madeline (I love her!) dolls, plastic rockets, plastic models, Brio blocks, Ty Beanie Babies (enough,
already!), and more.

Shipping: **$ $**   Navigation:

Amazon Auctions

http://auctions.amazon.com

Choose Toys & Games to see what's available. Shipping
rates vary depending on who's selling the item you want
to buy.

     Navigation:

Archie McPhee

www.mcphee.com ☆

Where else can you buy Amish punching puppets, angel
snot, and push-button aloha hula girls?! Okay, so these
toys aren't so much for kids necessarily, but it does help
to be immature to appreciate them. You can afford to stock
up at these prices! Shipping's a little steep, but suck it up.
These toys are worth it.

Shipping: **$ $ $**   Navigation: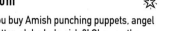

AuctionAddict.com
www.auctionaddict.com

Click the Toys link for deals on action figures, board games, marbles, model kits, and more. Shipping rates vary by seller.

 Navigation:

Auction Nation
www.auctionnation.com

Click the Toys link to find games, Beanie Babies, marbles, and more for auction. Note: Shipping costs may vary depending on who's selling the item you want to buy.

 Navigation:

Auctionscape
www.auctionscape.com

Click the Toys & Models link to see what's up for sale. You'll find action figures, Beanie Babies, dolls, games, models, and more. If it's video games you're after, check out the Video Games area instead. Note: shipping costs vary by seller.

 Navigation:

BabyAnt.com
www.babyant.com

Find baby toys, clothes, furniture, and more at BabyAnt.com. Prices are more than reasonable!

Shipping: **$ $** Navigation:

BabyCenter
www.babycenter.com

Visit BabyCenter's baby store for some good deals on toys. Check out the Clearance Center area for the best deals (the ducky rompers were my favorite).

Shipping: **$ $** Navigation:

Burlington Coat Factory Direct
www.coat.com/bcfdirect

In addition to finding (surprise!) coats at this site, you can hunt down some nice deals on toys.

Shipping: **$ $ $** Navigation:

BABIES AND KIDS

Children's Books
www.childsbooks.com/

Buy children's books at a discount here. Click the Products link to see what's on sale.

Shipping: **$ $** Navigation:

Costco Online
www.costco.com

You've probably heard of Costco, which is one of those warehouse clubs. Now Costco's online, offering members some great deals on some great merchandise (it costs a minimum of $40 to join, but if you shop there enough, prices will make up for it). Among other items, you'll find some nice prices on toys, including (whoo hoo!) Pokemon.

Shipping: **$ $** Navigation:

CyberShop
http://cybershop.com

Click the Departments tab and select Toys and Games to find deals on, well, toys and games. Up to 80 percent off original prices!

Shipping: **$ $** Navigation:

Discount Yo-Yos
http://st7.yahoo.com/yo-yo/index.html

Find tons of yo-yos and "yo-cessories" at this site, whose goal is to have the lowest yo-yo prices on the Web.

Shipping: **$** Navigation:

eBay
www.ebay.com

Click the Toys, Bean Bag Plush link to see what's available. During my last visit, this category featured 259,633 items! Note that shipping rates vary depending on who's selling the item you want to buy.

  Navigation:

edeal
www.edeal.com

Visit the Toys, Games & Hobbies area of this auction site to see what goodies are up for grabs. Note: shipping and handling charges may vary by seller.

  Navigation:

eswap

www.eswap.com

Click the Toys link to see what's up for grabs. Note that shipping rates may vary depending on who's selling the item you want to buy.

    Navigation:

etoys

www.etoys.com

This is the big daddy of toy sites; they're so sure about their prices that they'll refund the difference plus 10 percent if you find the item you bought cheaper at another site.

Shipping: **$ $**   Navigation:

FirstAuction

www.firstauction.com

The Toys category features loads of toys—Barbies, action figures, cars, trucks, trains, plush toys, and more—all up for auction. Note: Shipping costs will vary depending on the seller.

    Navigation:

For a Kid

www.forakid.com

For a Kid, which offers low prices on all sorts of toys, furniture, and baby accessories, is part of Buy It Now (see the chapter on agents and other shopping services for more information). Become a member of Buy It Now for special deals at For a Kid. Certain products ship free of charge (you'll see a Free Shipping tag on those items).

Shipping: **$ $**   Navigation:

Gameboard Online

www.gameboard.com

Still favor a rousing game of Risk in the real world over a virtual Doom experience? Then check out Gameboard Online, where you can find board games a-go-go.

Shipping: **$**   Navigation:

BABIES AND KIDS

Gund Outlet Stores

https://www.outletsonline.com/cgi-bin/SoftCart.exe/shop/gund/index.html?E+gund

Save up to 50 percent off of retail on snuggly stuffed animals when you order from this online catalog.

Shipping: $ $ $ Navigation:

iBaby.com

www.ibaby.com

iBaby.com has it all: toys, clothes, furniture, carriers, and more. Not everything's on sale, but good deals can be had.

Shipping: $ Navigation:

KBKids.com

www.kbkids.com

KBkids.com offers prices that are, on average, 60% less than the retail price AND shipping is free. This site rules.

Shipping: $ Navigation:

Kmart.com

www.kmart.com

Click the Baby of Mine link to find all sorts of baby goods—for sleepy time, feeding time, bath time, play time, learning time, and travel time—at low prices.

Shipping: $ $ Navigation:

Live and Learn

www.liveandlearn.com

This site's a little hard to get around, but you'll find all sorts of educational toys here, and at some more-than-nice prices.

Shipping: $ $ Navigation:

Online Smart Shopper

www.booneconsulting.com/general.htm

Select Toys from the drop-down list and click Search for below-wholesale prices. Selection is limited, and may vary.

Shipping: $ Navigation:

Owl's House

www.owlshouse.com

Find books, music, and toys for kids—all at 20 percent off. Be sure to check out the Sale area for even better deals.

Shipping: **$ $**   Navigation:

SellAndTrade.com

www.sellandtrade.com

Click Toys and Games to see what's on the auction block. Note that shipping charges will vary depending on the seller.

   Navigation:

Sellathon Auction Services

www.sellathon.com

Find collectible Hot Wheels, Beanies, Barbies, baseball cards, dolls, and more at this online auction. Note that shipping rates will vary by seller.

   Navigation:

Shop4.com

www.shop4.com

You must become a member to save on this site, but once you do, you'll find goods for as much as 60 percent off retail. Click the Toys link to find deals on all kinds of fun stuff. Click the Clearance link for the very best deals.

Shipping: **$ $**   Navigation:

Shoppers Advantage

www.shoppersadvantage.com

Click the Babies, Kids & Toys link for great savings. Note: you must register to become a member in order to cash in on the great savings on this site.

Shipping: **$ $**   Navigation:

Shopping.com

www.shopping.com

Click the Toys and Baby tab for deals on fun stuff for babies, toddlers, and big kids alike.

Shipping: **$ $**   Navigation:

SoldUSA.com

www.soldusa.com

You'll find lots of games and toys at this auction site, including action figures, dolls, board games, and vintage toys. Note that delivery charges may vary by seller.

  Navigation:

Sports 4 Kids

www.sports4kids.com

Find sporting goods for kids at discounted prices.

Shipping: **$ $**   Navigation:

toysmart.com

www.toysmart.com

Toysmart.com is so sure about its prices that it will refund 110% of the difference if you find an identical item with a lower price within 30 days of your purchase.

Shipping: **$ $ $** Navigation:

U Bid 4 It

www.ubid4it.com

Bid on toys—electronic, educational, and more—at this auction site. Note: Delivery rates vary by seller.

  Navigation:

Value America

www.valueamerica.com

If you're looking to buy something, there's a good chance Value America's looking to sell it—including toys and video games. Be sure to check out the hot buys! Become a member (it's free) and save even more.

Shipping: **$** Navigation:

Wal Mart Online

www.wal-mart.com

So there's no greeter, but that doesn't mean the online version of Wal Mart is a total bust. Click the Baby Shop and Toys & Hobby links for great prices on stuff for kids. Free shipping on some items (you'll know it when you see it).

Shipping: **$** Navigation:

Yahoo! Auctions
http://auctions.yahoo.com

Click the Toys & Games link to find goods like Beanie
Babies, video games, and other toys up for auction. Note
that shipping rates vary by seller.

Navigation: 👍

BARGAIN SHOPPING Online

Sports and Fitness

Apparel and Shoes

Amazon Auctions
http://auctions.amazon.com

Choose Sports & Recreation and select Apparel and Equipment to see what's available. Shipping rates vary depending on who's selling the item you want to buy.

    Navigation:

FirstAuction
www.firstauction.com   ☆

The Sports & Recreation category features loads of athletic shoes, camping and fishing gear, golf and tennis goodies, and necessities for the great outdoors—all up for auction. Note: shipping costs will vary depending on the seller.

    Navigation:

fogdog sports
www.fogdog.com   ☆

Visit the Super Deals area to save up to 50 percent on the sporting gear you need.

Shipping: **$**   Navigation:

gear.com
www.gear.com   ☆

Whether you're into skiing or tennis or kayaking, gear.com has the equipment you need at closeout prices.

Shipping: **$**   Navigation:

Just for Feet
www.feet.com

Find deals on athletic shoes of all types: cheerleading, aerobics, cross-training, and more. Be sure to visit the Combat Zone for savings of up to 70 percent! Shipping's a wee steep, but the savings make up for it.

Shipping: **$ $ $**   Navigation:

Live to Play Outdoor Sports Auction

www.livetoplay.com

Bid for apparel, bikes, camping equipment, climbing gear, eyewear, footwear, inline skates, backpacks, sleeping bags, skateboards, skis, snowboards, snowshoes, wetsuits, and more. Be sure to click the Today's Specials link for the best deals. This site features only new items supplied by select vendors.

    Navigation:

redtag.com

www.redtagoutlet.com

Find apparel, goodies for golfers, outdoor gear, and more.

Shipping: **$ $**   Navigation:

The Sports Place

www.thesportsplace.com
☆

The Sports Place, which offers low prices on all sorts of sporting goods, is part of Buy It Now (see the chapter on agents and other shopping services for more information). Become a member of Buy It Now for special deals at The Sports Place. Certain products ship free of charge (you'll see a Free Shipping tag on those items).

Shipping: **$ $**   Navigation:

The Urban Athlete

www.urban-athlete.com

Find tons of running shoes by makers like Asics, Brooks, and more, all at great prices. Free shipping!

Shipping: **$**   Navigation:

World Foot Locker

www.footlocker.com

Find shoes and togs for the sportsman, sportswoman, and sportskid at the supersite for Foot Locker, Lady Foot Locker, and Kids Foot Locker. Be sure to check out the Most Valuable Picks area for some seriously good deals!

Shipping: **$ $**   Navigation:

uBid Online Auction

www.ubid.com

Bid for sporting goods at this auction site. Note: Delivery charges may vary by seller.

 Navigation:

Value America

www.valueamerica.com

If you're looking to buy something, there's a good chance Value America's looking to sell it—including sporting goods. You'll find equipment for golf, baseball, football, basketball, soccer, camping, cycling, and more. Be sure to check out the hot buys! Become a member (it's free) and save even more.

Shipping: Navigation:

Yahoo! Auctions

http://auctions.yahoo.com

Click the Sports & Recreation link to find some serious sporting goods (last I checked, 36, 681 items were available in this area alone). Note that shipping rates vary by seller.

Navigation:

Billiards and Darts

Amazon Auctions
http://auctions.amazon.com

Choose Sports & Recreation and select Apparel and
Equipment to see what's available. Shipping rates vary
depending on who's selling the item you want to buy.

Navigation:

Costco Online
http://www.costco.com

You've probably heard of Costco, which is one of those
warehouse clubs. Now Costco's online, offering members
some great deals on some great merchandise (it costs a
minimum of $40 to join, but if you shop there enough,
prices will make up for it). Among other items, you'll find
some nice prices on sporting goods, including darts, bil-
liards supplies, and more.

Shipping: **$ $**
Navigation:

eBay
www.ebay.com ☆

Click the Miscellaneous link and check out the Sporting
Goods area to see what's for sale. Note that shipping rates
vary depending on who's selling the item you want to buy.

Navigation:

The Sports Place
www.thesportsplace.com ☆

The Sports Place, which offers low prices on all sorts of
sporting goods, is part of Buy It Now (see the chapter on
agents and other shopping services for more information). Become a member of Buy It Now for special deals at
The Sports Place. Certain products ship free of charge
(you'll see a Free Shipping tag on those items).

Shipping: **$ $** ⊕
Navigation:

uBid Online Auction

www.ubid.com

Bid for sporting goods at this auction site. Note: Delivery
charges may vary by seller.

          Navigation:

UsedSports.com

www.usedsports.com

Find tons of used sports equipment up for auction here.
Note that shipping rates vary by seller.

          Navigation:

Cycling

Amazon Auctions
http://auctions.amazon.com

Choose Sports & Recreation and select Apparel and Equipment to see what's available. Shipping rates vary depending on who's selling the item you want to buy.

   Navigation:

Bike Nashbar
www.bikenashbar.com

Bike Nashbar offers everything the cycling enthusiast could ever desire, much of which is at a pretty danged nice discount. Check out the Closeouts and Automatic Markdown areas for the best deals.

Shipping: **$ $**   Navigation:

Cambria Bicycle Outfitter
www.cambriabike.com

There's always a sale at this site, which gets its kicks blowing out cycling parts, apparel, and more. Shipping's a bit steep—especially if you live in the East—but prices may be good enough to make up for it, depending on what you buy.

Shipping: **$ $ $**   Navigation:

Costco Online
www.costco.com

You've probably heard of Costco, which is one of those warehouse clubs. Now Costco's online, offering members some great deals on some great merchandise (it costs a minimum of $40 to join, but if you shop there enough, prices will make up for it). Among other items, you'll find some nice prices on supplies and bikes.

Shipping: **$ $**   Navigation:

fogdog sports
www.fogdog.com

Visit the Super Deals area to save up to 50 percent on the sporting gear you need.

Shipping: **$**   Navigation:

gear.com
www.gear.com

If you're into cycling, gear.com has the equipment you need at closeout prices.

Shipping: **$**   Navigation:

Live to Play Outdoor Sports Auction
www.livetoplay.com

Bid for bikes and other cycling necessities. Be sure to click the Today's Specials link for the best deals. This site features only new items supplied by select vendors.

  Navigation:

Onsale.com
www.onsale.com

Click the Sports link under At Auction to find gear for cycling, as well as exercise equipment.

Shipping: **$ $**   Navigation:

Planet Bike Internet Auction
www.auction-land.com

Find bikes and parts—not to mention bags, racks, helmets, eyewear, and other cycling goodies—on the cheap at Planet Bike. This site is for serious cyclists and meanderers like me alike. Note that shipping rates vary by seller.

  Navigation:

PricePoint
www.pricepoint.com

Save up to 50 percent off suggested retail on bike parts, accessories, frames, clothing, shoes, and more. Be sure to check out the Internet specials.

Shipping: **$ $**   Navigation:

Recycler.com

www.recycler.com

Click the Sports & Hobbies link to browse the available items (there were 5,710 ads in this area last time I checked). Shipping rates vary by seller.

 Navigation:

REI Outlet

www.rei-outlet.com

Ah, REI. Who doesn't love that store? You'll be happy to know you can save big at the REI outlet on all your outdoor gear, including all the apparel you need for cycling. Shipping's cheap, too!

Shipping: **$** Navigation:

Shoppers Advantage

www.shoppersadvantage.com

Click the Sports & Health link for great savings on a huge variety of sporting goods for cycling. Note: you must register to become a member in order to cash in on the great savings on this site.

Shipping: **$ $** Navigation:

Shopping.com

www.shopping.com

Need a bike rack? Try clicking the Sports and Fitness tab to see what bargains are on Shopping.com. You're sure to find what you need.

Shipping: **$ $** Navigation:

Sporting Auction

www.sportingauction.com

No matter what your game is, you'll find the gear you need up for auction at this site. Note that delivery charges may vary by seller.

 Navigation:

The Sports Place

www.thesportsplace.com

The Sports Place, which offers low prices on all sorts of sporting goods, is part of Buy It Now (see the chapter on agents and other shopping services for more information). Become a member of Buy It Now for special deals at The Sports Place. Certain products ship free of charge (you'll see a Free Shipping tag on those items).

Shipping: **$ $** Navigation:

Tek Discount Warehouse

http://tekgallery.com

Click the Sports Goods link for deals on cycling equipment, rods, and reels.

Shipping: **$ $** Navigation:

uBid Online Auction

www.ubid.com

Bid for sporting goods for cycling at this auction site. Note: Delivery charges may vary by seller.

 Navigation:

Value America

www.valueamerica.com

If you're looking to buy something, there's a good chance Value America's looking to sell it—including sporting goods for cycling. Be sure to check out the hot buys! Become a member (it's free) and save even more.

Shipping: **$** Navigation:

Velo

www.velogear.com

Click the Specials button to find some nice prices on a variety of cycling apparel and collectibles. You won't find much in the way of parts and frames, but if you're in the market for a road racing mouse pad, this is the place to be.

Shipping: **$ $** Navigation:

UsedSports.com

www.usedsports.com

Find tons of used sports equipment for cycling up for auction here. Note that shipping rates vary by seller.

 Navigation:

Yahoo! Auctions

http://auctions.yahoo.com

Click the Sports & Recreation link to find some serious sporting goods (last I checked, 36, 681 items were available in this area alone). Note that shipping rates vary by seller.

Navigation:

Fitness Equipment

AuctionAddict.com

www.auctionaddict.com

Click the Sporting Goods link to see what fitness equipment is up for grabs. Shipping rates vary by seller.

 Navigation:

Bargain News Auctions Online

www.bnauctions.com

Click the Sporting Goods & Recreation link to find exercise equipment and more on the auction block. Delivery charges vary by seller.

 Navigation:

Buy It on the Web

www.buyitontheweb.com

Find your favorite "As-Seen-on-TV" sporting equipment (hello, Thigh Master) for sale here. Some items ship free!

Shipping: **$ $** Navigation:

eBay

www.ebay.com

Click the Miscellaneous link and check out the Sporting Goods area to see what's for sale. Note that shipping rates vary depending on who's selling the item you want to buy.

Navigation:

EZbid.com

www.ezbid.com

Visit the Sporting Goods area to find fitness equipment and more. Click the Rebate button to see which items on the site have rebates! Note: shipping and handling costs will differ depending on the seller.

 Navigation:

Fit-1.com

www.fit-1.com

Buy exercise equipment for your home (or if you happen
to own a health club, for your gym), including cardio
equipment, free weights, and accessories, at some nice
prices. Supplements are also available.

Shipping: **$ $**   Navigation:

Fitness Factory Outlet

www.fitnessfactory.com

Fitness Factory Outlet sells aerobic and strength-training
equipment, including a full line of free weights, weight
machines, treadmills, steppers, exercise bikes, home
gyms, and more. You'll save up to 50 percent on every
piece of high-quality strength training equipment they
carry. Free shipping on orders over $99 (except on iron
products).

Shipping: **$ $**   Navigation:

FitnessNet

www.fitnessnet.com

You'll find treadmills, steppers, stationary bikes, weight
machines, and more—all at prices lower than fitness
discounters'. Be sure to check out the Blowout Specials
area for some even better deals. Shipping may seem
steep, but remember that you're ordering things that
weigh a zillion pounds—and the good prices make up
for it, anyway.

Shipping: **$ $**   Navigation:

Fitness Wholesale

www.fwonline.com

Find equipment for all sorts of sporting endeavors, from
boxing to yoga (I confess—I ordered a yoga mat). Be sure
to check out the Clearance area!

Shipping: **$ $**   Navigation:

Onsale.com

www.onsale.com

Click the Sports link under At Auction to find exercise
equipment.

Shipping: **$ $**   Navigation:

SPORTS AND FITNESS

Recycler.com

www.recycler.com

Click the Sports & Hobbies link to browse the available items (there were 5,710 ads in this area last time I checked). Shipping rates vary by seller.

 Navigation:

Shoppers Advantage

www.shoppersadvantage.com

Click the Sports & Health link for great savings on a huge variety of fitness equipment. Note: you must register to become a member in order to cash in on the great savings on this site.

Shipping: **$ $**   Navigation:

Shopping.com

www.shopping.com

Need a even more exercise equipment? Try clicking the Sports and Fitness tab to see what bargains are on Shopping.com.

Shipping: **$ $**   Navigation:

Sporting Auction

www.sportingauction.com

No matter what your game is, you'll find the fitness equipment you need up for auction at this site. Note that delivery charges may vary by seller.

 Navigation:

uBid Online Auction

www.ubid.com

Bid for exercise equipment at this auction site. Note: Delivery charges may vary by seller.

 Navigation:

UsedSports.com

www.usedsports.com

Find tons of used fitness equipment up for auction here. Note that shipping rates vary by seller.

 Navigation:

Value America

www.valueamerica.com

If you're looking to buy something, there's a good chance Value America's looking to sell it—including fitness equipment. Be sure to check out the hot buys! Become a member (it's free) and save even more.

Shipping: **$**   Navigation:

Yahoo! Auctions

http://auctions.yahoo.com

Click the Sports & Recreation link to find some serious exercise equipment (last I checked, 36, 681 items were available in this area alone). Note that shipping rates vary by seller.

        Navigation:

SPORTS AND FITNESS

Golf

3D Auctions
www.3dauction.com

Find all sorts of goods at this auction site, which leans heavily toward golf (or at least it did last I visited). Shipping rates vary depending on who's selling the item you want to buy.

  Navigation:

Aberdeen Golf Inc.
www.aberdeengolfinc.com

Aberdeen Golf Inc.'s wholesale discounted golf prices are now available to the general public. Find woods, irons, putters, wedges, shafts, grips, and accessories here. Free shipping!

Shipping: **$** Navigation:

Amazon Auctions
http://auctions.amazon.com

Choose Sports & Recreation and select Apparel and Equipment to see what's available for golfers. Shipping rates vary depending on who's selling the item you want to buy.

  Navigation:

AuctionAddict.com
www.auctionaddict.com

Click the Sporting Goods link to see what golf gear is up for grabs. Shipping rates vary by seller.

  Navigation:

Bid.com

www.bid.com

Click the Sports link at this auction site for rock-bottom prices on equipment galore. Bids start at $1 for many items! Note: Charges for delivery vary by seller.

 Navigation:

chipshot.com

www.chipshot.com

Buy custom clubs by chipshot.com at about half the price of comparable brand-name clubs.

Shipping: **$ $** Navigation:

deals.com

www.deals.com

Click the Sports & Fitness link for deals on golf clubs and more.

Shipping: **$** Navigation:

Discount-Golf.com

www.discount-golf.com

Discount-golf.com sells high-quality golf equipment that is made with the same design and quality as big name brands, but for 60 percent less.

Shipping: **$ $** Navigation:

Drewco

www.drewcogolf.com

This site calls itself "The Pro Shop Liquidator," promising "Pro-Line Golf Equipment at Discount Pricing." Be sure to check out the closeout items and super specials for the best deals!

Shipping: **$ $** Navigation:

eBay

www.ebay.com ☆

Click the Miscellaneous link and check out the Sporting Goods area to see what's for sale. Note that shipping rates vary depending on who's selling the item you want to buy.

 Navigation:

Exclusively Golf

www.exclusivelygolf.com

For some good deals, check the Super Specials and Used Equipment areas of this site, which is devoted exclusively to golfing equipment for women.

Shipping: **$ $**   Navigation:

EZbid.com

www.ezbid.com

Visit the Sporting Goods area to find goods for golfers. Click the Rebate button to see which items on the site have rebates! Note: shipping and handling costs will differ depending on the seller.

     Navigation:

FirstAuction

www.firstauction.com

The Sports & Recreation category features loads of golf goodies and other necessities—all up for auction. Note: shipping costs will vary depending on the seller.

     Navigation:

fogdog sports

www.fogdog.com

Visit the Super Deals area to save up to 50 percent on the golf gear you need.

Shipping: **$**   Navigation:

gear.com

www.gear.com

If you're into golf, gear.com has the equipment you need at closeout prices.

Shipping: **$**   Navigation:

Golf Auction USA

www.golfauctionusa.com

New and used irons, woods, wedges, putters, accessories, and more—all up for auction. Note: Costs for shipping and handling vary by seller.

     Navigation:

Golf Bargains
www.golfbargains.com

Golf Bargains features quality golf equipment at amazing prices. You'll find gear from makers like Adams, Bag Boy, Callaway, Cleveland, Cobra, Lynx, Mizuno, Odyssey, Pole Kat, Ping, Sun Mountain, Top Flite, Taylor Made, Titleist, Tommy Armour, Wilson and more. Free shipping in the USA!

Shipping: **$**   Navigation:

Golf Club Exchange
www.golfclubexchange.com

Buy used golf clubs from other golfers here. Costs for shipping and handling vary by seller.

Navigation:

Golf Clubs Fore Less
www.clubs4less.com

At Golf Clubs Fore Less, you'll find a line of golf clubs manufactured with the highest-quality materials, and excellent design, but at a fraction of the price of name brands (as in 40 to 60 percent less). Their club heads, shafts and grips are made of the exact same materials as the major brands and are manufactured in the same foundries.

Shipping: **$ $**   Navigation:

Golf Manufacturers Outlet
www.golfsoutlet.com

This site's golf products, which are manufacturers overstocks, are 30 percent off retail at a minimum! Click the Clearance link for the best deals. Free shipping for online orders.

Shipping: **$**   Navigation:

GolfBalls.com
www.golfballs.com   ☆

Find new and used golf balls at deep discounts. Click the Our Best Deals link for, uh, their best deals.

Shipping: **$ $**   Navigation:

GolfBids.com
www.golfbids.com

Find golf equipment and apparel for men, women, and kids, all up for auction. Costs for shipping and handling will vary by seller. Also check out the travel packages to see what's up for grabs!

Navigation:

GolfDiscount.com
www.golfdiscount.com

GolfDiscount.com is an authorized reseller of new equipment from all the name-brand manufacturers, including Callaway, Taylor Made, Cobra, Orlimar, Titleist, Ping, Top-Flite, Adams, Power/Bilt, and so on. No "copy cat" clubs here.

Shipping: $ $ Navigation:

GolfOutlet.com
www.golfoutlet.com

Buy all the golf paraphernalia you could ever want, for less. Click the Monthly Specials link for the best deals.

Shipping: $ $ Navigation:

GolfPeddler.com
www.golfpeddler.com   ☆

Save up to 50 percent on new and used golf clubs, bags, and other golf equipment. Sellers pay shipping charges, meaning you don't have to!

Shipping: $ Navigation:

iGo International Golf Outlet
www.igogolf.com

Before you hit the links, check out this site for deals on equipment and paraphernalia. Be sure to check out the Bargain Barrel.

Shipping: $ $ 🌐   Navigation:

Joe's Golf House
www.joegolf.com

Check out Joe's Golf House for low prices on the finest in golf equipment. Be sure to check out the Hot Specials!

Shipping: $ $ $ Navigation: 👎

New York Golf Center

www.newyorkgolf.com

New York Golf Center superstores have gone online; they offer golf clubs and accessories at discount prices. Be sure to click the Specials link for the best deals.

Shipping: **$ $**   Navigation:

Northway 8 Golf Shop

www.northway8golf.com

Find golf shoes, clubs, bags, and accessories here at some very nice prices. Be sure to check out the Hot Deals area!

Shipping: **$ $**   Navigation:

Onsale.com

www.onsale.com

Click the Sports link under At Auction to find gear for golf and other sporting equipment.

Shipping: **$ $**   Navigation:

Recycler.com

www.recycler.com

Click the Sports & Hobbies link to browse the available items (there were 5,710 ads in this area last time I checked). Shipping rates vary by seller.

    Navigation:

redtag.com

www.redtagoutlet.com

Find apparel and goodies for golfers.

Shipping: **$ $**   Navigation:

Shoppers Advantage

www.shoppersadvantage.com

Click the Sports & Health link for great savings on a huge variety of golf equipment. Note: you must register to become a member in order to cash in on the great savings on this site.

Shipping: **$ $**   Navigation:

Shopping.com
www.shopping.com

Need a new set of clubs? Try clicking the Sports and Fitness tab to see what bargains are on Shopping.com.

Shipping: **$ $**   Navigation:

Sporting Auction
www.sportingauction.com

No matter what your game is, you'll find the gear you need up for auction at this site. Note that delivery charges may vary by seller.

          Navigation:

The Sports Place
www.thesportsplace.com

The Sports Place, which offers low prices on all sorts of sporting goods, is part of Buy It Now (see the chapter on agents and other shopping services for more information). Become a member of Buy It Now for special deals at The Sports Place. Certain products ship free of charge (you'll see a Free Shipping tag on those items).

Shipping: **$ $**   🌐   Navigation:

Tek Discount Warehouse
http://tekgallery.com

Click the Sports Goods link for deals on golf clubs.

Shipping: **$ $**   Navigation:

TGW.com
www.tgw.com

Save a bundle on clubs, balls, shoes, bags, books, videos, and more.

Shipping: **$ $**   🌐   Navigation:

uBid Online Auction
www.ubid.com

Bid for sporting goods at this auction site. Note: Delivery charges may vary by seller.

          Navigation:

UsedSports.com
www.usedsports.com

Find tons of used sports equipment up for auction here.
Note that shipping rates vary by seller.

 Navigation:

Value America
www.valueamerica.com

If you're looking to buy something, there's a good chance
Value America's looking to sell it—including equipment
for golf. Be sure to check out the hot buys! Become a
member (it's free) and save even more.

Shipping: **$**   Navigation:

Virtual Fairway
www.virtual-fairway.com

Virtual Fairway sells quality, high grade, used golf balls—
typically at 50 percent off retail prices for new balls.

Shipping: **$ $**   Navigation:

Yahoo! Auctions
http://auctions.yahoo.com

Click the Sports & Recreation link to find some serious
sporting goods (last I checked, 36, 681 items were available in this area alone). Note that shipping rates vary by
seller.

Navigation:

Inline Skating and Skateboarding

Amazon Auctions

http://auctions.amazon.com

Choose Sports & Recreation and select Apparel and Equipment to see what's available. Shipping rates vary depending on who's selling the item you want to buy.

 Navigation: 👍

The Cheap Skater

www.cheapskater.com

Find great prices on past-season skates and gear. Free shipping on orders over $25!

Shipping: **$** Navigation: ✋

Costco Online

www.costco.com

You've probably heard of Costco, which is one of those warehouse clubs. Now Costco's online, offering members some great deals on some great merchandise (it costs a minimum of $40 to join, but if you shop there enough, prices will make up for it). Among other items, you'll find some nice prices on sporting goods, including skateboards.

Shipping: **$ $** Navigation: 👍

eBay

www.ebay.com ☆

Click the Miscellaneous link and check out the Sporting Goods area to see inline skates and skateboards for sale. Note that shipping rates vary depending on who's selling the item you want to buy.

 Navigation: 👍

fogdog sports

www.fogdog.com

Visit the Super Deals area to save up to 50 percent on the skating gear you need.

Shipping: **$**   Navigation:

gear.com

www.gear.com

Whether you're into inline skating or skateboarding, gear.com has the equipment you need at closeout prices.

Shipping: **$**   Navigation:

Live to Play Outdoor Sports Auction

www.livetoplay.com

Bid for apparel, inline skates, backpacks, skateboards, snowboards, and more. Be sure to click the Today's Specials link for the best deals. This site features only new items supplied by select vendors.

      Navigation:

Recycler.com

www.recycler.com

Click the Sports & Hobbies link to browse the available items (there were 5,710 ads in this area last time I checked). Shipping rates vary by seller.

      Navigation:

Shoppers Advantage

www.shoppersadvantage.com

Click the Sports & Health link for great savings on a huge variety of inline skating and skateboarding items. Note: you must register to become a member in order to cash in on the great savings on this site.

Shipping: **$ $**   Navigation:

Shopping.com

www.shopping.com

Need a snowboard? Try clicking the Sports and Fitness tab to see what bargains are on Shopping.com.

Shipping: **$ $**   Navigation:

SPORTS AND FITNESS

Sporting Auction

www.sportingauction.com

No matter what your game is, you'll find the gear you need up for auction at this site. Note that delivery charges may vary by seller.

 Navigation:

The Sports Place

www.thesportsplace.com

The Sports Place, which offers low prices on all sorts of sporting goods, is part of Buy It Now (see the chapter on agents and other shopping services for more information). Become a member of Buy It Now for special deals at The Sports Place. Certain products ship free of charge (you'll see a Free Shipping tag on those items).

Shipping: **$ $**   Navigation:

UsedSports.com

www.usedsports.com

Find tons of used sports equipment up for auction here. Note that shipping rates vary by seller.

 Navigation:

Yahoo! Auctions

http://auctions.yahoo.com

Click the Sports & Recreation link to find some serious sporting goods (last I checked, 36, 681 items were available in this area alone). Note that shipping rates vary by seller.

 Navigation:

Outdoors

American Wilderness Gear Online

www.awgear.com

Find packs, tents, and more outdoor gear at this nice-looking site. Be sure to visit the On Sale area!

Shipping: **$ $**   Navigation:

Amazon Auctions

http://auctions.amazon.com

Choose Sports & Recreation and select Apparel and Equipment to see what outdoor gear is available. Shipping rates vary depending on who's selling the item you want to buy.

     Navigation:

Armed Forces Merchandise Outlet

www.afmo.com

Save big on survival and outdoor gear, courtesy of your U.S. armed forces. (Heck, your tax dollars are probably paying for the discount, so you may as well take advantage of it.) New and used items available.

Shipping: **$ $ $**   Navigation:

AuctionAddict.com

www.auctionaddict.com

Click the Sporting Goods link to see what's up for grabs. Subcategories include Fishing and Hunting, Golf, and more. Shipping rates vary by seller.

     Navigation:

Backcountry Gear

www.backcountrygear.com   ☆

Find outdoor apparel, backpacks, tents, sleeping bags, hydration systems, accessories, and more at this comprehensive site. Be sure to check out the Clearance area.

Shipping: **$**   Navigation: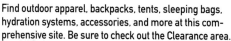

SPORTS AND FITNESS

The Backcountry Store

www.bcstore.com

Buy tents, sleeping bags, packs, stoves, cookware, and that yucky dehydrated food here. Be sure to check out the sales. Free shipping!

Shipping: **$**   Navigation:

Blowout Knives

www.blowoutknives.com

Save 40 to 50 percent on knives at this site.

Shipping: **$ $**   Navigation:

Campmor

www.campmor.com

Find tons of camping gear here—first aid equipment, packs, sleeping gear, water filtration systems, and more. Be sure to visit the Web Bargains area!

Shipping: **$ $**   Navigation:

Costco Online

www.costco.com

You've probably heard of Costco, which is one of those warehouse clubs. Now Costco's online, offering members some great deals on some great merchandise (it costs a minimum of $40 to join, but if you shop there enough, prices will make up for it). Among other items, you'll find some nice prices on sporting goods and camping gear.

Shipping: **$ $**   Navigation:

DDLures.com

www.ddlures.com

Check out DDLures.com to buy lures direct from the D&D Lures or Venom Manufacturing. This site promises top-quality lures at the lowest prices on the Internet. Shipping's a bit steep, but the prices may make up for it.

Shipping: **$ $ $**   Navigation:

eBay

www.ebay.com

Click the Miscellaneous link and check out the Sporting Goods area to see what outdoor gear is for sale. Note that shipping rates vary depending on who's selling the item you want to buy.

 Navigation:

EZbid.com

www.ezbid.com

Visit the Sporting Goods area to outdoor gear. Click the Rebate button to see which items on the site have rebates! Note: shipping and handling costs will differ depending on the seller.

 Navigation:

FirstAuction

www.firstauction.com

The Sports & Recreation category features loads camping and fishing gear, and necessities for the great outdoors—all up for auction. Note: shipping costs will vary depending on the seller.

 Navigation:

fogdog sports

www.fogdog.com

Visit the Super Deals area to save up to 50 percent on the outdoor gear you need.

Shipping: **$**   Navigation:

gear.com

www.gear.com

If you're into camping, gear.com has the equipment you need at closeout prices.

Shipping: **$**   Navigation:

Just Good Books

www.justgoodbooks.com

Just Good Books has one of the largest inventories of new and used sporting books (site categories include Fly Fishing, Hunting, Guns, and Dogs). Shipping's a bit steep, but if you're looking for these hard-to-find books, it may still be worth it.

Shipping: **$ $ $** Navigation:

Kirkham's Outdoor Products

www.kirkhams.com

Find cool outdoor products at a discount. Be sure to check out the Cool Stuff—Less Bucks area!

Shipping: **$ $** Navigation:

Live to Play Outdoor Sports Auction

www.livetoplay.com

Bid for apparel, bikes, camping equipment, climbing gear, eyewear, footwear, inline skates, backpacks, sleeping bags, skateboards, skis, snowboards, snowshoes, wetsuits, and more. Be sure to click the Today's Specials link for the best deals. This site features only new items supplied by select vendors.

  Navigation:

NRS

www.nrsweb.com

Find everything you need for river sports—life jackets, kayaks, oars, and paddles—and camping. Be sure to check out the great deals under the Sale area.

Shipping: **$ $**   Navigation:

The Outdoor Gear Exchange

www.gearx.com

Save 20 to 50 percent on used, closeout, and seconds gear for backpacking, climbing, mountaineering, and camping gear.

Shipping: **$ $**   Navigation:

Out In Style
http://order.outinstyle.com

Out In Style has a tremendous inventory of camping, hunting, law enforcement, and military supplies—they stock a large inventory of military surplus goods. Be sure to hit the monthly specials.

Shipping: **$ $**   Navigation:

Rail Riders
www.railriders.com

Thrifty adventure seekers, look no farther. Rail Riders offers apparel for the ballsy members of our species. If your desire is to climb Everest or to enter one of those adventure race events they always feature on the Discovery Channel, this is the site for you. Be sure to see what's on clearance.

Shipping: **$ $**   Navigation:

Recycler.com
www.recycler.com

Click the Sports & Hobbies link to browse classified ads for used items (there were 5,710 ads in this area last time I checked). Shipping rates vary by seller.

Navigation:

redtag.com
www.redtagoutlet.com

Find apparel and outdoor gear here.

Shipping: **$ $**   Navigation:

REI Outlet
www.rei-outlet.com   ☆

Ah, REI. Who doesn't love that store? You'll be happy to know you can save big at the REI outlet on all your outdoor gear. Shipping's cheap, too!

Shipping: **$**   Navigation:

Shoppers Advantage
www.shoppersadvantage.com   ☆

Click the Sports & Health link for great savings on a huge variety of outdoor gear. Note: you must register to become a member in order to cash in on the great savings on this site.

Shipping: **$ $**   Navigation:

Shopping.com

www.shopping.com

Need a tent? Try clicking the Sports and Fitness tab to see what bargains are on Shopping.com.

Shipping: **$ $**   Navigation:

SoldUSA.com

www.soldusa.com

You'll find lots of items for hunters and fishermen at this auction site. Note that delivery charges may vary by seller.

Shipping: **$ $**   Navigation:

Sporting Auction

www.sportingauction.com

No matter what your game is, you'll find the gear you need up for auction at this site. Note that delivery charges may vary by seller.

                    Navigation:

Sport Knives

http://sportknives.com

Find some great prices on knives for hunting, fishing, and the like! Be sure to click the Specials link for the best deals.

Shipping: **$ $ $**   Navigation:

The Sportsman's Guide

www.sportsmansguide.com

All you hunting, fishing, and camping types will really dig this site,.It offers gear and clothes at rock bottom prices.

Shipping: **$ $ $**   Navigation:

Tek Discount Warehouse

http://tekgallery.com

Click the Sports Goods link for deals on rods and reels.

Shipping: **$ $**   Navigation:

Tents4Less.com
www.tents4less.com

Like the site says: name-brand Coleman tents at discount prices.

Shipping: **$ $**

Navigation:

uBid Online Auction
www.ubid.com

Bid for sporting goods at this auction site. Note: Delivery charges may vary by seller.

 Navigation:

UsedSports.com
www.usedsports.com ☆

Find tons of used outdoor equipment up for auction here. Note that shipping rates vary by seller.

 Navigation:

Value America
www.valueamerica.com

If you're looking to buy something, there's a good chance Value America's looking to sell it—including equipment for camping. Be sure to check out the hot buys! Become a member (it's free) and save even more.

Shipping: **$**

Navigation:

Yahoo! Auctions
http://auctions.yahoo.com

Click the Sports & Recreation link to find some serious sporting goods (last I checked, 36, 681 items were available in this area alone). Note that shipping rates vary by seller.

 Navigation:

Team Sports

A.D. Starr

www.adstarr.com

A.D. Starr is a great place to shop for baseball and softball equipment whether you run a league with a zillion teams or run a household with a single kid. They ship everything factory direct and free.

Shipping: **$** Navigation:

Amazon Auctions

http://auctions.amazon.com

Choose Sports & Recreation and select Apparel and Equipment to see what's available. Shipping rates vary depending on who's selling the item you want to buy.

 Navigation:

Bid.com

www.bid.com

Click the Sports link at this auction site for rock-bottom prices on equipment galore. Bids start at $1 for many items! Note: Charges for delivery vary by seller.

 Navigation:

Bids Wanted

www.bidswanted.com

Click the Sports & Fitness links for auction bargains on equipment and memorabilia. Charges for delivery vary by seller.

 Navigation:

Big Toe Sports

www.bigtoesports.com

Find clothing, shoes, and equipment for soccer. Check the Bargain Basement for the best deals!

Shipping: **$ $** Navigation:

eBay

www.ebay.com

Click the Miscellaneous link and check out the Sporting Goods area to see what's for sale. Note that shipping rates vary depending on who's selling the item you want to buy.

 Navigation:

fogdog sports

www.fogdog.com

Visit the Super Deals area to save up to 50 percent on the sporting gear you need.

Shipping: **$** Navigation:

gear.com

www.gear.com

Whether you're into skiing or tennis or kayaking, gear.com has the equipment you need at closeout prices.

Shipping: **$** Navigation:

Onsale.com

www.onsale.com

Click the Sports link under At Auction to find gear for golf, tennis, cycling, and team sports, not to mention exercise equipment.

Shipping: **$ $** Navigation:

Shoppers Advantage

www.shoppersadvantage.com

Click the Sports & Health link for great savings on a huge variety of sporting goods. Note: you must register to become a member in order to cash in on the great savings on this site.

Shipping: **$ $** Navigation:

Shopping.com

www.shopping.com

Need a bike rack? What about a snowboard? Try clicking the Sports and Fitness tab to see what bargains are on Shopping.com.

Shipping: **$ $** Navigation:

Soccer Partners' Discount Soccer
http://st7.yahoo.com/discountsoccer/index.html

Save on soccer jerseys, balls, bags, and other cool stuff.

Shipping: **$ $**   Navigation:

Sporting Auction
www.sportingauction.com ☆

No matter what your game is, you'll find the gear you
need up for auction at this site. Note that delivery charges
may vary by seller.

Navigation:

The Sports Place
www.thesportsplace.com ☆

The Sports Place, which offers low prices on all sorts of
sporting goods, is part of Buy It Now (see the chapter on
agents and other shopping services for more information). Become a member of Buy It Now for special deals at
The Sports Place. Certain products ship free of charge
(you'll see a Free Shipping tag on those items).

Shipping: **$ $**   Navigation:

uBid Online Auction
www.ubid.com

Bid for sporting goods at this auction site. Note: Delivery
charges may vary by seller.

Navigation:

UsedSports.com
www.usedsports.com ☆

Find tons of used sports equipment up for auction here.
Note that shipping rates vary by seller.

Navigation:

Value America
www.valueamerica.com

If you're looking to buy something, there's a good chance
Value America's looking to sell it—including sporting goods.
You'll find equipment for golf, baseball, football, basketball,
soccer, camping, cycling, and more. Be sure to check out the
hot buys! Become a member (it's free) and save even more.

Shipping: **$**   Navigation:

Yahoo! Auctions
http://auctions.yahoo.com

Click the Sports & Recreation link to find some serious
sporting goods (last I checked, 36, 681 items were available in this area alone). Note that shipping rates vary by
seller.

   Navigation:

Tennis

Amazon Auctions
http://auctions.amazon.com

Choose Sports & Recreation and select Apparel and Equipment to see what tennis gear is available. Shipping rates vary depending on who's selling the item you want to buy.

 Navigation:

Bid.com
www.bid.com

Click the Sports link at this auction site for rock-bottom prices on tennis equipment. Bids start at $1 for many items! Note: Charges for delivery vary by seller.

Navigation:

EZbid.com
www.ezbid.com

Visit the Sporting Goods area to find tennis equipment. Click the Rebate button to see which items on the site have rebates! Note: shipping and handling costs will differ depending on the seller.

Navigation:

FirstAuction
www.firstauction.com ☆

The Sports & Recreation category features loads of tennis goodies—all up for auction. Note: shipping costs will vary depending on the seller.

Navigation:

fogdog sports
www.fogdog.com ☆

Visit the Super Deals area to save up to 50 percent on the tennis gear you need.

Shipping: $ ⊕ Navigation:

gear.com

www.gear.com

If you're into tennis, gear.com has the equipment you need at closeout prices.

Shipping: **$** Navigation: 👍

Onsale.com

www.onsale.com

Click the Sports link under At Auction to find gear for tennis, as well as exercise equipment.

Shipping: **$ $** Navigation: 👍

Recycler.com

www.recycler.com

Click the Sports & Hobbies link to browse the available items (there were 5,710 ads in this area last time I checked). Shipping rates vary by seller.

 Navigation: 👍

Shoppers Advantage

www.shoppersadvantage.com

Click the Sports & Health link for great savings on a huge variety of tennis gear. Note: you must register to become a member in order to cash in on the great savings on this site.

Shipping: **$ $** Navigation: 👍

The Sports Place

www.thesportsplace.com

Click the Sports Place, which offers low prices on all sorts of sporting goods, is part of Buy It Now (see the chapter on agents and other shopping services for more information). Become a member of Buy It Now for special deals at The Sports Place. Certain products ship free of charge (you'll see a Free Shipping tag on those items).

Shipping: **$ $** Navigation: 👍

Tek Discount Warehouse

http://tekgallery.com

Click the Sports Goods link for deals on tennis rackets.

Shipping: **$ $** Navigation:

uBid Online Auction

www.ubid.com

Bid for tennis gear at this auction site. Note: Delivery charges may vary by seller.

 Navigation:

UsedSports.com

www.usedsports.com

Find tons of used tennis equipment up for auction here. Note that shipping rates vary by seller.

 Navigation:

Yahoo! Auctions

http://auctions.yahoo.com

Click the Sports & Recreation link to find some serious sporting goods (last I checked, 36, 681 items were available in this area alone). Note that shipping rates vary by seller.

Navigation:

Water Sports

Amazon Auctions
http://auctions.amazon.com

Choose Sports & Recreation and select Apparel and Equipment to see what water sports equipment is available. Shipping rates vary depending on who's selling the item you want to buy.

 Navigation:

eBay
www.ebay.com ☆

Click the Miscellaneous link and check out the Sporting Goods area to see what's for sale. Note that shipping rates vary depending on who's selling the item you want to buy.

 Navigation:

fogdog sports
www.fogdog.com ☆

Visit the Super Deals area to save up to 50 percent on the water sports gear you need.

Shipping: $ Navigation:

gear.com
www.gear.com ☆

If you're into kayaking, gear.com has the equipment you need at closeout prices.

Shipping: $ Navigation:

Live to Play Outdoor Sports Auction
www.livetoplay.com ☆

Bid for apparel, eyewear, wetsuits, and more. Be sure to click the Today's Specials link for the best deals. This site features only new items supplied by select vendors.

 Navigation:

SPORTS AND FITNESS

Recycler.com

www.recycler.com

Click the Sports & Hobbies link to browse the available items (there were 5,710 ads in this area last time I checked). Shipping rates vary by seller.

 Navigation:

Shoppers Advantage

www.shoppersadvantage.com

Click the Sports & Health link for great savings on a huge variety of water sport goods. Note: you must register to become a member in order to cash in on the great savings on this site.

Shipping: **$ $** Navigation:

Shopping.com

www.shopping.com

Try clicking the Sports and Fitness tab to see what watersport-related bargains are on Shopping.com.

Shipping: **$ $** Navigation:

Sporting Auction

www.sportingauction.com

No matter what your game is, you'll find the gear you need up for auction at this site. Note that delivery charges may vary by seller.

 Navigation:

The Sports Place

www.thesportsplace.com

The Sports Place, which offers low prices on all sorts of sporting goods, is part of Buy It Now (see the chapter on agents and other shopping services for more information). Become a member of Buy It Now for special deals at The Sports Place. Certain products ship free of charge (you'll see a Free Shipping tag on those items).

Shipping: **$ $** Navigation:

UsedSports.com
www.usedsports.com

Find tons of used water sports equipment up for auction here. Note that shipping rates vary by seller.

 Navigation:

Yahoo! Auctions
http://auctions.yahoo.com

Click the Sports & Recreation link to find some serious sporting goods (last I checked, 36, 681 items were available in this area alone). Note that shipping rates vary by seller.

Navigation:

Winter Sports

Amazon Auctions
http://auctions.amazon.com

Choose Sports & Recreation and select Apparel and Equipment to see what's available. Shipping rates vary depending on who's selling the item you want to buy.

 Navigation:

Cheap Snowboards
www.cheapsnowboards.com/base.htm

This site's name says it all. Find cheap snowboards and snowboard-related items (apparel, accessories, and the like) for auction or for sale. Shipping is a bit steep, but prices are low enough that it may still be worth your while to shop here.

Shipping: **$ $ $** Navigation:

eBay
www.ebay.com

Click the Miscellaneous link and check out the Sporting Goods area to see what winter gear is for sale. Note that shipping rates vary depending on who's selling the item you want to buy.

 Navigation:

Eternal
www.eternalsnow.com

At Eternal, you'll find snowboards, snowboard clothing, gloves, goggles, bindings, bags, boots, t-shirts, ball caps, accessories, and other snowboard related items—all at great prices.

Shipping: **$ $** Navigation:

fogdog sports

www.fogdog.com

Visit the Super Deals area to save up to 50 percent on the winter sports gear you need.

Shipping: **$** Navigation: 👍

gear.com

www.gear.com

If you're into skiing, gear.com has the equipment you need at closeout prices.

Shipping: **$** Navigation: 👍

Live to Play Outdoor Sports Auction

www.livetoplay.com

Bid for apparel, skis, snowboards, snowshoes, and more. Be sure to click the Today's Specials link for the best deals. This site features only new items supplied by select vendors.

🔨 Navigation: 👍

MountainSlayer.com

www.mountainslayer.com

Save big on apparel for skiing and snowboarding here. Shipping's a little bit steep, but the prices make up for it.

Shipping: **$ $ $**   Navigation: 👍

Peak Ski and Sport Lifestyles

www.peakski.com

Buy all the apparel you need to hit the slopes in style. At this site, you'll find outerwear, thermals, hats, headbands, helmets, gloves, goggles, avalanche gear, ski and boot bags, racks, and more. Be sure you hit the Clearance Center.

Shipping: **$ $ $** Navigation: 👍

Performance Snowboarding

www.performancesnowboards.com

Dude, you gotta check out this snowboard site, where you'll find snowboards (well duh), bindings, boots, clothing, and accessories at some kind prices. Be sure to check out the Smokin' Deals.

Shipping: **$ $** Navigation: 👍

Recycler.com

www.recycler.com

Click the Sports & Hobbies link to browse the available items (there were 5,710 ads in this area last time I checked). Shipping rates vary by seller.

 Navigation:

REI Outlet

www.rei-outlet.com

Ah, REI. Who doesn't love that store? You'll be happy to know you can save big at the REI outlet on all your outdoor gear, including all the apparel you need for skiing and snowboarding. Shipping's cheap, too!

Shipping: **$**   Navigation:

Shoppers Advantage

www.shoppersadvantage.com

Click the Sports & Health link for great savings on a huge variety of winter sports goods. Note: you must register to become a member in order to cash in on the great savings on this site.

Shipping: **$ $**   Navigation:

Shopping.com

www.shopping.com

What about a snowboard? Try clicking the Sports and Fitness tab to see what bargains are on Shopping.com.

Shipping: **$ $**   Navigation:

The Sports Place

www.thesportsplace.com

The Sports Place, which offers low prices on all sorts of sporting goods, is part of Buy It Now (see the chapter on agents and other shopping services for more information). Become a member of Buy It Now for special deals at The Sports Place. Certain products ship free of charge (you'll see a Free Shipping tag on those items).

Shipping: **$ $**   Navigation:

Tek Discount Warehouse
http://tekgallery.com

Click the Sports Goods link for deals on skis.

Shipping: **$ $**　　　　　　　　Navigation:

UsedSports.com
www.usedsports.com

Find tons of used sports equipment up for auction here.
Note that shipping rates vary by seller.

　　Navigation:

Yahoo! Auctions
http://auctions.yahoo.com

Click the Sports & Recreation link to find some serious
sporting goods (last I checked, 36, 681 items were available in this area alone). Note that shipping rates vary by
seller.

　　Navigation:

BARGAIN SHOPPING Online

Antiques and Collectibles

Antiques

Antique Alley
http://bmark.com/aa

Click Search Antique Alley and select from the Category list to find what you're looking for. Antique Alley is actually a network of individual vendors, so prices and shipping policies will vary depending on the vendor.

Navigation:

AuctionFloor.com
www.auctionfloor.com

Click the Collectibles tab to see what antiques are up for auction. Note that shipping prices may vary depending on who's selling the item you want to buy.

 Navigation:

AuctionPage.com
http://auctionpage.com

Find antiques for auction at this site. Note that shipping rates vary depending on who's selling the item you want to buy.

 Navigation:

AuctionPort
www.auctionport.com

Find antiques and all sorts of collectibles at this auction site. Note: shipping rates and policies vary by seller.

 Navigation:

Auctionscape
www.auctionscape.com

Click the Antiques & Arts link to see what's up for auction. Shipping costs vary by seller.

 Navigation:

Auction Ware

www.auctionware.com

Check out the Collecting area to see what antiques are on the auction block. Note that delivery charges vary by seller.

 Navigation:

Boxlot

www.boxlot.com

You'll find a little of everything on the auction block here—but collectibles are available in spades. Bid on a variety of antiques and more. Note that shipping rates vary by seller.

 Navigation:

Classifieds 2000

www.classifieds2000.com

Click the Collectibles link to search for thousands of auction and classified ads for collectibles. You'll find everything from Beanie Babies to trading cards, including antiques. Note: Shipping charges vary by vendor.

Navigation:

collectit.net

www.collectit.net

Check out both the auction and the classified links to see what antiques are out there. Note that delivery charges vary by seller.

 Navigation:

eBay

www.ebay.com   ☆

eBay's the big daddy of the auction sites. When you see how many items are for sale there, you'll see why. Last I checked, 58,857 items were for auction in the Antiques area. Note that shipping rates vary depending on who's selling the item you want to buy.

 Navigation:

edeal

www.edeal.com

Find antiques at this site. Note: Delivery charges will vary by seller.

 Navigation:

ANTIQUES AND COLLECTIBLES

eswap.com

www.eswap.com

Click the Antiques link to see what's for sale. Note that shipping prices may vary depending on who's selling the item you want to buy.

 Navigation:

goMainLine.com
www.gomainline.com

At this auction site, you'll find a variety of antiques to choose from. Costs for shipping and handling will vary by seller).

 Navigation:

The Internet Antique Shop
www.tias.com

Select from the category list to see what's available. The Internet Antique Shop is actually a network of individual vendors, so prices and shipping policies will vary depending on which vendor is selling the item you want.

Navigation:

SoldUSA.com
www.soldusa.com

You'll find a nice selection of antiques items at this auction site. Note that delivery charges vary by seller.

 Navigation:

Trade Hall
www.tradehall.com

At this auction site, you'll find antiques on the auction block. Note that shipping charges will vary by seller.

 Navigation:

USAuctions.com
www.usauctions.com

Click the Collectibles link to see what's available in the way of antiques. Note that shipping rates will vary depending on who is selling the item you want to buy.

 Navigation:

Autographs

AuctionFloor.com
www.auctionfloor.com

Click the Collectibles tab to see what autographs are up for auction. Note that shipping prices may vary depending on who's selling the item you want to buy.

 Navigation:

Auction Nation
www.auctionnation.com

Click the Autographs link to see what items are up for auction. Note that shipping costs may vary depending on who's selling the item you want to buy.

 Navigation:

Auction Universe
www.auctionuniverse.com

Click the Autographs & Paper links for items you like to collect. Shipping rates may vary by vendor.

 Navigation:

Bargain News Auctions Online
www.bnauctions.com

Click the Books, Autographs & Paper link to see what's on the auction block. Delivery charges vary by seller.

 Navigation:

Classifieds 2000
www.classifieds2000.com

Click the Collectibles link to search for thousands of autographs from just about anyone who can write. Note: Shipping charges vary by vendor.

Navigation:

Collectors Universe

www.collectorsuniverse.com

This auction site, a collector's nirvana, acts as a gateway
to more than a dozen collector auctions, including auctions for autographs. Search individual auction sites or
search Collectors Universe in its entirety for the items you
want! Shipping rates vary by seller.

 Navigation:

eBay

www.ebay.com

eBay's the big daddy of the auction sites. When you see
how many items are for sale there, you'll see why. Click
the Collectibles link to find the autographs. Note that shipping rates vary depending on who's selling the item you
want to buy.

 Navigation:

Sports Trade

www.sportstrade.com

Find items autographed by your favorite NFL and MLB
players, plus loads of other sports memorabilia at this
auction site. Note that delivery charges may vary by seller.

 Navigation:

Trade Hall

www.tradehall.com

At this auction site, you'll find a variety autographs. Note
that shipping charges will vary by seller.

 Navigation:

USAuctions.com

www.usauctions.com

Click the Collectibles link to see what's available in the
way of autographs. Note that shipping rates will vary
depending on who is selling the item you want to buy.

 Navigation:

Beanie Babies

Auction Adventures
www.auctionadventures.net

You'll find all sorts of collectibles, including Beanie Babies, at this auction site. Note: shipping costs vary by seller.

 Navigation:

AuctionPage.com
http://auctionpage.com

Find Beanie Babies and a variety of other collectibles for auction at this site. Note that shipping rates vary depending on who's selling the item you want to buy.

 Navigation:

Auction Universe
www.auctionuniverse.com

Click the Beanies and More Beans link to find the items you like to collect. Shipping rates may vary by vendor.

 Navigation:

Auction Ware
www.auctionware.com

Check out the Collecting area to see what Beanies are on the auction block. Note that delivery charges vary by seller.

 Navigation:

Bargain News Auctions Online
www.bnauctions.com

Click the Beanies and More Beans link to see what's on the auction block. Delivery charges vary by seller.

 Navigation:

Classifieds 2000
www.classifieds2000.com

Click the Collectibles link to search for thousands of auction and classified ads for collectibles. You'll find Beanie Babies. Note: Shipping charges vary by vendor.

Navigation:

Collectors Universe

www.collectorsuniverse.com

This auction site, a collector's nirvana, acts as a gateway to more than a dozen collector auctions, including auctions for Beanie Babies. Search individual auction sites, or search Collectors Universe in its entirety for the items you want! Shipping rates vary by seller.

 Navigation:

edeal

www.edeal.com

Find tons of Beanies here. Note: Delivery charges vary by seller.

 Navigation:

One Web Place

www.onewebplace.com

This site offers Beanies and other collectibles. Go crazy! Note: Delivery rates will vary by vendor.

 Navigation:

Trade Hall

www.tradehall.com

At this auction site, you'll find Beanie Babies, along with autographs, comics, dolls, toys, models, memorabilia, trading cards, stamps, coins, and currency. Note that shipping charges will vary by seller.

Navigation:

Up 4 Sale

www.up4sale.com

Check out the Antiques and Collectibles area to bid on Beanies. Note that shipping rates will vary by seller.

 Navigation:

USAuctions.com

www.usauctions.com

Click the Collectibles link to see what's available in the way of Beanies. Note that shipping rates will vary depending on who is selling the item you want to buy.

 Navigation:

Coins and Currency

Amazon Auctions
http://auctions.amazon.com

Choose Coins & Stamps to see what's available. Shipping
rates vary depending on who's selling the item you want
to buy.

    Navigation:

AuctionAddict.com
www.auctionaddict.com

Click the Coins & Currency link to see what's up for grabs.
Shipping rates vary by seller.

    Navigation:

Auction Adventures
www.auctionadventures.net

You'll find all sorts of collectibles—including coins—at
this site. Note: shipping costs vary by seller.

    Navigation:

AuctionFloor.com
www.auctionfloor.com

Click the Collectibles tab to see which coins and currency
are up for auction. Note that shipping prices may vary
depending on who's selling the item you want to buy.

    Navigation:

Auction Nation
www.auctionnation.com

Click the Coins link to see what collectibles are up for auction. Note that shipping costs may vary depending on
who's selling the item you want to buy.

    Navigation:

AuctionPage.com
http://auctionpage.com

Find coins and other collectibles for auction at this site.
Note that shipping rates vary depending on who's selling
the item you want to buy.

 Navigation:

Auction Universe
www.auctionuniverse.com

Click the Stamps, Coins, & Currency link to find those items
you like to collect. Shipping rates may vary by vendor.

 Navigation:

Bargain News Auctions Online
www.bnauctions.com

Click the Stamps, Coins & Currency link to see what's on
the auction block. Delivery charges vary by seller.

 Navigation:

Boxlot
www.boxlot.com

You'll find a little of everything on the auction block here—
but collectibles are available in spades. Bid on coins and
currency. Note that shipping rates vary by seller.

 Navigation:

cce-auction.com
www.cce-auction.com

Numismatics unite! Find coins galore for auction here.
Note that delivery charges may vary depending on who's
doing the selling.

 Navigation:

Classifieds 2000
www.classifieds2000.com

Click the Collectibles link to search for thousands of auction and classified ads for collectibles. You'll find the coins
and currency you have been looking for. Note: Shipping
charges vary by vendor.

Navigation:

collectit.net
www.collectit.net

Check out both the auction and the classified links to see what collectibles are out there. You'll find coins and currency, memorabilia, and more. Note that delivery charges vary by seller.

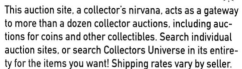 Navigation:

Collectors Universe
www.collectorsuniverse.com

This auction site, a collector's nirvana, acts as a gateway to more than a dozen collector auctions, including auctions for coins and other collectibles. Search individual auction sites, or search Collectors Universe in its entirety for the items you want! Shipping rates vary by seller.

 Navigation:

eBay
www.ebay.com

eBay's the big daddy of the auction sites. When you see how many items are for sale there, you'll see why. Click the Coins & Stamps link to see what's available. Note that shipping rates vary depending on who's selling the item you want to buy.

 Navigation:

edeal
www.edeal.com

Check out the Currency & Stamps area to see what's up for grabs. Note: Delivery charges will vary by seller.

 Navigation:

eswap.com
www.eswap.com

Click the Coins link to see what's up for sale. Note that shipping prices may vary depending on who is selling the item you want to buy.

Navigation:

FirstAuction
www.firstauction.com

The Collectibles category features loads of coins, stamps, and more—all up for auction. Note: shipping costs will vary depending on the seller.

 Navigation:

ANTIQUES AND COLLECTIBLES

goMainLine.com

www.gomainline.com

At this auction site, you'll find coins, stamps, collectibles, and more. Costs for shipping and handling will vary by seller.

  Navigation:

One Web Place

www.onewebplace.com

This site offers coins and other collectibles for auction. Go crazy! Note: Delivery rates will vary by vendor.

  Navigation:

Teletrade Auctions

www.teletrade.com

Find a variety of coins and more on the auction block.

  Navigation:

Trade Hall

www.tradehall.com

At this auction site, you'll find coins and currency, memorabilia, and more. Note that shipping charges will vary by seller.

  Navigation:

Up 4 Sale

www.up4sale.com

Check out the Antiques and Collectibles area and find a variety of coins to bid on. Note that shipping rates will vary by seller.

  Navigation:

USAuctions.com

www.usauctions.com

Click the Collectibles link to see what's available in the way of coins and currency, memorabilia, and other collectibles. Note that shipping rates will vary depending on who is selling the item you want to buy.

  Navigation:

Comic Books

Amazon Auctions

http://auctions.amazon.com

Choose Comics, Cards & Science Fiction to see what's available. Shipping rates vary depending on who's selling the item you want to buy.

   Navigation:

Auction Adventures

www.auctionadventures.net

You'll find all sorts of collectibles—including comic books—at this auction site. Note: shipping costs vary by seller.

   Navigation:

AuctionComic.com

www.auctioncomic.com

This auction sells only comic books and comic paraphernalia. Note that shipping rates may vary by seller.

   Navigation:

Auction Nation

www.auctionnation.com

Click the Comic Books link to see what collectibles are up for auction. Note that shipping costs may vary depending on who's selling the item you want to buy.

   Navigation:

Auction Universe

www.auctionuniverse.com

Click the Comics, Cards, Figures, Sci-Fi link to find the items you like to collect. Shipping rates may vary by vendor.

   Navigation:

Auction Ware

www.auctionware.com

Check out the Collecting area to see what comics are on the auction block. Note that delivery charges vary by seller.

 Navigation:

Bargain News Auctions Online

www.bnauctions.com

Click the Comics, Cards, Figures, Sci-Fi link to see what's available for bidding. Delivery charges vary by seller.

 Navigation:

Classifieds 2000

www.classifieds2000.com

Click the Collectibles link to search for thousands of auction and classified ads for collectibles. You'll find everything from Beanie Babies to trading cards, including comic books. Note: Shipping charges vary by vendor.

Navigation:

collectit.net

www.collectit.net

Check out both the auction and the classified links to see what collectibles are out there. You'll find comics and more. Note that delivery charges vary by seller.

 Navigation:

Comic Exchange

http://www.ComicExchange.net

Comic Exchange calls itself "The largest online comic auction"; more than 2,500 items were listed last I checked! So, if you can't live without that mint-condition Superman #75 platinum edition, try looking here. Note: Delivery charges will vary by sender.

 Navigation:

eBay

www.ebay.com

eBay's the big daddy of the auction sites. When you see how many items are for sale there, you'll see why. Click the Collectibles link to find the comic books. Note that shipping rates vary depending on who's selling the item you want to buy.

  Navigation:

goMainLine.com

www.gomainline.com

At this auction site, you'll find comics and more. Costs for shipping and handling will vary by seller.

  Navigation:

One Web Place

www.onewebplace.com

This site offers a variety of comics to bid on. Go crazy! Note: Delivery rates will vary by vendor.

Navigation:

SoldUSA.com

www.soldusa.com

You'll find collectible items at this auction site, including comic books, memorabilia, and other collectibles. Note that delivery charges vary by seller.

  Navigation:

Teletrade Auctions

www.teletrade.com

Find comic books and more on the auction block at Teletrade Auctions.

  Navigation:

Trade Hall

www.tradehall.com

This site offers comic books for auction. You'll find the items you've been searching for here. Note that shipping charges will vary by seller.

  Navigation:

Dolls and Figures

Auction Adventures

www.auctionadventures.net

You'll find all sorts of collectibles at this site—dolls, glass, porcelain, you name it. Note: shipping costs vary by seller.

 Navigation:

AuctionFloor.com

www.auctionfloor.com

Click the Collectibles tab to see dolls and figures up for auction. Note that shipping prices may vary depending on who's selling the item you want to buy.

 Navigation:

Auction Nation

www.auctionnation.com

Click the Dolls/Figures link to see what collectibles are up for auction. Note that shipping costs may vary depending on who's selling the item you want to buy.

 Navigation:

Auction Ware

www.auctionware.com

Check out the Collecting area to see what figures and dolls are on the auction block. Note that delivery charges vary by seller.

 Navigation:

Boxlot

www.boxlot.com

You'll find a little of everything on the auction block here—but collectibles are available in spades. Bid on dolls, figurines, and more. Note that shipping rates vary by seller.

 Navigation:

Classifieds 2000
www.classifieds2000.com

Click the Collectibles link to search for thousands of auction and classified ads for collectibles. You'll find everything from Beanie Babies to trading cards, including dolls. Note: Shipping charges vary by vendor.

Navigation:

Collectors Universe
www.collectorsuniverse.com

This auction site, a collector's nirvana, acts as a gateway to more than a dozen collector auctions, including auctions for dolls. Search individual auction sites, or search Collectors Universe in its entirety for the items you want! Shipping rates vary by seller.

 Navigation:

eBay
www.ebay.com

eBay's the big daddy of the auction sites. When you see how many items are for sale there, you'll see why. Click the Dolls, Figures link to see what's available. Note that shipping rates vary depending on who's selling the item you want to buy.

 Navigation:

edeal
www.edeal.com

Check out the Dolls area at this auction site to see what's on the block. Note: Delivery charges will vary by seller.

 Navigation:

FirstAuction
www.firstauction.com

The Collectibles category features loads dolls, figurines, and more—all up for auction Note: shipping costs will vary depending on the seller.

 Navigation:

goMainLine.com

www.gomainline.com

At this auction site, you'll find, dolls and memorabilia. Costs for shipping and handling will vary by seller.

 Navigation:

One Web Place

www.onewebplace.com

This site offers dolls, Beanies, memorabilia, and more. Go crazy! Note: Delivery rates will vary by vendor.

 Navigation:

Trade Hall

www.tradehall.com

At this auction site, you'll find dolls galore! Note that shipping charges will vary by seller.

 Navigation:

Up 4 Sale

www.up4sale.com

Check out the Antiques and Collectibles area to bid on figurines, and other collectibles. Note that shipping rates will vary by seller.

 Navigation:

Militaria

Auction Nation
www.auctionnation.com

Click the Militaria link to see what collectibles are up for
auction. Note that shipping costs may vary depending on
who's selling the item you want to buy.

 Navigation:

eBay
www.ebay.com

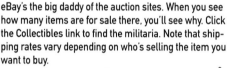

eBay's the big daddy of the auction sites. When you see
how many items are for sale there, you'll see why. Click
the Collectibles link to find the militaria. Note that shipping rates vary depending on who's selling the item you
want to buy.

 Navigation:

SoldUSA.com
www.soldusa.com

You'll find collectible items at this auction site, including
militaria. Note that delivery charges vary by seller.

 Navigation:

SpeedBid
www.speedbid.com

You'll find an extensive collection of militaria at this auction site. Note that shipping charges may vary by seller.

Navigation:

Up 4 Sale
www.up4sale.com

Check out the Antiques and Collectibles area to bid on
militaria. Note that shipping rates will vary by seller.

 Navigation:

USAuctions.com

www.usauctions.com

Click the Collectibles link to see what's available in the
way of militaria. Note that shipping rates will vary
depending on who is selling the item you want to buy.

         Navigation:

Yahoo! Auctions

http://auctions.yahoo.com

Click the Antiques & Collectibles and Trading Cards links
to scour collectible goods up for auction. You'll find memorabilia, militaria, and more. Note that shipping rates vary
by seller.

Movie and Music Memorabilia

AuctionAddict.com

www.auctionaddict.com

Click the Memorabilia link to see what's up for grabs.
Shipping rates vary by seller.

 Navigation:

Auction Nation

www.auctionnation.com

Click the Autographs and Memorabilia links to see what
collectibles are up for auction. Note that shipping costs
may vary depending on who's selling the item you want to
buy.

 Navigation:

Classifieds 2000

www.classifieds2000.com

Click the Collectibles link to search for thousands of auction and classified ads for collectibles. You'll find everything from Beanie Babies to trading cards, including
movie memorabilia. Note: Shipping charges vary by
vendor.

Navigation:

eBay

www.ebay.com

eBay's the big daddy of the auction sites. When you see
how many items are for sale there, you'll see why. Click
the Collectibles link to find the movie memorabilia. Note
that shipping rates vary depending on who's selling the
item you want to buy.

 Navigation:

erock.net
www.erock.net

This site calls itself "The World's Premier Rock-n-Roll Memorabilia Auction Site." Choose from auction categories like The Beatles, Elvis Presley, Kiss Memorabilia, and more. Shipping rates vary by seller.

  Navigation:

eswap.com
www.eswap.com

Click the Memorabilia link to see what's up for sale. Note that shipping prices may vary depending on who is selling the item you want to buy.

  Navigation:

goMainLine.com
www.gomainline.com

At this auction site, you'll find loads of antiques and memorabilia. Costs for shipping and handling will vary by seller).

  Navigation:

The Hollywood Backlot Auction
www.dvdexpress.com

Click the Auctions link on the DVD Express home page to visit the Hollywood Backlot Auction. There, you'll find countless one-of-a-kind items. The last time I visited, items for sale included signed photos from "Battlestar Galactica," the dinosaur T-shirt Michelle Pfeiffer wore in "One Fine Day," a "Roseanne" script autographed by the entire cast, and Yoko Ono autographed stationery!

    Navigation:

One Web Place
www.onewebplace.com

This site offers tons of memorabilia, stamps, and more. Go crazy! Note: Delivery rates will vary by vendor.

  Navigation:

SoldUSA.com

www.soldusa.com

You'll find collectible items at this auction site, including tons of memorabilia items. Note that delivery charges vary by seller.

 Navigation:

Teletrade Auctions

www.teletrade.com

Teletrade Auctions has loads of memorabilia on the auction block.

 Navigation:

Trade Hall

www.tradehall.com

At this auction site, you'll find the memorabilia and other collectible items you've been searching for. Note that shipping charges will vary by seller.

 Navigation:

Yahoo! Auctions

http://auctions.yahoo.com

Click the Antiques & Collectibles and Trading Cards links to scour collectible goods up for auction. You'll find memorabilia, militaria, and more. Note that shipping rates vary by seller.

 Navigation:

ANTIQUES AND COLLECTIBLES

Sports Memorabilia and Trading Cards

AuctionAddict.com

www.auctionaddict.com

Click the Memorabilia and Trading Cards links to see what's up for grabs. Shipping rates vary by seller.

 Navigation:

AuctionFloor.com

www.auctionfloor.com

Click the Collectibles tab to see what sports memorabilia and trading cards are up for auction. Note that shipping prices may vary depending on who's selling the item you want to buy.

 Navigation:

Auction Nation

www.auctionnation.com

Click the Autographs, Memorabilia, and Trading Cards links to see what collectibles are up for auction. Note that shipping costs may vary depending on who's selling the item you want to buy.

 Navigation:

AuctionPage.com

http://auctionpage.com

Find trading cards and other sports memorabilia for auction at this site. Note that shipping rates vary depending on who's selling the item you want to buy.

 Navigation:

Auction Universe

www.auctionuniverse.com

Click the Autographs & Paper and Sports Cards & Collectibles links to find items you want. Shipping rates may vary by vendor.

 Navigation:

Auction Ware

www.auctionware.com

Check out the Collecting area to see what goodies are on the auction block. Note that delivery charges vary by seller.

 Navigation:

Bargain News Auctions Online

www.bnauctions.com

Click the Sports Cards & Collectibles link to see available for bidding. Delivery charges vary by seller.

 Navigation:

Boxlot

www.boxlot.com

You'll find a little of everything on the auction block here— but collectibles are available in spades. Check out the selection of trading cards to bid on. Note that shipping rates vary by seller.

 Navigation:

Classifieds 2000

www.classifieds2000.com

Click the Collectibles link to search for thousands of auction and classified ads for collectibles. You'll find everything from memorabilia to autographs to trading cards. Note: Shipping charges vary by vendor.

Navigation:

collectit.net

www.collectit.net

Check out both the auction and the classified links to see what collectibles are out there. You'll find sports cards and other sports memorabilia. Note that delivery charges vary by seller.

 Navigation:

Collectors Universe

www.collectorsuniverse.com

This auction site, a collector's nirvana, acts as a gateway to more than a dozen collector auctions, including auctions for trading cards. Search individual auction sites, or search Collectors Universe in its entirety for the items you want! Shipping rates vary by seller.

 Navigation:

Curran's

www.curranscards.com

Find trading cards for baseball, hockey, football, basketball, and NASCAR; other memorabilia also available. Note that delivery charges will vary from seller to seller.

 Navigation:

eBay

www.ebay.com

eBay's the big daddy of the auction sites. When you see how many items are for sale there, you'll see why. Click the Collectibles link to find trading cards and autographs. Note that shipping rates vary depending on who's selling the item you want to buy.

 Navigation:

edeal

http://www.edeal.com

Check out the Sports Memorabilia area at this site to see what's on the block. Note: Delivery charges will vary by seller.

 Navigation:

eswap.com

www.eswap.com

Click the Memorabilia and Trading Cards links to see what's up for sale. Note that shipping prices may vary depending on who is selling the item you want to buy.

 Navigation:

goMainLine.com

www.gomainline.com

☆

You'll find trading cards, sports memorabilia, and other collectible items at this auction site. Costs for shipping and handling will vary by seller).

 Navigation:

SoldUSA.com

www.soldusa.com

You'll find collectible items at this auction site, including memorabilia, trading cards, and more. Note that delivery charges vary by seller.

 Navigation:

The Sporting News Auction House

www.auctions.sportingnews.com

Find sports collectibles and other trading cards for every sport you can imagine—including yachting, bowling, and snooker—up on the auction block. Note that delivery charges may vary by seller.

Navigation:

Sports Auction

www.sportsauction.com

Find trading cards, autographed items, and other sports memorabilia at this auction site. Note that delivery charges may vary by sender.

 Navigation:

Sports Trade

www.sportstrade.com

Find items autographed by your favorite NFL and MLB players, plus loads of other sports memorabilia at this auction site. Note that delivery charges may vary by seller.

Navigation:

Teletrade Auctions

www.teletrade.com

Find a variety of trading cards and other sports memorabilia on the auction block.

 Navigation:

ANTIQUES AND COLLECTIBLES

Trade Hall

www.tradehall.com

This auction site offers autographs, memorabilia, and trading cards. Note that shipping charges will vary by seller.

 Navigation:

Up 4 Sale

www.up4sale.com

Check out the Antiques and Collectibles area to bid on trading cards and more. Note that shipping rates will vary by seller.

 Navigation:

Yahoo! Auctions

http://auctions.yahoo.com

Click the Antiques & Collectibles and Trading Cards links to scour collectible goods up for auction. You'll find memorabilia, and more. Note that shipping rates vary by seller.

 Navigation:

USAuctions.com

www.usauctions.com

Click the Collectibles link to see what's available in the way of sports memorabilia and more. Note that shipping rates will vary depending on who is selling the item you want to buy.

 Navigation:

Stamps

Amazon Auctions
http://auctions.amazon.com

Choose Coins & Stamps to see what's available. Shipping
rates vary depending on who's selling the item you want
to buy.

 Navigation:

AuctionAddict.com
www.auctionaddict.com

Click the Stamps link to see what's up for grabs. Shipping
rates vary by seller.

 Navigation:

Auction Adventures
www.auctionadventures.net

You'll find all sorts of stamps and other collectibles at
Auction Adventures. Note: shipping costs vary by seller.

Navigation:

Auction Nation
www.auctionnation.com

Click the Stamps link to see what stamps and other collectibles are up for auction. Note that shipping costs may
vary depending on who's selling the item you want to buy.

 Navigation:

AuctionPage.com
http://auctionpage.com

Find stamps, coins, and more for auction at this site. Note
that shipping rates vary depending on who's selling the
item you want to buy.

 Navigation:

Auction Universe

www.auctionuniverse.com

Click Stamps, Coins, & Currency link to find those items you like to collect. Shipping rates may vary by vendor.

 Navigation:

Auction Ware

www.auctionware.com

Check out the Collecting area to see what goodies are on the auction block. Note that delivery charges vary by seller.

 Navigation:

Bargain News Auctions Online

www.bnauctions.com

Click the Stamps, Coins & Currency link to see what's on the auction block. Delivery charges vary by seller.

 Navigation:

Boxlot

www.boxlot.com

You'll find a little of everything on the auction block here—but collectibles are available in spades. Bid on a wide range of stamps and more. Note that shipping rates vary by seller.

 Navigation:

Classifieds 2000

www.classifieds2000.com

Click the Collectibles link to search for thousands of auction and classified ads for collectibles. You'll find everything from Beanie Babies to trading cards, including stamps. Note: Shipping charges vary by vendor.

Navigation:

collectit.net

www.collectit.net

Check out both the auction and the classified links to see what stamps and collectibles are out there. Note that delivery charges vary by seller.

 Navigation:

Collectors Universe

www.collectorsuniverse.com

This auction site, a collector's nirvana, acts as a gateway to more than a dozen collector auctions, including auctions for stamps. Search individual auction sites or search Collectors Universe in its entirety for the items you want! Shipping rates vary by seller.

 Navigation:

eBay

www.ebay.com

eBay's the big daddy of the auction sites. When you see how many items are for sale there, you'll see why. Click the Coins & Stamps link to see what's available. Note that shipping rates vary depending on who's selling the item you want to buy.

 Navigation:

edeal

www.edeal.com

Check out the Coins, Currency & Stamps area of this site to see what's on the block. Note: Delivery charges will vary by seller.

 Navigation:

eswap.com

www.eswap.com

Click Stamps link to see what's up for sale. Note that shipping prices may vary depending on who is selling the item you want to buy.

 Navigation:

FirstAuction

www.firstauction.com

The Collectibles category features loads of coins , stamps, and more—all up for auction Note: shipping costs will vary depending on the seller.

 Navigation:

goMainLine.com

www.gomainline.com

At this auction site, you'll find stamps, coins and other collectibles. Costs for shipping and handling will vary by seller.

 Navigation:

One Web Place

www.onewebplace.com

This site offers loads of stamps and collectibles. Go crazy! Note: Delivery rates will vary by vendor.

 Navigation:

SoldUSA.com

www.soldusa.com

You'll find collectible items at this auction site, including stamps, coins, and more. Note that delivery charges vary by seller.

 Navigation:

Teletrade Auctions

www.teletrade.com

Find stamps and memorabilia on the auction block at Teletrade Auctions.

 Navigation:

Trade Hall

www.tradehall.com

At this auction site, you'll find a wide variety of stamps and other collectibles. Note that shipping charges will vary by seller.

 Navigation:

Up 4 Sale

www.up4sale.com

Check out the Antiques and Collectibles area to bid on stamps and more. Note that shipping rates will vary by seller.

 Navigation:

USAuctions.com

www.usauctions.com

Click the Collectibles link to see what's available in the way of stamps and other collectibles. Note that shipping rates will vary depending on who is selling the item you want to buy.

 Navigation:

Office Supplies

AtYourOffice.com

www.atyouroffice.com

This site sells more than 26,000 office products and promises to have the lowest prices. Shipping's a bargain, too.

Shipping: **$**   Navigation:

Bid.com

www.bid.com

Click the Office Products link at this auction site for rock-bottom prices—bids start at $1 for many items! Note: Charges for delivery vary by seller.

                             Navigation:

Business Products Express

www.supplies-computer.com

Save on office supplies galore. Be sure to click the Specials link for the best deals.

Shipping: **$**   Navigation:

Carrot's Ink Cartridges

www.carrotbunch.com

Buy ink cartridges for your printer at 60 percent off name brand prices.

Shipping: **$ $**   Navigation:

Costco Online

www.costco.com

You've probably heard of Costco, which is one of those warehouse clubs. Now Costco's online, offering members some great deals on some great merchandise (it costs a minimum of $40 to join, but if you shop there enough, prices will make up for it). Among other items, you'll find office machines and supplies at Costco.

Shipping: **$ $**   Navigation:

CyberSupply

www.cybersupply.com

More than 10,000 products—including paper products, pens, tape, fasteners, staplers, toner cartridges, and more—are available from this site, which offers sale specials and volume discounts. Shipping is free for orders over $50!

Shipping: **$ $**   Navigation:

ExpressSupplies.com

www.ExpressSupplies.Com

ExpressSupplies.com offers a wide selection of supplies for Hewlett-Packard, Epson, Canon, Lexmark, Xerox, IBM, and other inkjet and laser printers.

Shipping: **$ $**   Navigation:

FaxOutlet

www.faxoutlet.com

Buy faxes and other office machines at some serious discounts here. You'll find machines by Brother, Canon, Jetfax, Okidata, Panasonic, Ricoh, and Xerox.

Shipping: **$ $ $**   Navigation:

GE CSN Business Equipment Center

www.gecsn.com/xerox/at_top.html

Buy certified, pre-owned office equipment here.

Shipping: **$ $**   Navigation:

Hertz Furniture Systems Corp.

www.hertzfurniture.com

Hertz offers furniture for offices, schools, and churches at some big discounts (up to 55 percent below list price). Be sure to check out the Blowout Specials section.

Shipping: **$ $**   Navigation:

J&R

www.jandr.com

Good deals on home office equipment, including phones, copiers, fax machines, answering machines, paper shredders, and more.

Shipping: **$ $**   Navigation:

Keysan

www.keysan.com

Office supplies a-go-go —binders, files, computer equipment, chairs, file cabinets, easels, you name it. The downside: A minimum order of $85 is required, so if all you need are some rubber bands, it'd probably be best to look elsewhere.

Shipping: **$ $**   Navigation:

Office Base

www.officebase.com

Office Base has thousands of items to choose from, at discount prices. Be sure to check out the specials. One downside: shipping's a bit steep, and takes about three weeks.

Shipping: **$ $ $**   Navigation:

Office Furniture Outlet

www.officefurniture.net/

Buy new and pre-owned office furnishings here! Find desks, seating, storage, boardroom tables, bookcases, and more (try to overlook the fact that they spelled "Accessories" with only one "S"). Shipping's way steep, but the prices make up for it.

Shipping: **$ $ $**   Navigation:

OfficeMax.com

www.officemax.com

Find office supplies for even less than at the OfficeMax retail stores. OfficeMax takes their low-price guarantee seriously in a big way. If you find an item you've purchased advertised at a lower price within 7 days of your purchase (certain items excluded), OfficeMax will refund the difference plus 55 percent (up to $55).

Shipping: **$**   Navigation:

Panasonic Refurbished Product Retail Outlet

www.pasc.panasonic.com/Refurb/default.asp

Buy refurbished Panasonic, Technics, and Quasar office equipment on the cheap. Parts are also available.

Shipping: **$ $**   Navigation:

Photocopiers.com
www.photocopiers.com

Find copiers, fax machines, printers, and more at this site, which sells imaging equipment and supplies to the public at wholesale prices. Be sure to check out the Closeout area!

Shipping: **$**   Navigation:

Quill
www.quillcorp.com

Find a bazillion office-supply products on sale here, at some very low prices. Be sure to check out the Clearance Zone, where you'll save up to 90 percent off list prices.

Shipping: **$**   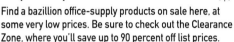   Navigation:

Staples
www.staples.com

A zillion office items, all at low prices! Be sure to check the Specials area for the best deals. Shipping is free if you spend more than $50.

Shipping: **$**   Navigation:

Value America
www.valueamerica.com

If you're looking to buy something, there's a good chance Value America's looking to sell it—including office products. Be sure to check out the hot buys! Become a member (it's free) and save even more.

Shipping: **$**   Navigation:

Viking Office Products Online
www.vikingop.com

Save up to 69 percent off the list price when you buy office supplies from Viking. Shipping is free on orders over $25.

Shipping: **$**   Navigation:

Wal Mart Online
www.wal-mart.com

So there's no greeter, but that doesn't mean the online version of Wal Mart is a total bust. Click the Electronics & Office link for great prices on office equipment. Free shipping on some items (you'll know it when you see it).

Shipping: **$**   Navigation:

Web Emporium

www.webporium.com

You'll find a bit of everything here at Web Emporium—including office supplies, tools, and more—all at nice prices.

Shipping: **$ $**   Navigation:

Electronics

Cameras and Camcorders

1-888-Camcorder

www.888camcorder.com/l

Find camcorders and other AV equipment here. The downside: You must call to order (you can't order online).

Shipping: **$ $ $**   Navigation:

24-7 Outlet

www.7-24outlet.com

Click the Cameras link to check out discounted equipment. Selection is limited; if you don't see what you like, check back. This site is frequently updated.

Shipping: **$ $**   ⊕   Navigation:

800.com

http://www.800.com

You'll find some good prices on electronics here, including cameras and camcorders. If your purchase costs less than $100, shipping is free!

Shipping: **$**   Navigation:

Access Discount & Video

www.accesscamera.com

Not every item on this site is at deep discount, but you can find some good deals on camera equipment. Be sure to check out the Sale Items link.

Shipping: **$ $**   Navigation:

Amazon Auctions

http://auctions.amazon.com

Choose Electronics & Photography to see what's up for auction. Shipping rates vary depending on who's selling the item you want to buy.

          Navigation:

Auction Universe
www.auctionuniverse.com

Click the Electronics link to find audio and video equipment, cameras, and more. Delivery charges may vary by vendor.

 Navigation:

Auction World
www.a-world.com

Click the Consumer Electronics link to check out the cameras and video equipment up for auction. Be sure to check the Pick of the Week, Dollar Mania, Steals & Deals, and Out of This World areas for the best bargains! Shipping rates vary by seller.

 Navigation:

AuctioNet.com
www.auctionet.com

Click the Consumer Electronics link to find a variety of cameras and other electronic equipment—all for auction. Note that shipping rates vary depending on who's selling the item you want to buy.

 Navigation:

AuctionFloor.com
www.auctionfloor.com

Click the Electronics tab to see what cameras and camcorders are up for auction. Note that shipping prices may vary depending on who's selling the item you want to buy.

 Navigation:

AudioExcellence.com
www.audioexcellence.com

High-end audio and video products on the cheap. Click the Hot Deals link for the best deals.

Shipping: $ $ Navigation:

AudioVideo.com
www.audiovideo.com

Camcorders, digital cameras, and more. You'll even find karaoke machines (whoo hoo!).

Shipping: $ $ Navigation:

ELECTRONICS

Bargain News Auctions Online
www.bnauctions.com

Click the Electronics link to see what gadgets are on the auction block. Delivery charges vary by seller.

  Navigation:

Bid.com
www.bid.com

Click the Cameras & Optics link at this auction site for rock-bottom prices—bids start at $1 for many items! Note: Charges for delivery vary by seller.

  Navigation:

BidHit.com
www.bidhit.com

At this auction site, you'll find camcorders, digital cameras, and more. Shipping and handling charges vary by seller.

  Navigation:

Bids Wanted
www.bidswanted.com

Click the Electronics and SOHO links to see what gadgets for home, office, and auto are on the auction block! Charges for delivery vary by seller.

  Navigation:

Camera World
www.cameraworld.com

Camera World has a vast selection of, well, cameras—but that's not all. You'll also find camcorders, TVs, stereo equipment, DVD players, VCRs, and more, at prices way lower than the suggested retail price. One irritating caveat: For certain items, you must call for prices (not their fault—the manufacturer demands it).

Shipping: **$** Navigation:

Cameras Etcetera
www.cameras-etc.com

Cameras Etcetera offers quality used photo equipment at fair prices. Click the Specials button for the best deals!

Shipping: **$ $** Navigation:

Classifieds 2000

www.classifieds2000.com

Click the General Merchandise link and choose
Electronics & Gadgets to find thousands of auction
and classified ads for, well, electronics and gadgets.
Note: If you're looking for photography equipment,
check under Just for Fun. Shipping charges may vary
by vendor.

Navigation:

CompUSANet.com

www.compusanet.com

You'll find a nice selection of digital cameras here at
CompUSANet, and you won't even have to take off your
bunny slippers to browse.

Shipping: **$ $**　　　　　　Navigation:

Consumer Direct Warehouse

www.consumer-direct.com

Choose from a variety of cameras and other electronic
merchandise at this discount site.

Shipping: **$ $ $**　　　Navigation:

Costco Online

www.costco.com

You've probably heard of Costco, which is one of those
warehouse clubs. Now Costco's online, offering
members some great deals on some great merchandise
(it costs a minimum of $40 to join, but if you shop
there enough, prices will make up for it). Among other
items, you'll find audio equipment and cameras at
Costco.

Shipping: **$ $**　　　Navigation:

CyberShop

www.cybershop.com

Up to 80 percent of original prices! Click the Departments
tab and select Electronics to find deals on cameras. Click
the CyberBargains link for the best prices on a variety of
items.

Shipping: **$ $**　　　Navigation:

DealDeal.com
www.dealdeal.com

Find cameras, gaming systems, phones and faxes, and more—all up for auction. Note: Delivery charges will vary from seller to seller.

 Navigation:

deals.com
www.deals.com

Click the Electronics link for deals on camcorders and other electronic equipment.

Shipping: **$** Navigation:

Digital Camera Mall
www.vbizmall.com

Save on digital cameras and accessories here. Free shipping on orders over $100!

Shipping: **$** Navigation:

eBay
www.ebay.com

Click the Photo & Electronics link to see what's available (last time I visited, 45,613 items were up for auction in this category). Note that shipping rates vary depending on who's selling the item you want to buy.

 Navigation:

edeal
www.edeal.com

Visit the Photo & Electronics area of this auction site to see what gadgets are up for grabs. Note: shipping and handling charges may vary by seller.

 Navigation:

Electronic Central
www.electroniccentral.com

Electronic Central, which offers low prices on a variety of consumer electronics, is part of Buy It Now (see the chapter on agents and other shopping services for more information). Become a member of Buy It Now for special deals at Electronic Central. Certain products ship free of charge (you'll see a Free Shipping tag on those items).

Shipping: **$ $** Navigation:

Electronics By Web

www.ebyweb.com

Find camcorders, cameras (traditional and digital) at some pretty nice prices here.

Shipping: **$ $**   Navigation:

Electronics.net

www.electronics.net/

Click the links under Electronics for deals on camcorders, cameras, and more. Check out the auction while you're there to see what's up for grabs!

Shipping: **$ $**   Navigation:

EZbid.com

www.ezbid.com

Find camcorders, cameras, and more—all up for auction. Click the Rebate button to see which items on the site have rebates! Note: shipping and handling costs will differ depending on the seller.

    Navigation:

FirstAuction

www.firstauction.com   ☆

The Electronics category features loads of gadgets up for auction, including cameras, camcorders, and more. Note: Shipping costs will vary depending on the seller.

    Navigation:

Focus

www.focuscamera.com

Photography equipment galore, all at a discount. More than 32,000 items in stock.

Shipping: **$ $**   Navigation:

GiantSavings.com

www.giantsavings.com

Name brands at discounted prices. Find electronic goodies like camcorders, cameras, and more.

Shipping: **$ $**   Navigation:

ELECTRONICS

Cameras and Camcorders   281

J&R

www.jandr.com

Good deals on cameras/optics, audio and video equipment, and more.

Shipping: **$ $**   Navigation:

Kodak Factory Outlet

www.kodak.com/US/en/store/catalog/Category.jhtml?CATID=5

Save up to 25 percent on reconditioned traditional and digital cameras by Kodak.

Shipping: **$ $**   Navigation:

MiniMax Electronics

www.miniprice.com

MiniMax purchases high quality electronic products direct from the manufacturers in large quantities, which means that you save big on cameras and camcorders. Plus, it offers nice deals on Walkmans, radios, scanners, digital watches, binoculars, pagers, cellular phones, and other electronic gadgets.

Shipping: **$**   Navigation:

RedTag.com

www.redtagoutlet.com

Find cameras, camcorders, and more.

Shipping: **$ $**   Navigation:

Shop4.com

www.shop4.com

You must become a member to save on this site, but once you do, you'll find goods for as much as 60 percent off retail. You'll find audio/video equipment, cameras, phones, and more. Click the Clearance link for the very best deals.

Shipping: **$ $**   Navigation:

Shoppers Advantage
www.shoppersadvantage.com

Click the Electronics & Cameras link for great savings on all sorts of goodies. Note: you must register to become a member in order to cash in on the great savings on this site.

Shipping: **$ $**   Navigation:

Shopping.com
www.shopping.com

Click the Home Electronics tab for some serious deals on cameras, camcorders, and other electronic gadgets.

Shipping: **$ $**   Navigation:

State Street Direct Online
www.ssdonline.com   ☆

One of the biggest and best bargain sites for every kind of personal electronic device you can think of. With the shipping costs clearly stated for each item on sale and the cut-rate pricing, this site is a must see.

Shipping: **$ $**   Navigation:

Supreme Video and Electronics
www.supremevideo.com

Low prices on cameras, camcorders, video-editing equipment, and more. Check the Specials area for the best deals. An irritating caveat: because certain manufacturers forbid pricing information to be posted on Web sites, you must call for prices on certain items.

Shipping: **$ $**   Navigation:

Tek Discount Warehouse
http://tekgallery.com

Click the Electronics tab for deals on audio and video equipment, cameras, and more.

Shipping: **$ $**   Navigation:

ELECTRONICS

The SpiderGear Connection
www.spidergear.com

Click the appropriate links to find home audio and video products, as well as cameras and palm devices—all at a discount. Site members get first stab at new products.

Shipping: **$ $ $**   Navigation: 👍

ThinkBid.com
www.thinkbid.com

At this auction site, you'll find a wide variety of camcorders to choose from. Note that delivery charges will vary by seller.

                    Navigation: 👍

uBid Online Auction
www.ubid.com

Bid for consumer electronic products, including audio/video equipment, digital satellites, and more at this auction site. Note: Delivery charges may vary by seller.

Shipping: **$ $**   Navigation: 👍

Value America
www.valueamerica.com

If you're looking to buy something, there's a good chance Value America's looking to sell it—including electronics. Be sure to check out the hot buys! Become a member (it's free) and save even more.

Shipping: **$**   Navigation: 👍

Wal Mart Online
www.wal-mart.com

So there's no greeter, but that doesn't mean the online version of Wal Mart is a total bust. Click the Electronics & Office link for great prices on, well, electronics and office equipment. Free shipping on some items (you'll know it when you see it).

Shipping: **$**   Navigation: 👍

Web Emporium
www.webporium.com

You'll find a bit of everything here at Web Emporium—
including camcorders —at nice prices.

Shipping: **$ $**   Navigation:

Wholesale Advantage
www.wholesaleadvantage.com

Wholesale Advantage offers wholesale prices on electronics equipment, with an emphasis on cameras and
video equipment.

Shipping: **$ $ $**   Navigation:

Yahoo! Auctions
http://auctions.yahoo.com

Click the Electronics & Camera link to scour the goods up
for auction (last I checked, this category had 8,813 items
up for sale). You'll find deals on camera equipment, audio
and video stuff, and more. Note that shipping rates vary by
seller.

                Navigation:

ELECTRONICS

Home Theater

1-888-Camcorder
www.888camcorder.com/l

Find camcorders and other AV equipment here. The downside: You must call to order (you can't order online).

Shipping: **$ $ $**   Navigation:

800.com
www.800.com

You'll find some good prices on electronics here. If your purchase costs less than $100, shipping is free!

Shipping: **$**   Navigation:

Amazon Auctions
auctions.amazon.com

Choose Electronics & Photography to see what's up for auction. Shipping rates vary depending on who's selling the item you want to buy.

    Navigation:

Auction Universe
www.auctionuniverse.com

Click the Electronics link to find audio and video equipment and other electronic must-have items. Delivery charges may vary by vendor.

    Navigation:

Auction World
www.a-world.com

Click the Consumer Electronics link to check out the home theater goods up for auction. Be sure to check the Pick of the Week, Dollar Mania, Steals & Deals, and Out of This World areas for the best bargains! Shipping rates vary by seller.

    Navigation:

AuctioNet.com

www.auctionet.com

Click the Consumer Electronics link to find VCRs, DVDs, speakers, you name it—all for auction. Note that shipping rates vary depending on who's selling the item you want to buy.

 Navigation:

AuctionFloor.com

www.auctionfloor.com

Click the Electronics tab to see what home theater items are up for auction. Note that shipping prices may vary depending on who's selling the item you want to buy.

 Navigation:

AudioExcellence.com

www.audioexcellence.com

High-end audio and video products on the cheap. Click the Hot Deals link for the best deals.

Shipping: **$ $** Navigation:

AudioVideo.com

www.audiovideo.com

Buy DVD players, stereo equipment, and more. You'll even find karaoke machines (whoo hoo!).

Shipping: **$ $** Navigation:

Bargain News Auctions Online

www.bnauctions.com

Click the Electronics link to see what gadgets are on the auction block. Delivery charges vary by seller.

 Navigation:

Ben's House

www.emrkt.com/estore/ben/

At this site, you'll find stereo equipment, telephone equipment, radar detectors and other gadgets, VHS and DVD players, and more. Be sure to check out the Hot Deals area.

Shipping: **$ $** Navigation:

Bid.com

www.bid.com

Click the Electronics link at this auction site for rock-bottom prices—bids start at $1 for many items! Note: Charges for delivery vary by seller.

 Navigation:

BidHit.com

www.bidhit.com

At this auction site, you'll find TVs, VCRs, power tools, stereo equipment, DVD and laser disc players, camcorders, digital cameras, and more. Shipping and handling charges vary by seller.

Shipping: $ $ $ Navigation:

Bids Wanted

www.bidswanted.com

Click the Electronics and SOHO links to see what gadgets for home, office, and auto are on the auction block! Charges for delivery vary by seller.

 Navigation:

Classifieds 2000

www.classifieds2000.com

Click the General Merchandise link and choose Electronics & Gadgets to find thousands of auction and classified ads for, well, electronics and gadgets. Shipping charges may vary by vendor.

Navigation:

Consumer Direct Warehouse

www.consumer-direct.com

Buy satellites, TVs, DVD players, phones, and more from this discount site.

Shipping: $ $ $ Navigation:

Costco Online

www.costco.com

You've probably heard of Costco, which is one of those warehouse clubs. Now Costco's online, offering members some great deals on some great merchandise (it costs a minimum of $40 to join, but if you shop there enough, prices will make up for it). Among other items, you'll find audio equipment, home theater goodies, and phones at Costco.

Shipping: $ $ Navigation:

CyberShop

www.cybershop.com

Up to 80 percent of original prices! Click the Departments tab and select Electronics to find deals on TVs, and other home theatre equipment. Click the CyberBargains link for the best prices on a variety of items.

Shipping: **$ $**   Navigation:

DealDeal.com

www.dealdeal.com

Find gaming systems, home audio and hi-fi systems, satellite dishes, VCRs, DVD players, and more—all up for auction. Note: Delivery charges will vary from seller to seller.

     Navigation:

deals.com

www.deals.com   ☆

Click the Electronics link for deals on stereos, palm devices, TVs, video games, and more.

Shipping: **$**   Navigation:

DishDirect

www.dishonline.com

Find the best satellite, TV, and home theater products at an unbeatable price. Be sure to check out the Current Promotions area.

Shipping: **$ $ $**   Navigation:

DVD City

www.dvdcity.com

DVDs themselves aren't sold here, but the players are. You'll find more than reasonable prices.

Shipping: **$ $ $**   Navigation:

eBay

www.ebay.com   ☆

Click the Photo & Electronics link to see what's available (last time I visited, 45,613 items were up for auction in this category). Note that shipping rates vary depending on who's selling the item you want to buy.

     Navigation:

ELECTRONICS

edeal
www.edeal.com

Visit the Photo & Electronics area of this auction site to
see what gadgets are up for grabs. Note: shipping and
handling charges may vary by seller.

 Navigation:

Electronic Central
www.electroniccentral.com

Electronic Central, which offers low prices on a variety
of consumer electronics, is part of Buy It Now (see the
chapter on agents and other shopping services for more
information). Become a member of Buy It Now for special deals at Electronic Central. Certain products ship
free of charge (you'll see a Free Shipping tag on those
items).

Shipping: **$ $** Navigation:

Electronics By Web
www.ebyweb.com

Find home audio, telephones, portable audio systems,
TVs, VCRs, car stereos, and DVD players at some pretty
nice prices here.

Shipping: **$ $** Navigation:

Electronics.net
www.electronics.net/

Click the links under Electronics for deals on TVs, stereos,
camcorders and more. Check out the auction while you're
there to see what's up for grabs!

Shipping: **$ $** Navigation:

EZbid.com
www.ezbid.com

Find home theater and stereo equipment, phones, and
more—all up for auction. Click the Rebate button
to see which items on the site have rebates! Note: shipping and handling costs will differ depending on the
seller.

 Navigation:

FirstAuction

www.firstauction.com

The Electronics category features loads of gadgets
(digital satellites, stereo equipment, photo and video
equipment, phones, and more) up for auction.
Note: Shipping costs will vary depending on the
seller.

 Navigation: 👍

GiantSavings.com

www.giantsavings.com

Name brands at discounted prices. Find electronic
goodies like telephones, CD players, camcorders,
PDAs, DVD players, TVs, and more.

Shipping: **$ $**　　　　　　　　Navigation: 👍

J&R

www.jandr.com

Good deals on cameras/optics, audio and video equipment, and more.

Shipping: **$ $**　　　　　　　　Navigation: 👍

MiniMax Electronics

www.miniprice.com

MiniMax purchases high quality electronic products direct
from the manufacturers in large quantities, which means
that you save big on TVs, VCRs, CD players, cameras, camcorders, Walkmans, radios, scanners, digital watches,
binoculars, pagers, cellular phones, and other electronic
gadgets.

Shipping: **$**　　　　　　　　Navigation: 👎

RedTag.com

www.redtagoutlet.com

Find a variety of home theater items, stereo equipment
phones, and more.

Shipping: **$ $**　　　　　　　　Navigation: 👍

ELECTRONICS

Shop4.com
www.shop4.com

You must become a member to save on this site, but once you do, you'll find audio/video equipment for as much as 60 percent off retail. Click the Clearance link for the very best deals.

Shipping: **$ $**   Navigation:

Shoppers Advantage
www.shoppersadvantage.com

Click the Electronics & Cameras link for great savings on all sorts of goodies. Note: you must register to become a member in order to cash in on the great savings on this site.

Shipping: **$ $**   Navigation:

Shopping.com
www.shopping.com/store/

Click the Home Electronics tab for some serious deals on TVs, gaming stations, stereo equipment, and more.

Shipping: **$ $**   Navigation:

State Street Direct Online
www.ssdonline.com

One of the biggest and best bargain sites for every kind of personal electronic device you can think of. With the shipping costs clearly stated for each item on sale and the cut rate pricing, this site is a must see.

Shipping: **$ $**   Navigation:

Supreme Video and Electronics
www.supremevideo.com

Low prices on VCRs, DVD players, TVs, video-editing equipment, and more. Check the Specials area for the best deals. An irritating caveat: because certain manufacturers forbid pricing information to be posted on Web sites, you must call for prices on certain items.

Shipping: **$ $**   Navigation:

Tek Discount Warehouse
http://tekgallery.com

Click the Electronics tab for deals on audio and video equipment and other home theatre items.

Shipping: **$ $**   Navigation:

The SpiderGear Connection
www.spidergear.com

Click the appropriate links to find home audio and video products, as well as palm devices—all at a discount. Site members get first stab at new products.

Shipping: **$ $ $**   Navigation:

ThinkBid.com
www.thinkbid.com

At this auction site, you'll find VCRs, TVs, stereo equipment, and phones. Note that delivery charges will vary by seller.

Navigation:

uBid Online Auction
www.ubid.com

Bid for consumer electronic products, including audio/video equipment, digital satellites, and more at this auction site. Note: Delivery charges may vary by seller.

Shipping: **$ $**   Navigation:

Value America
www.valueamerica.com

If you're looking to buy something, there's a good chance Value America's looking to sell it—including electronics. Be sure to check out the hot buys! Become a member (it's free) and save even more.

Shipping: **$**   Navigation:

Wal Mart Online
www.wal-mart.com

So there's no greeter, but that doesn't mean the online version of Wal Mart is a total bust. Click the Electronics & Office link for great prices on electronics. Free shipping on some items (you'll know it when you see it).

Shipping: **$**   Navigation:

ELECTRONICS

Web Emporium
www.webporium.com

You'll find a bit of everything here at Web Emporium—including home theater goodies — all at nice prices.

Shipping: **$ $**   Navigation:

WebAuction.com
www.webauction.com

Bid on home theater equipment, telephones, stereo equipment, and more.

 Navigation:

Wholesale Advantage
www.wholesaleadvantage.com

Wholesale Advantage offers wholesale prices on a variety of home theatre and electronics equipment.

Shipping: **$ $ $** Navigation:

Wholesell.com
www.wholesell.com

Find DVD players, VCRs, and more here.

Shipping: **$ $ $** Navigation:

Yahoo! Auctions
http://auctions.yahoo.com

Click the Electronics & Camera link to scour the goods up for auction (last I checked, this category had 8,813 items up for sale). You'll find deals on audio and video stuff. Note that shipping rates vary by seller.

 Navigation:

Palm Devices

Amazon Auctions
http://auctions.amazon.com

Choose Electronics & Photography and click Consumer
Electronics see what PDAs are up for auction. Shipping
rates vary depending on who's selling the item you want
to buy.

    Navigation:

Classifieds 2000
www.classifieds2000.com

Click the General Merchandise link and choose
Electronics & Gadgets to find thousands of auction and
classified ads for, well, electronics and gadgets. Shipping
charges may vary by vendor.

Navigation:

CompUSANet.com
www.compusanet.com

You'll find a nice selection of palm devices here at
CompUSANet. Buying one will make you seem very
important.

Shipping: $ $ Navigation:

Costco Online
www.costco.com

You've probably heard of Costco, which is one of those
warehouse clubs. Now Costco's online, offering members
some great deals on some great merchandise (it costs a
minimum of $40 to join, but if you shop there enough,
prices will make up for it). Among other items, you'll find
palm devices here (check under the Computers &
Peripherals link).

Shipping: $ $ Navigation:

deals.com

www.deals.com

Click the Electronics link for deals on a variety of palm devices, along with loads of other electronic gadgets.

Shipping: **$**   Navigation:

Electronic Central

www.electroniccentral.com

Electronic Central, which offers low prices on a variety of consumer electronics, is part of Buy It Now (see the chapter on agents and other shopping services for more information). Become a member of Buy It Now for special deals at Electronic Central. Certain products ship free of charge (you'll see a Free Shipping tag on those items).

Shipping: **$ $**   Navigation:

Electronics By Web

www.ebyweb.com

Find palm devices, among other gadgets, at some pretty nice prices here.

Shipping: **$ $**   Navigation:

GiantSavings.com

www.giantsavings.com

Name brands at discounted prices. Find electronic goodies like PDAs and more.

Shipping: **$ $**   Navigation:

State Street Direct Online

www.ssdonline.com

One of the biggest and best bargain sites for every kind of personal electronic device you can think of. With the shipping costs clearly stated for each item on sale and the cut-rate pricing, this site is a must see.

Shipping: **$ $**   Navigation:

The SpiderGear Connection

www.spidergear.com

Click the appropriate links to find palm devices at a discount. Site members get first stab at new products.

Shipping: **$ $ $**   Navigation:

Phones

Bargain News Auctions Online

www.bnauctions.com

Click the Electronics link to see what gadgets are on the auction block. Delivery charges vary by seller.

 Navigation:

Ben's House

www.emrkt.com/estore/ben/

At this site, you'll find telephone equipment, radar detectors and other gadgets. Be sure to check out the Hot Deals area.

Shipping: **$ $** Navigation:

Bid.com

www.bid.com

Click the Electronics link at this auction site for rock-bottom prices—bids start at $1 for many items! Note: Charges for delivery vary by seller.

 Navigation:

Bids Wanted

www.bidswanted.com

Click the Electronics and SOHO links to see what phones for home, office, and auto are on the auction block! Charges for delivery vary by seller.

 Navigation:

Cellular Depot

www.cellulardepot.com

Find discount wireless phones and accessories here. Be sure to check out the Red Hot Specials area. Free shipping!

Shipping: **$** Navigation:

ELECTRONICS

Classifieds 2000
www.classifieds2000.com

Click the General Merchandise link and choose Electronics & Gadgets to find thousands of auction and classified ads for, well, electronics and gadgets. Shipping charges may vary by vendor.

Navigation:

CompareNet
www.comparenet.com

CompareNet compares prices for goods in seven different categories, one of which is Electronics. Before you buy, check here to see who's offering the best prices on the goods you want.

Navigation:

Consumer Direct Warehouse
www.consumer-direct.com

Choose from a variety of phones and other electronic equipment from this discount site.

Shipping: $ $ $ Navigation:

Costco Online
www.costco.com

You've probably heard of Costco, which is one of those warehouse clubs. Now Costco's online, offering members some great deals on some great merchandise (it costs a minimum of $40 to join, but if you shop there enough, prices will make up for it). Among other items, you'll find audio equipment, home theater goodies, phones, and cameras at Costco.

Shipping: $ $ Navigation:

CyberShop
www.cybershop.com

Up to 80 percent off original prices! Click the Departments tab and select Electronics to find deals on phones. Click the CyberBargains link for the best prices on a variety of items.

Shipping: $ $ Navigation:

DealDeal.com

www.dealdeal.com

Find phones and faxes, and other electronic gadgets —all up for auction. Note: Delivery charges will vary from seller to seller.

 Navigation:

deals.com

www.deals.com

Click the Electronics link for deals on phones.

Shipping: **$** Navigation:

eBay

www.ebay.com

Click the Photo & Electronics link to see what's available (last time I visited, 45,613 items were up for auction in this category). Note that shipping rates vary depending on who's selling the item you want to buy.

 Navigation:

edeal

www.edeal.com

Visit the Photo & Electronics area of this auction site to see what gadgets are up for grabs. Note: shipping and handling charges may vary by seller.

 Navigation:

Electronic Central

www.electroniccentral.com

Electronic Central, which offers low prices on a variety of consumer electronics, is part of Buy It Now (see the chapter on agents and other shopping services for more information). Become a member of Buy It Now for special deals at Electronic Central. Certain products ship free of charge (you'll see a Free Shipping tag on those items).

Shipping: **$ $** Navigation:

ELECTRONICS

Electronics By Web

www.ebyweb.com

Find telephones at some pretty nice prices here.

Shipping: **$ $** Navigation:

EZbid.com
www.ezbid.com

Find phones up for auction here. Click the Rebate button to see which items on the site have rebates! Note: shipping and handling costs will differ depending on the seller.

 Navigation: 👍

FirstAuction
www.firstauction.com

The Electronics category features loads of phone and other electronic gadgets up for auction. Note: Shipping costs will vary depending on the seller.

 Navigation: 👍

MiniMax Electronics
www.miniprice.com

MiniMax purchases high quality electronic products direct from the manufacturers in large quantities, which means that you save big on cellular phones, Walkmans, radios, scanners, digital watches, binoculars, pagers, and other electronic gadgets.

Shipping: $ Navigation:

Panasonic Refurbished Product Retail Outlet
www.pasc.panasonic.com/Refurb/default.asp

Buy refurbished Panasonic, Technics, and Quasar products on the cheap. Parts are also available.

Shipping: $ $ Navigation:

Point.com
www.point.com

At Point.com, you can compare side by side virtually all brand name phones and service plans in your market, find compatible accessories for your phone, and buy certain items online.

Shipping: $ $ Navigation:

RedTag.com
www.redtagoutlet.com

Find a variety of phones for sale here.

Shipping: **$ $**   Navigation:

Shop4.com
www.shop4.com

You must become a member to save on this site, but once you do, you'll find goods for as much as 60 percent off retail. You'll find phones and loads of other electronic equipment. Click the Clearance link for the very best deals.

Shipping: **$ $**   Navigation:

Shoppers Advantage
www.shoppersadvantage.com

Click the Electronics & Cameras link for great savings on all sorts of goodies. Note: you must register to become a member in order to cash in on the great savings on this site.

Shipping: **$ $**   Navigation:

Shopping.com
www.shopping.com/store/

Click the Home Electronics tab for some serious deals on phones.

Shipping: **$ $**   Navigation:

State Street Direct Online
www.ssdonline.com   ☆

One of the biggest and best bargain sites for every kind of personal electronic device you can think of. With the shipping costs clearly stated for each item on sale and the cut rate pricing, this site is a must see.

Shipping: **$ $**   Navigation:

ThinkBid.com
www.thinkbid.com

At this auction site, you'll find some nice deals on phones. Note that delivery charges will vary by seller.

               Navigation:

ELECTRONICS

Value America

www.valueamerica.com

If you're looking to buy something, there's a good chance Value America's looking to sell it—including phones and other electronics. Be sure to check out the hot buys! Become a member (it's free) and save even more.

Shipping: **$**   Navigation: 👍

Stereo Equipment

800.com
www.800.com

You'll find some good prices on electronics here, including stereo equipment. If your purchase costs less than $100, shipping is free!

Shipping: $ Navigation:

Auction Universe
www.auctionuniverse.com

Click the Electronics link to find audio equipment. Delivery charges may vary by vendor.

     Navigation:

Auction World
www.a-world.com

Click the Consumer Electronics link to check out the stereo equipment up for auction. Be sure to check the Pick of the Week, Dollar Mania, Steals & Deals, and Out of This World areas for the best bargains! Shipping rates vary by seller.

     Navigation:

AuctioNet.com
www.auctionet.com

Click the Consumer Electronics link to find stereo equipment and speakers, among other things—all for auction. Note that shipping rates vary depending on who's selling the item you want to buy.

     Navigation:

AuctionFloor.com
www.auctionfloor.com

Click the Electronics tab to see what stereo equipment is up for auction. Note that shipping prices may vary depending on who's selling the item you want to buy.

    Navigation:

AudioExcellence.com
www.audioexcellence.com

High-end audio and video products on the cheap. Click the Hot Deals link for the best deals.

Shipping: **$ $**   Navigation:

AudioVideo.com
www.audiovideo.com

AudioVideo.com offers a wide range of stereo equipment. You'll even find karaoke machines (whoo hoo!).

Shipping: **$ $**   Navigation:

Bargain News Auctions Online
www.bnauctions.com

Click the Electronics link to see what gadgets are on the auction block. Delivery charges vary by seller.

    Navigation:

Ben's House
www.emrkt.com/estore/ben/

At this site, you'll find stereo equipment and accessories. Be sure to check out the Hot Deals area.

Shipping: **$ $**   Navigation:

Bid.com
www.bid.com

Click the Electronics link at this auction site for rock-bottom prices—bids start at $1 for many items! Note: Charges for delivery vary by seller.

Navigation:

BidHit.com
www.bidhit.com

At this auction site, you'll find stereo equipment, DVD and laser disc players, and more. Shipping and handling charges vary by seller.

Navigation:

Bids Wanted

www.bidswanted.com

Click the Electronics and SOHO links to see what gadgets for home, office, and auto are on the auction block! Charges for delivery vary by seller.

 Navigation:

Classifieds 2000

www.classifieds2000.com

Click the General Merchandise link and choose Electronics & Gadgets to find thousands of auction and classified ads for stereo equipment, as well as other electronics and gadgets. Shipping charges may vary by vendor.

Navigation:

Consumer Direct Warehouse

www.consumer-direct.com

Buy stereo equipment at this discount site.

Shipping: **$ $ $**   Navigation:

Costco Online

www.costco.com

You've probably heard of Costco, which is one of those warehouse clubs. Now Costco's online, offering members some great deals on some great merchandise (it costs a minimum of $40 to join, but if you shop there enough, prices will make up for it). Among other items, you'll find a nice selection of audio equipment to choose from

Shipping: **$ $**   Navigation:

CyberShop

http://cybershop.com

Up to 80 percent of original prices! Click the Departments tab and select Electronics to find deals on stereo equipment. Click the CyberBargains link for the best prices on a variety of items.

Shipping: **$ $**   Navigation:

DealDeal.com
www.dealdeal.com

Find home audio and hi-fi sytems, along with other
electronic equipment —all up for auction. Note: Delivery
charges will vary from seller to seller.

  Navigation:

deals.com
www.deals.com

Click the Electronics link to check out a variety of stereo
equipment to choose from.

Shipping: $ Navigation:

eBay
www.ebay.com

Click the Photo & Electronics link to see what's
available (last time I visited, 45,613 items were up for
auction in this category). Note that shipping rates
vary depending on who's selling the item you want
to buy.

 Navigation:

edeal
www.edeal.com

Visit the Photo & Electronics area of this auction site to
see what stereo equipment is up for grabs. Note: shipping
and handling charges may vary by seller.

 Navigation:

Electronic Central
www.electroniccentral.com

Electronic Central, which offers low prices on a variety
of consumer electronics, is part of Buy It Now (see the
chapter on agents and other shopping services for
more information). Become a member of Buy It Now
for special deals at Electronic Central. Certain products
ship free of charge (you'll see a Free Shipping tag on
those items).

Shipping: $ $ Navigation:

Electronics By Web

www.ebyweb.com

Find car stereos and portable audio systems at some pretty nice prices here.

Shipping: **$ $**   Navigation:

Electronics.net

www.electronics.net/

Click the links under Electronics for deals on stereos. Check out the auction while you're there to see what's up for grabs!

Shipping: **$ $** Navigation:

EZbid.com

www.ezbid.com

Find stereo equipment up for auction here. Click the Rebate button to see which items on the site have rebates! Note: shipping and handling costs will differ depending on the seller.

  Navigation:

FirstAuction

www.firstauction.com ☆

The Electronics category features loads of stereo equipment and other electronic gadgets up for auction. Note: Shipping costs will vary depending on the seller.

  Navigation:

GiantSavings.com

www.giantsavings.com

Name brands at discounted prices. Find electronic goodies like telephones, CD players, camcorders, PDAs, cameras, DVD players, TVs, and more.

Shipping: **$ $** Navigation:

J&R

www.jandr.com

Good deals on audio and video equipment and more.

Shipping: **$ $** Navigation:

MiniMax Electronics

www.miniprice.com

MiniMax purchases high quality electronic products direct from the manufacturers in large quantities, which means that you save big on stereo equipment, Walkmans, radios, and other electronic gadgets.

Shipping: **$**　　　　　　　　　　Navigation:

Panasonic Refurbished Product Retail Outlet

www.pasc.panasonic.com/Refurb/default.asp

Buy refurbished Panasonic, Technics, and Quasar products on the cheap. Parts are also available.

Shipping: **$ $**　　　　　　　　Navigation:

RedTag.com

www.redtagoutlet.com

Find a variety of stereo equipment and other electronic gadgets here.

Shipping: **$ $**　　　　　　　　Navigation:

Shop4.com

www.shop4.com

You must become a member to save on this site, but once you do, you'll find goods for as much as 60 percent off retail. including stereo equipment. Click the Clearance link for the very best deals.

Shipping: **$ $**　　　　　　　　Navigation:

Shoppers Advantage

www.shoppersadvantage.com

Click the Electronics & Cameras link for great savings on all sorts of goodies. Note: you must register to become a member in order to cash in on the great savings on this site.

Shipping: **$ $**　　　　　　　　Navigation:

Shopping.com

www.shopping.com/store/

Click the Home Electronics tab for some serious deals on stereo equipment.

Shipping: **$ $**　　　　　　　　Navigation:

State Street Direct Online
www.ssdonline.com

One of the biggest and best bargain sites for every kind of personal electronic device you can think of. With the shipping costs clearly stated for each item on sale and the cut rate pricing, this site is a must see.

Shipping: **$ $** Navigation:

Tek Discount Warehouse
http://tekgallery.com

Click the Electronics tab for deals on audio equipment.

Shipping: **$ $** Navigation:

The SpiderGear Connection
www.spidergear.com

Click the appropriate links to find home audio products at a discount. Site members get first stab at new products.

Shipping: **$ $ $** Navigation:

ThinkBid.com
www.thinkbid.com

At this auction site, you'll find loads of stereo equipment. Note that delivery charges will vary by seller.

  Navigation:

uBid Online Auction
www.ubid.com

Bid for consumer electronic products, including audio/video equipment, at this auction site. Note: Delivery charges may vary by seller.

Shipping: **$ $** Navigation:

Value America
www.valueamerica.com

If you're looking to buy something, there's a good chance Value America's looking to sell it—including stereo equipment. Be sure to check out the hot buys! Become a member (it's free) and save even more.

Shipping: **$** Navigation:

ELECTRONICS

Wal Mart Online

www.wal-mart.com

So there's no greeter, but that doesn't mean the online version of Wal Mart is a total bust. Click the Electronics & Office link for great prices on, well, stereo equipment and other electronics. Free shipping on some items (you'll know it when you see it).

Shipping: **$**   Navigation:

Web Emporium

www.webporium.com

You'll find a bit of everything here at Web Emporium—including stereo equipment —all at nice prices.

Shipping: **$ $**   Navigation:

WebAuction.com

www.webauction.com

Bid on stereo goodies and other electronic equipment here.

                    Navigation:

Yahoo! Auctions

http://auctions.yahoo.com

Click the Electronics & Camera link to scour the goods up for auction (last I checked, this category had 8,813 items up for sale). You'll find deals on audio stuff and more. Note that shipping rates vary by seller.

Navigation:

Video Games

Amazon Auctions
http://auctions.amazon.com

Choose Electronics & Photography to see what video games are up for auction. Shipping rates vary depending on who's selling the item you want to buy.

     Navigation:

Auction Universe
www.auctionuniverse.com

Click the Electronics link to find video games. Delivery charges may vary by vendor.

     Navigation:

Bargain News Auctions Online
www.bnauctions.com

Click the Electronics link to see what games are on the auction block. Delivery charges vary by seller.

     Navigation:

Buy Rite Video Games
www.buyrite1.com

Buy Rite has video games at some seriously low prices. Be sure to check out the specials. Shipping's a little steep, but it's a flat fee, so the more you order the better.

Shipping: **$ $ $**   Navigation:

Classifieds 2000
www.classifieds2000.com

Click the General Merchandise link and choose Electronics & Gadgets to find thousands of auction and classified ads for video games. Shipping charges may vary by vendor.

    Navigation:

CD World

www.cdworld.com

CD World calls itself "The World's Largest Discount Entertainment Store." You'll find some nice prices on video games.

Shipping: $ $ ⊕   Navigation: 👍

CompUSANet.com

www.compusanet.com

Regress! Buy a Nintendo or Sega system here. Prices are low enough that your allowance might even cover it.

Shipping: $ $ ⊕   Navigation: 👍

DealDeal.com

www.dealdeal.com

Find gaming systems and more—all up for auction. Note: Delivery charges will vary from seller to seller.

      Navigation: 👍

deals.com

www.deals.com

Click the Electronics link for deals on video games.

Shipping: $ Navigation: 👍

The Dragon's Den

www.dragon.ca/

Find games for your PC, Sony Playstation, Nintendo 64, and Gameboy here —all at some nice prices. Be sure to visit the On Sale area.

Shipping: $ $ ⊕   Navigation: 👍

DVD Express

www.dvdexpress.com

You wouldn't think that a site called DVD Express would have video games, but it does. Prices are decent, and shipping's pretty danged cheap, too.

Shipping: $ ⊕   Navigation: 👍

Electronic Arts

www.eastore.ea.com

Find some good prices on video games for PCs, Macs, Sony Playstations, and Nintendo 64s. Plus hint books and other merchandise. Be sure to check the Hot Deals area.

Shipping: $ $ Navigation:

Electronics Boutique

www.ebworld.com

Find countless video games here for PCs, Macs, PlayStation, Dreamcast, Nintendo 64, Game Boy, and more—not to mention the game consoles themselves. You'll also find strategy guides and accessories.

Shipping: $ $ Navigation:

Electronics By Web

www.ebyweb.com

Find game systems at some pretty nice prices here.

Shipping: $ $ Navigation:

Shopping.com

www.shopping.com/store/

Click the Home Electronics tab for some serious deals on gaming stations.

Shipping: $ $ Navigation:

Value America

www.valueamerica.com

If you're looking to buy something, there's a good chance Value America's looking to sell it—including video games. Be sure to check out the hot buys! Become a member (it's free) and save even more.

Shipping: $ Navigation:

Wal Mart Online

www.wal-mart.com

So there's no greeter, but that doesn't mean the online version of Wal Mart is a total bust. Click the Electronics & Office link for great prices on video games. Free shipping on some items (you'll know it when you see it).

Shipping: $ Navigation:

ELECTRONICS

Computers

Hardware

24-7 Outlet

www.7-24outlet.com

Click the Computer Hardware link to check out deals on, well, computer hardware. This site changes frequently, so bookmark it and check it often.

Shipping: **$ $** Navigation:

3D Auction

www.3dauction.com

Find all sorts of goods at this auction site, including computer equipment. Shipping rates vary depending on who's selling the item you want to buy.

 Navigation:

2apex.com

www.2apex.com

Buy everything you need to build your own machine here, or get one ready-made.

Shipping: **$ $** Navigation:

2BuyPC

www.2buypc.com

2BuyPC has more than 80,000 boxed hardware and software items and over 130,000 downloadable software items at wholesale prices.

Shipping: **$ $** Navigation:

A+ Printers

www.printers123.com

Find inkjet, laser, even dot-matrix printers here—not to mention monitors, modems, and books—at some very nice prices. Be sure to check out the specials. Shipping's pretty cheap, too!

Shipping: **$** Navigation:

Access Micro

www.accessmicro.com

If you are shopping for peripherals or computers you really must try Access Micro. Of note are their Specials drop down boxes right on the front page. All of the items there were especially tempting to me, even though I don't need them.

Shipping: **$ $**   Navigation:

AllMonitors.com

www.allmonitors.com

All Monitors, All the Time. Everything's discounted, but click the Liquidation link for the very best deals. You can also buy refurbished monitors on the cheap.

Shipping: **$ $**   Navigation:

Amazon Auctions

http://auctions.amazon.com

Choose Computers & Software to see what's available. Shipping rates vary depending on who's selling the item you want to buy.

          Navigation:

American PC

www.americanpc.com

I'm willing to overlook that this site had misspelled "Clearance" when I was there last, simply because the items in that area really were a steal.

Shipping: **$ $**   Navigation:

American Starlex

www.starlex.com

This company specializes in new and refurbished laptops. Free ground shipping!

Shipping: **$**   Navigation:

Applied Computer Online

www.applied-computer.com

Find tons of hardware at great prices.

Shipping: **$ $**   Navigation:

COMPUTERS

Auction First

www.auctionfirst.com

Find computer hardware (among other things) for auction here. Note that shipping rates may vary depending on who's selling the item you want to buy.

 Navigation:

Auction IT

www.auction-it.net

By mainframes, mid-range machines, workstations, servers, networking equipment, and PCs. Dealers pay shipping, meaning you don't have to!

Shipping: **$** Navigation:

Auction Nation

www.auctionnation.com

Click the Computers link to find disk media, printers, hardware, modems, monitors, and more for auction. Note: Shipping costs may vary depending on who's selling the item you want to buy.

 Navigation:

Auction Sales

www.auction-sales.com

Find loads of hardware (laptops, PCs, Macs, digital cameras, and more), and miscellaneous goodies (computer books, electronics, and such) for auction here. Click the $1 Directory link to find all the auctions starting at $1. Note: Shipping rates vary depending on the vendor.

 Navigation:

Auction Universe

www.auctionuniverse.com

Click the Computers link to find PCs, laptops, Macs, and more. Delivery charges may vary by vendor.

 Navigation:

Auction Ware

www.auctionware.com

Check out the Computer Related area to see what hardware is on the auction block. Note that delivery charges vary by seller.

 Navigation:

Auction World

www.a-world.com

Click the Hardware and Software links to check out the goods up for auction. Be sure to check the Pick of the Week, Dollar Mania, Steals & Deals, and Out of This World areas for the best bargains! Shipping rates vary by seller.

 Navigation:

Auction-Warehouse.com

www.auction-warehouse.com

Click the Computer Hardware and Computer Software links to see what goodies are on the auction block. Note: Delivery charges may vary depending on who's selling the item you want.

 Navigation:

AuctionAddict.com

www.auctionaddict.com

Click the Computers link to see what's up for grabs. Shipping rates vary by seller.

 Navigation:

AuctioNet.com

www.auctionet.com

Find computer systems, peripherals, printers, notebooks, storage, and monitors for auction here. Note that shipping rates vary depending on who's selling the item you want to buy.

 Navigation:

AuctionFloor.com

www.auctionfloor.com

Click the Computers tab to see what's up for auction. Note that shipping prices may vary depending on who's selling the item you want to buy.

 Navigation:

AuctionMAX

www.auctionmax.com

AuctionMax is a warehouse outlet for new computer stuff (no used or refurbished here). Click the PriceDrop link for some interesting deals—the more people buy an item, the less it costs. Shipping rates and policies vary by seller.

 Navigation:

AuctionPage.com

http://auctionpage.com

Find computers for auction at this site. Note that shipping rates vary depending on who's selling the item you want to buy.

 Navigation:

Auctionscape

www.auctionscape.com

Click the Computers link to see what's on the auction block. You'll find Macs, PCs, peripherals, and more. Note that shipping prices vary by seller.

 Navigation:

Bargain News Auctions Online

www.bnauctions.com

Click the Computers link to see what goodies are on the auction block. Delivery charges vary by seller.

 Navigation:

BestPricePC.com

www.bestpricepc.com

BestPricePC.com is committed to providing the best prices on the Web on the widest variety of computer products.

Shipping: **$ $**   Navigation:

Beyond.com

www.beyond.com

This site is especially useful in that it is one of the few who list their price versus list price. While their newer item's prices are not the best on the Web, their closeout and last year model prices are. They are definitely worth a stop when shopping for computer hardware. Note that they are mainly a peripheral and parts supplier as opposed to dealing in whole systems.

Shipping: **$ $**   Navigation:

Bid.com

www.bid.com

Click the Computers, Notebooks, Monitors, and Upgrades & Accessories links at this auction site for rock-bottom prices—bids start at $1 for many items! Note: Charges for delivery vary by seller.

    Navigation:

BidHit.com

www.bidhit.com/auction/

At this auction site, you'll find PCs, laptops, monitors, printers, scanners, processors, modems, sound and video cards, drives, and more. Shipping and handling charges vary by seller.

    Navigation:

Bids Wanted

www.bidswanted.com

Click the Computers link to see what's for sale. Charges for delivery vary by seller.

    Navigation:

Buy.com

www.buy.com

You'll find great deals on computers and peripherals here. This site's handy Compare Price feature makes for safe bargain shopping.

Shipping: **$ $**   Navigation:

CableMakers
www.cablemakers.com

Now you propeller-heads out there can buy cables, adapters, and switches on the cheap.

Shipping: **$ $** Navigation:

CDW.com
www.cdw.com

An extremely robust site with hundreds of low priced name brands and third-party manufacturers of PC's, laptops, peripherals and parts. They have been around for a while and are one of the mega-hardware sites on the net.

Shipping: **$ $**   Navigation:

Classifieds 2000
www.classifieds2000.com

Click Computers & Software to search for auction and classified ads for computers. Note: Shipping charges may vary by vendor.

Navigation:

CNET Auctions
http://auctions.cnet.com

CNET Auctions is THE place for refurbished, discontinued, and new computers, peripherals, and software. Not only does CNET give you access to great products at great prices, but it empowers you to make informed purchasing decisions. Note: Shipping rates vary from seller to seller.

  Navigation:

Compaq Factory Outlet Superstore
http://worksstore.compaqworks.com

Find refurbished and new Compaq servers, laptops, and desktop computers here.

Shipping: **$ $ $** Navigation:

CompUSANet.com
www.compusanet.com

You've probably seen one of these stores in the real world; now you can get Comp USA deals without taking off your bunny slippers. You'll find notebooks, systems, peripherals, networking tools, accessories, and more. Be sure to check out the Xtreme Buys and Clearance areas.

Shipping: **$ $**   Navigation:

The Computer Geeks Discount Outlet
www.compgeeks.com

The Computer Geeks Discount Outlet purchases manufacturers' excess, overstock, and slightly obsolete inventories in huge quantities, allowing it to offer products at very low prices.

Shipping: **$ $**   Navigation:

Computer Shopper
www.zdnet.com/computershopper/

Visit Computer Shopper's Basement Store for some very fine prices on miscellaneous overstocked and refurbished computer hardware. Note that items featured on Computer Shopper's site are in fact sold by other vendors; shipping rates vary by seller.

Navigation:

Computers 4Sure
www.computers4sure.com

An excellent collection of name-brand and not-name-brand computers and peripherals at extremely discounted prices. A must stop if you are looking to upgrade your computing experience. They also have the most generous return and guarantee program that I have seen yet, right down to arranging and paying for the shipping in the advent of a return. With no restocking fee on the return, this site must be shooting for a customer service award!

Shipping: **$**   Navigation:

Costco Online
www.costco.com

You've probably heard of Costco, which is one of those warehouse clubs. Now Costco's online, offering members some great deals on some great merchandise (it costs a minimum of $40 to join, but if you shop there enough, prices will make up for it). Among other items, you'll find computers and peripherals, electronics, and more.

Shipping: **$ $**   Navigation:

Cyber Swap
www.cyberswap.com

Find hardware, software, and peripherals on the auction block here. Delivery charges will vary from seller to seller.

     Navigation:

COMPUTERS

CyberWarehouse.com
www.cyberwarehouse

Look for great bargains on "factory renewed" items (man-ufacturer's overstocks, customer refusals, closeouts, and so on, which have been recertified by the manufacturer and are in full compliance with the original specification).

Shipping: **$**   Navigation:

DealDeal.com
www.dealdeal.com

Click the Computer Products link to find CPUs, hard drives, keyboards, memory, modems, monitors, motherboards, laptops, printers, servers, and more—all up for auction. Note: Delivery charges will vary from seller to seller.

    Navigation:

Dell
www.dell.com

Build a computer with exactly—and only—the features you need at Dell! Alternatively, check out the refurbished machines for sale.

Shipping: **$ $ $**   Navigation:

DellAuction.com
www.dellauction.com

Buy and sell used PCs, notebooks, servers, peripherals, and accessories. Dell previously leased and factory-refurbished systems are available here. Note that ship-ping rates vary by seller.

    Navigation:

Digital Auction
www.digital-auction.com

Buy PCs, hard drives, CPUs, motherboards, modems, video cards, monitors, and more from this auction site. Note: Delivery charges vary by seller.

    Navigation:

Dirt Cheap Drives
www.dirtcheapdrives.com

Find hard drives, CD drives and recorders, tape drives, and related products that are, uh, dirt cheap. Be sure to check out the Internet specials and closeouts.

Shipping: **$ $**   Navigation:

eBay

www.ebay.com

Last I checked, eBay was offering 85,802 items for auction in the Computers area. Note that shipping rates vary depending on who's selling the item you want to buy.

 Navigation:

eCOST.com

www.ecost.com

eCost sells thousands of computer hardware products, including notebooks, digital cameras, and more, at or below wholesale. Plus it offers free shipping to boot!

Shipping: **$** Navigation:

edeal

www.edeal.com

Visit the Computers area of this auction site to see what's up for grabs. Note: shipping and handling charges may vary by seller.

 Navigation:

Egghead Surplus Auctions

www.surplusauction.com

Maybe it's because I'm blonde, but I had a hard time navigating this auction site. But if you can figure it out, good deals can be had on computers, peripherals, and accessories. Check the Surplus area for items that aren't up for auction, but are up for sale cheap.

Shipping: **$ $**   Navigation:

electronics.net

www.electronics.net/

Click the links under Home Office for deals on computer hardware.

Shipping: **$ $** Navigation:

eswap

www.eswap.com

Click the Computers link to see what's up for auction. Note that shipping prices may vary depending on who's selling the item you want to buy.

 Navigation:

EZbid.com

www.ezbid.com

Find cards, desktop computers, handhelds, modems, monitors, motherboards, notebooks, printers, scanners, speakers, storage, and more up for auction. Click the Rebate button to see which items on the site have rebates! Note: shipping and handling costs will differ depending on the seller.

 Navigation:

FirstAuction

www.firstauction.com

The Computers category features loads of accessories and upgrades, desktop computers, drives, processors, modems, monitors, laptops, printers, scanners, and more—all up for auction. Note: shipping costs will vary depending on the seller.

 Navigation:

FirstSource.com

www.firstsource.com

FirstSource.com acts as a storefront for multiple nation-wide distributors, enabling them to offer low prices on thousands of items.

Shipping: $ $ Navigation:

Gateway

www.Gateway.com

Customize a machine through Gateway, and avoid paying for features no one in your house would even dream of using.

Shipping: $ $ $ Navigation:

Going Once

www.goingonce.net

Categories at this auction site include, among others, memory, modems, monitors, motherboards, notebooks, printers, scanners, and servers. Note: Costs for shipping and handling will vary by seller.

 Navigation:

Haggle Online
www.haggle.com

Haggle Online offers so many different types of computer
equipment for auction, the category is broken in two:
Computers and More Computers (you'll even find "Antique
Computers" listed). Note: shipping and handling charges
will vary by seller.

 Navigation:

HardwareStreet.com
www.hardwarestreet.com

Select from a wide selection of discounted hardware,
including input devices, storage devices, memory and
processors, and more.

Shipping: **$ $**   Navigation:

Insight
www.insight.com

Find deals on brand-name computer equipment, including hardware, and accessories. Be sure to check the
Specials area for the best deals.

Shipping: **$ $ $**   Navigation:

Internet Shopping Outlet
www.shoplet.com

Find hardware, games, and more at 20 to 70 percent off
retail prices.

Shipping: **$ $**   Navigation:

J&R
www.jandr.com

Good deals on hardware—including Macs—and software.

Shipping: **$ $**   Navigation:

Lynn Computer Products
www.lynncomp.com ☼

While the site look is not as polished as some of the larger
online vendors, Lynn Computer Products is the real deal.
Having ordered an AMD CPU from them and having gotten
it at a fabulous price, I can safely recommend them. They
do not sell name brand desktop computers or laptops, but
for parts and accessories, Lynn is a must stop.

Shipping: **$ $**   Navigation:

COMPUTERS

Micro Warehouse
www.warehouse.com

While not all of Micro Warehouse's items are at bargain prices, the ones that are are the real deal. Probably a site for an individual who already knows the ballpark price of what they are looking for and can therefore, compare. They get a nod for having perhaps the largest selection of hardware that I have seen online.

Shipping: **$ $**   Navigation:

MicronPC.com
www.micronpc.com/l\

Buy desktops, notebooks, and servers here—using only those components you want. No more paying extra for features you'll never use!

Shipping: **$ $ $**   Navigation:

NC Buy
www.ncbuy.com

Buy computer systems and peripherals here, at some nice prices.

Shipping: **$ $**   Navigation:

NECX
www.necx.com

Find everything you need to get your computer up and running here. Click the Outlet Center link for even better deals.

Shipping: **$**   Navigation:

One Web Place
www.onewebplace.com

Click the Computers & Electronics link to get your fill of software and hardware—all on the auction block. Delivery rates vary by seller.

    Navigation:

OnSale.com
www.onsale.com

Find wholesale prices on leading computer brand names, for both hardware and software. This site rocks. You'll notice a definite difference in prices at this site compared to the others! Be sure to check out their auction area, as well.

Shipping: **$ $**   Navigation:

Outpost.com

www.outpost.com

Prices throughout the site are decent but check out the Bargain Basement area for more savings. (Stop by the auction area, too!) Avoid shipping sticker shock by shopping here, where shipping within the U.S. is always free.

Shipping: **$** Navigation: 👍

PC Connection

www.pcconnection.com

This site began as a mail-order catalog in 1982, and has been offering discounted equipment ever since. Click the Hot Deals and Clearance tabs for special savings.

Shipping: **$ $ $** Navigation: ✋

PC Shopping Planet

www.shoppingplanet.com

Not every item on this Web site is dirt cheap, but try clicking the Hot Buys link for the occasional blowout.

Shipping: **$ $** Navigation: ✋

ProVantage

www.provantage.com

Buy computer hardware, and books at this site.

Shipping: **$ $** Navigation: 👍

Recycler.com

www.recycler.com

Click the Computers & Accessories link to browse the available items (there were 2,977 in this area last time I checked). Shipping rates may vary depending on who's selling the item you want to buy.

 Navigation: 👍

SellAndTrade.com

www.sellandtrade.com

Click the Computer Hardware and Computer Software links to see what's on the auction block. Note that shipping charges will vary depending on the seller.

  Navigation: ✋

Shop4.com
www.shop4.com

You must become a member to save on this site, but once you do, you'll find hardware for as much as 60 percent off retail. You'll find hardware, software, and more. Click the Clearance link for the very best deals.

Shipping: **$ $**   Navigation:

Shoppers Advantage
www.shoppersadvantage.com

Click the Computers & Software link for great savings. Note: you must register to become a member in order to cash in on the great savings on this site.

Shipping: **$ $**   Navigation:

Shopping.com
www.shopping.com

Click the Computers and Office tab to find great deals on hardware.

Shipping: **$ $**   Navigation:

SoftwareSoftware.com
www.softwaresoftware.com

Buy computer systems, input devices, storage devices, memory and processors, power-protection devices, printers, and more at this site

Shipping: **$ $**   Navigation:

The SpiderGear Connection
www.spidergear.com

Click the Computers link to find printers, laptops, and scanners at a discount. Site members get first stab at new products, and better prices.

Shipping: **$ $ $**   Navigation:

State Street Direct Online
www.ssdonline.com

With a huge selection, bargain prices, and the shipping cost listed right along with the product, this site is worth looking at.

Shipping: **$ $**   Navigation:

TC Computers
www.tccomputers.com

Geek out here, where you'll find everything you need to build your own machine (for you techno-wimps out there, ready-made systems are also available). TC's specialty is motherboards.

Shipping: **$ $**   Navigation:

TechShopper
www.techshopper.com

TechShopper, from CMP's TechWeb, can help you research and purchase hardware for your PC. You can't actually buy here, but it's worth a visit because of the information it offers.

Navigation:

Tek Discount Warehouse
http://tekgallery.com

Click the Electronics link for deals on computer equipment.

Shipping: **$ $**   Navigation:

ThinkBid.com
www.thinkbid.com

At this auction site, you'll find accessories, memory upgrades, modems, monitors, motherboards and cases, laptops, printers, scanners, CPUs, and more. Note that delivery charges will vary by seller.

          Navigation:

U Bid 4 It
www.ubid4it.com

Bid on computer equipment—systems, notebooks, storage, printers, and more—at this auction site. Note: Delivery charges vary by seller.

          Navigation:

uBid Online Auction
www.ubid.com

Bid for computer products, including monitors, printers, and more at this auction site. Note: Delivery charges may vary by seller.

          Navigation:

COMPUTERS

Up 4 Sale

www.up4sale.com

Bid on Apple products, PCs, drives, memory, mice
and keyboards, modems, monitors, motherboards,
laptops, printers, scanners, servers, cards, and more
at Up 4 Sale. Note that shipping rates will vary
by seller.

    Navigation:

USAuctions.com

www.usauctions.com

Click the Computers and Software links to see what's
available. Note that shipping rates vary depending on
who's selling the item you want to buy.

    Navigation:

The Used Computer Mall

www.usedcomputer.com

If you don't really care about being the fastest, biggest, or
best, The Used Computer Mall is the place for you. Find
items up for auction, as well as classified ads peddling
used equipment on the cheap. Note that shipping rates
vary by seller.

    Navigation:

Value America

www.valueamerica.com

If you're looking to buy something, there's a good
chance Value America's looking to sell it—including
computers, and accessories. Be sure to check out the
hot buys! Become a member (it's free) and save even
more.

Shipping: **$**   Navigation:

Voltex

www.voltexcomputers.com

Find everything you need to put together the jigsaw that is
a computer—cables, cases, drives, memory, modems,
mice/keyboards, monitors, motherboards, and more. The
downside? Shipping's a bit steep.

Shipping: **$ $ $**   Navigation:

Wal Mart Online
www.wal-mart.com

So there's no greeter, but that doesn't mean the online version of Wal Mart is a total bust. Click the Computers & Software link for great prices on computers. Free shipping on some items (you'll know it when you see it).

Shipping: **$**   Navigation:

WebAuction.com
www.webauction.com

Bid on desktop computers, laptops, digital cameras, printers, monitors, storage, modems, and more.

 Navigation:

Web Emporium
www.webporium.com

You'll find a bit of everything here at Web Emporium—computer hardware electronics, and more—all at nice prices.

Shipping: **$ $**   Navigation:

Wholesell.com
www.wholesell.com

Find desktop PCs, laptops, servers, printers, and more.

Shipping: **$ $ $**   Navigation:

Yahoo! Auctions
http://auctions.yahoo.com

Click the Computers link to find great deals on hardware and software (last I checked, this area featured 36,145 ads). Note that shipping rates vary by seller.

 Navigation:

Zones.com
www.zones.com

Find computer hardware, whether you're a Macophile or a PC-head. Be sure to click the Super Values link to find the best deals!

Shipping: **$ $**   Navigation:

Software

24-7 Outlet
www.7-24outlet.com

Click the Software link to check out some serious software bargains. Selection is limited, but you should bookmark this site and check back often.

Shipping: **$ $**   Navigation:

3D Auction
www.3dauction.com

Find all sorts of goods at this auction site, including computer software. Shipping rates vary depending on who's selling the item you want to buy.

  Navigation:

2BuyPC
www.2buypc.com

2BuyPC has more than 80,000 boxed hardware and software items and over 130,000 downloadable software items at wholesale prices.

Shipping: **$ $** Navigation:

999software.com
www.999software.com

All software sold at this site costs just $9.99.

Shipping: **$ $** Navigation:

Access Micro
www.accessmicro.com

In your search for the cheapest source of software, Access Micro is a definite stop. With a large selection to choose from at cut-throat prices, you can't really go wrong.

Shipping: **$ $** Navigation:

Amazon Auctions

http://auctions.amazon.com

Choose Computers & Software to see what's available.
Shipping rates vary depending on who's selling the item
you want to buy.

 Navigation:

Applied Computer Online

www.applied-computer.com

Find tons of software at great prices.

Shipping: **$ $** Navigation:

Auction Adventures

www.auctionadventures.net

Click the Computer Stuff link to see what's up for auction
on this site. Shipping rates vary by seller.

 Navigation:

Auction First

www.auctionfirst.com

Find computer software (among other things) for auction
here. Note that shipping rates may vary depending on
who's selling the item you want to buy.

 Navigation:

Auction Nation

www.auctionnation.com

Click the Computers link to find software and other computer must-have items for auction. Note: Shipping costs
may vary depending on who's selling the item you want to
buy.

 Navigation:

Auction Sales

www.auction-sales.com

Find loads of software and miscellaneous goodies (computer books, electronics, and such) for auction here. Click
the $1 Directory link to find all the auctions starting at $1.
Note: Shipping rates vary depending on the vendor.

 Navigation:

COMPUTERS

Auction Universe

www.auctionuniverse.com

Click the Computers link to find a wide variety of software
and other computer necessities. Delivery charges may
vary by vendor.

 Navigation:

Auction Ware

www.auctionware.com

Check out the Computer Related area to see software is
on the auction block. Note that delivery charges vary by
seller.

 Navigation:

Auction World

www.a-world.com

Click the Hardware and Software links to check out the
goods up for auction. Be sure to check the Pick of the
Week, Dollar Mania, Steals & Deals, and Out of This World
areas for the best bargains! Shipping rates vary by seller.

 Navigation:

Auction-Warehouse.com

www.auction-warehouse.com

Click the Computer Software link to see what goodies are
on the auction block. Note: Delivery charges may vary
depending on who's selling the item you want.

 Navigation:

AuctionAddict.com

www.auctionaddict.com

Click the Computers link to see what's up for grabs.
Shipping rates vary by seller.

 Navigation:

AuctioNet.com

www.auctionet.com

Find software, peripherals and other computer must-
have items for auction here. Note that shipping rates vary
depending on who's selling the item you want to buy.

 Navigation:

AuctionFloor.com
www.auctionfloor.com

Click the Computers tab to see what's up for auction. Note that shipping prices may vary depending on who's selling the item you want to buy.

Navigation:

AuctionMAX
www.auctionmax.com

AuctionMax is a warehouse outlet for new computer stuff (no used or refurbished here). Click the PriceDrop link for some interesting deals—the more people buy an item, the less it costs. Shipping rates and policies vary by seller.

Navigation:

AuctionPage.com
http://auctionpage.com

Find loads of software for auction at this site. Note that shipping rates vary depending on who's selling the item you want to buy.

Navigation:

Auctionscape
www.auctionscape.com

Click the Computers link to see what software's on the auction block. Note that shipping prices vary by seller.

Navigation:

Bargain News Auctions Online
www.bnauctions.com

Click the Computers link to see what goodies are on the auction block. Delivery charges vary by seller.

Navigation:

Barnes&Noble.com
www.barnesandnoble.com

In addition to the books you'd expect to find here, you'll also find one helluva selection of software. Click the Bargains tab for even hotter deals.

Shipping: **$ $**

Navigation:

Bid.com
www.bid.com

This auction site sports some rock-bottom prices—bids start at $1 for many items, including software! Note: Charges for delivery vary by seller.

 Navigation:

BidHit.com
www.bidhit.com/auction/

At this auction site, you'll software and other computer necessities. Shipping and handling charges vary by seller.

 Navigation:

Bids Wanted
www.bidswanted.com

Click the Computers link to see what's for sale. Charges for delivery vary by seller.

 Navigation:

Buy.com
www.buy.com

You'll find great deals on software. Use the Compare Price feature to make sure you're getting the best bargain.

Shipping: **$ $**   Navigation:

CD World
www.cdworld.com

CD World calls itself "The World's Largest Discount Entertainment Store." You'll find some nice prices on software.

Shipping: **$ $**   Navigation:

CDW.com
www.cdw.com

As one of the mega-computer shopping sites on the network, they appropriately offer a wide selection of cut-rate priced software. A great place to shop for almost any software need.

Shipping: **$ $**   Navigation:

Classifieds 2000

www.classifieds2000.com

Click the Computers & Software link to search for thousands of auction and classified ads for software. Note: Shipping charges may vary by vendor.

Navigation:

CNET Auctions

http://auctions.cnet.com

CNET Auctions is THE place for software. Not only does CNET give you access to great products at great prices, but it empowers you to make informed purchasing decisions. Note: Shipping rates vary from seller to seller.

                    Navigation:

CNET Download

http://download.com

This site is a huge resource for downloadable software, including a ton of freeware (read: free software) and shareware (read: cheap or free software).

Navigation:

Columbia House

www.columbiahouse.com

Columbia House offers as many clubs as you'll find in a golf bag—one for music, one for videos, one for DVDs, and one for CD-ROMs. Shipping and handling's a bit steep, but being a member does have its advantages.

Shipping: **$ $ $**   Navigation:

CompUSANet.com

www.compusanet.com

You've probably seen one of these stores in the real world; now you can get Comp USA deals without taking off your bunny slippers. You'll find all sorts of software goodies here. Be sure to check out the Xtreme Buys and Clearance areas.

Shipping: **$ $**   Navigation:

COMPUTERS

The Computer Geeks Discount Outlet
www.compgeeks.com

The Computer Geeks Discount Outlet purchases manufacturers' excess, overstock, and slightly obsolete inventories in huge quantities, allowing it to offer products at
very low prices.

Shipping: **$ $**   Navigation:

Costco Online
www.costco.com

You've probably heard of Costco, which is one of those
warehouse clubs. Now Costco's online, offering members
some great deals on some great merchandise, including
software (it costs a minimum of $40 to join, but if you shop
there enough, prices will make up for it)

Shipping: **$ $**   Navigation:

Cyber Swap
www.cyberswap.com

Find some nice software deals on the auction block here.
Delivery charges will vary from seller to seller.

   Navigation:

CyberWarehouse.com
www.cyberwarehouse

Look for great bargains on "factory renewed" items
(manufacturer's overstocks, customer refusals, closeouts, and so on, which have been recertified by the manufacturer and are in full compliance with the original
specification).

Shipping: **$**   Navigation:

DealDeal.com
www.dealdeal.com

Click the Computer Products link to software and other
computer must-have items —all up for auction. Note:
Delivery charges will vary from seller to seller.

   Navigation:

DellAuction.com
www.dellauction.com

Buy and sell used software and other computer necessities. Dell previously leased and factory-refurbished systems are available here. Note that shipping rates vary by seller.

 Navigation:

DownloadDrive.com
www.downloaddrive.com

Find downloadable software on the cheap at this site.

Navigation:

eBay
www.ebay.com

Last I checked, eBay was offering 85,802 items for auction in the Computers area. Note that shipping rates vary depending on who's selling the item you want to buy.

 Navigation:

edeal
www.edeal.com

Visit the Computers area of this auction site to see what's up for grabs. Note: shipping and handling charges may vary by seller.

Navigation:

Egghead Surplus Auctions
www.surplusauction.com

Maybe it's because I'm blonde, but I had a hard time navigating this auction site. But if you can figure it out, good deals can be had on software and other computer-related items. Check the Surplus area for items that aren't up for auction, but are up for sale cheap.

Shipping: **$ $**   Navigation:

eswap
www.eswap.com

Click the Computers link to see what's up for auction. Note that shipping prices may vary depending on who's selling the item you want to buy.

Navigation:

EZbid.com

www.ezbid.com

Find a variety of software and other computer must-have items, all up for auction. Click the Rebate button to see which items on the site have rebates! Note: shipping and handling costs will differ depending on the seller.

    Navigation:

FirstAuction

www.firstauction.com

The Computers category features loads software —all up for auction. Note: shipping costs will vary depending on the seller.

    Navigation:

Going Once

www.goingonce.net

Categories at this auction site include, among others, memory, modems, monitors, motherboards, notebooks, printers, scanners, servers, and software. Note: Costs for shipping and handling will vary by seller.

    Navigation:

Haggle Online

www.haggle.com

Haggle Online offers so many different types of computer equipment for auction, the category is broken in two: Computers and More Computers (you'll even find "Antique Computers" listed). Note: shipping and handling charges will vary by seller.

    Navigation:

Insight

www.insight.com

Find deals on brand-name computer equipment, including a nice selection of software. Be sure to check the Specials area for the best deals.

Shipping: **$ $ $**   Navigation:

Internet Shopping Outlet
www.shoplet.com

Find a variety of software items to choose from, at 20 to 70 percent off retail prices.

Shipping: **$ $**   Navigation:

J&R
www.jandr.com

Good deals on software to be found here.

Shipping: **$ $**   Navigation:

Kmart.com
www.kmart.com

Click the Software Selections link to find all sorts of software titles at low prices.

Shipping: **$ $**   Navigation:

The Learning Company
www.new.shoptlc.com

Find discounted software here. Be sure to check out the Bargains area. Join the TLC Advantage Club for even better savings.

Shipping: **$ $**   Navigation:

NC Buy
www.ncbuy.com

Buy software out of the box or in download form here.

Shipping: **$ $**   Navigation:

NECX
www.necx.com

Find everything you need to get your computer up and running here. Click the Outlet Center link for even better deals.

Shipping: **$**   Navigation:

COMPUTERS

One Web Place

www.onewebplace.com

Click the Computers & Electronics link to get your fill of software —all on the auction block. Delivery rates vary by seller.

 Navigation:

Outpost.com

www.outpost.com

Prices throughout the site are decent; check out the Bargain Basement area for more savings. (Check out the auction, too!) Avoid shipping sticker shock by shopping here, where shipping within the U.S. is always free.

Shipping: **$** Navigation:

PC Magazine's Shareware Library

www.zdnet.com/pcmag/downloads/

Find plenty of downloadable software. Click the Free Utilities link to download any number of free applications.

Navigation:

ProVantage

www.provantage.com

Choose from a variety of computer software items at this site.

Shipping: **$ $** Navigation:

Recycler.com

www.recycler.com

Click the Computers & Accessories link to browse the available items (there were 2,977 in this area last time I checked). Shipping rates may vary depending on who's selling the item you want to buy.

Navigation:

SellAndTrade.com

www.sellandtrade.com

Click the Computer Software link to see what's on the auction block. Note that shipping charges will vary depending on the seller.

 Navigation:

Shop4.com

www.shop4.com

You must become a member to save on this site, but once you do, you'll find goods for as much as 60 percent off retail. You'll find loads of software. Click the Clearance link for the very best deals.

Shipping: **$ $**   Navigation:

Shoppers Advantage

www.shoppersadvantage.com

Click the Computers & Software link for great savings. Note: you must register to become a member in order to cash in on the great savings on this site.

Shipping: **$ $**   Navigation:

Shopping.com

www.shopping.com

Click the Computers and Office tab to find great deals on software.

Shipping: **$ $**   Navigation:

Software Auction Online

www.gosao.com

Find software for your PC and Mac on the auction block. Note that shipping costs will vary by seller.

                    Navigation:

SoftwareCloseouts.com

www.softwarecloseouts.com

If you're not the type of person who always needs the newest software, then this is the site for you. Find "new old stock" of software here, at very deep discounts!

Shipping: **$ $**   Navigation:

SoftwareSoftware.com

www.softwaresoftware.com

Buy software for business, education, graphics and design, home finance, networking, programming, and more at this site.

Shipping: **$ $**   Navigation:

SoftwareStreet.com
www.softwarestreet.com

Select from a wide selection of discounted software for Macs and PCs.

Shipping: **$ $**   Navigation: 👍

TC Computers
www.tccomputers.com

Geek out here, where you'll find tons of software at some nice prices.

Shipping: **$ $** Navigation: 👍

ThinkBid.com
www.thinkbid.com

At this auction site, you'll find the software you've been search for and more. Note that delivery charges will vary by seller.

 Navigation: 👍

U Bid 4 It
www.ubid4it.com

Bid on computer equipment—systems, notebooks, storage, printers, software and more—at this auction site. Note: Delivery rates vary by seller.

 Navigation: 👍

uBid Online Auction
www.ubid.com

Bid for computer products, including software and more at this auction site. Note: Delivery charges may vary by seller.

 Navigation: 👍

Up 4 Sale
www.up4sale.com

Bid on a wide selection of software. Note that shipping rates will vary by seller.

 Navigation: ✋

USAuctions.com

www.usauctions.com

Click the Computers and Software links to see what's available. Note that shipping rates vary depending on who's selling the item you want to buy.

  Navigation:

Value America

www.valueamerica.com

If you're looking to buy something, there's a good chance Value America's looking to sell it—including computers, accessories, and software (video games, too!). Be sure to check out the hot buys! Become a member (it's free) and save even more.

Shipping: **$** Navigation:

Wal Mart Online

www.wal-mart.com

So there's no greeter, but that doesn't mean the online version of Wal Mart is a total bust. Click the Computers & Software link for great prices on, well, computers and software. Free shipping on some items (you'll know it when you see it).

Shipping: **$** Navigation:

WebAuction.com

www.webauction.com

Bid on software and other computer must-have items.

  Navigation:

Web Emporium

www.webporium.com

You'll find a bit of everything here at Web Emporium—but look for computer software for some great deals.

Shipping: **$ $** Navigation:

Wholesell.com

www.wholesell.com

Find the software item you've been searching for here.

Shipping: **$ $ $** Navigation:

COMPUTERS

Yahoo! Auctions

http://auctions.yahoo.com

Click the Computers link to find great deals on hardware and software (last I checked, this area featured 36,145 ads). Note that shipping rates vary by seller.

 Navigation:

Zones.com

www.zones.com

Find computer software, whether you're a Macophile or a PC-head. Be sure to click the Super Values link to find the best deals!

Shipping: **$ $**   Navigation:

BARGAIN SHOPPING Online

Comparison Shopper

Comparison Shopper

Acses

www.acses.com

This shopping agent checks book prices, availability, shipping time, and costs of books, CDs, and movies at over 20 online stores.

Navigation:

Add All Book Searching and Price Comparison

www.bookarea.com

How great is THIS? Enter in your shipping destination; the currency you use; and the title, author, ISBN, or keyword of the book you want to find, and this site compares the pricing and services at 39 stores (at present) to find the cheapest offering. Stop here before you buy to make sure you get the best deal!

Navigation:

Auction Watchers

www.auctionwatchers.com

Auction Watchers' advanced search bots find the best deals on computer equipment currently available from major online auctions.

 Navigation:

Bargain Dog

www.bargaindog.com

Join Bargain Dog and receive a free, customized email newsletter that updates you on sales, clearances, and great deals at leading online merchants.

Navigation:

BestBookBuys.com
www.bestbookbuys.com

Type the title, author, keyword, or ISBN of the book you want to find, click Search, and let BestBookBuys.com do the legwork for you! It searches 25 stores (at present) for the best price. This database is fast and comprehensive!

Navigation: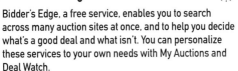

Bidder's Edge
www.biddersedge.com ☆

Bidder's Edge, a free service, enables you to search across many auction sites at once, and to help you decide what's a good deal and what isn't. You can personalize these services to your own needs with My Auctions and Deal Watch.

 Navigation:

BidFind
www.bidfind.com ☆

This World Wide Web auction search site indexes thousands of items from popular auction sites every day. If you're looking to buy something specific from an auction, check out this site first to see where it's available for the lowest price!

 Navigation:

BookFinder.com
www.bookfinder.com

This online bookstore comparison shopping agent scans several of the top online booksellers' databases to find new, used, rare, and out of print books. Results are returned within seconds!

Navigation:

BottomDollar
www.bottomdollar.com

BottomDollar searches for deals on items in 20 product categories: Auction, Books, Electronics, Flowers, Fragrances, Gifts, Hardware, Health/Beauty, Home/Garden, Kitchen, Magazines, Movies, Music, Office Products, Pro-Audio, Software, Sports, Toys, Video Games, and Other.

Navigation:

COMPARISON SHOPPER

BrandsForLess.com
www.brandsforless.com

BrandsForLess calls itself an "e-partment store," and takes pride in offering great prices, great service, and name brands you know. You'll link to other sites to find apparel, items for babies and kids, accessories and cosmetics, items for your home and garden, computers, software, office supplies, electronics, books, pet supplies, and more.

Shipping: $ Navigation:

Buy It Now
www.buyitnow.com

BuyItNow.com houses a collection of stores available on the Web that offer great brand names along with unique, hard-to-find items at guaranteed low prices. Join Buy It Now to receive special sale prices year round.

Shipping: $ $ Navigation:

Catalog City
www.catalogcity.com

This catalog-shopping portal offers a wide range of products sold through thousands of catalogs including Brookstone, Critic's Choice, Hammacher Schlemmer, Harry and David, J. Jill, Neiman Marcus, Patagonia, and more. Not everything's a bargain, but they can be found here. Note that shipping costs depend on which catalog you order from.

Navigation:

CNET Shopper
www.shopper.com

Whether you're looking for complete desktops or notebooks, or just components or software, this is the place to visit first. CNET Shopper compares about a gazillion (that's a technical term) sites to see who's offering the best prices on the items you want.

Navigation:

CompareNet
www.comparenet.com

CompareNet compares prices for goods in seven different categories: Electronics, Automotive, Baby Care, Computing, Home Appliances, Home Office, and Sports and Leisure.

Navigation:

Consumer World

www.consumerworld.org

Find product comparisons, reviews, and a pricing service at this site.

Navigation:

ebates.com

www.ebates.com

Here's a new one: ebates pays you up to 25 percent cash back on every purchase you make through its site. Whatever you're looking to buy, stop by here first! Plus you'll find loads of affiliate stores with some great bargains.

Navigation:

eSmarts

www.esmarts.com

eSmarts offers bots and shopping agents for bargain shopping on the Web. At this site, you'll find listings of discounts, merchant reports, and buying guides covering auctions, banks, books, brokers, cars, computers, electronics, flowers, groceries, long distance, music, toys, travel, and more.

Navigation:

Excite Shopping Channel

www.excite.com/shopping

This is a good place to begin your search for the merchandise you want. Not only are items categorized and searchable, but a list of featured merchants will also help you find what you seek!

Navigation:

imall

www.imall.com

Shop for bargains on quality products and services by product or by store.

Navigation:

InShop.com
www.inshop.com

If you love sales, you'll really love InShop.com. This free service clues you into all the sales, deals, and bargains online, in catalogs, and on the street. They prefer to list sites (whether apparel, accessories, or furniture) with discounts of at least 50 percent off retail.

Navigation:

The Internet Auction List
http://www.internetauctionlist.com

This portal to the auction community enables you to find the best bargains amidst the hundreds of online auction sites. With IAL's product search service, you can search more than 200 auction sites at once!

 Navigation:

The Internet Resale Directory
www.secondhand.com

With more than 40,000 secondhand, surplus, and salvage stores listed, the Internet Resale Directory is the Internet's largest information source for resale shopping.

Navigation:

Lycos Shopping
www.lycos.com/shopnet

This site, which includes an impressive list of shopping categories as well as special features, is a good point of entry for online shoppers.

Navigation:

My Simon
www.mysimon.com

My Simon can search thousands of merchants in hundreds of product categories in real time, so he always finds the right products at the best price. Major product categories include Apparel & Accessories; Book, Music & Movies, Computers & Software; Consumer Electronics; Family, Health & Beauty; Flowers & Gifts; Gourmet & Groceries; Hobby & Leisure; Holiday & Seasonal; Home & Garden; Office Supplies; Sports & Recreation; and Toys & Collectibles.

Navigation:

NowOnSpecial.com

www.nowonspecial.com

Visit NowOnSpecial.com regularly to see what's on sale at a variety of sites around the Web. You'll find goods from ibaby.com, barnesandnoble.com, outletmall.com, and more! Note that this site doesn't sell things; it only lists sale items on other sites. Shipping charges vary by seller.

Navigation:

Planet Retail

www.planetretail.com

This superstore bot search and shopping guide is way huge; you can shop for apparel, books, electronics, gifts, movies, and more, from a huge variety of retailers.

Navigation:

PriceScan

www.pricescan.com ☆

This site rules. PriceSCAN helps take the hassle out of shopping by hunting down the best prices on the goods you want to buy, be they books, movies, music, computers, office supplies, home electronics, toys, baby goods, home improvement items, sporting goods, gifts, home items, or whatever. Don't search a zillion sites looking for the cheapest prices on the goods you want. Instead, visit PriceScan.

Navigation:

RoboShopper

www.roboshopper.com

RoboShopper makes online shopping fast and easy—just tell it what you're looking for (books, music, movies, computer hardware, computer software, toys, sporting goods, or auctions) and it will query online stores and then display the results.

Navigation:

SalesSales.com

www.salessales.com

SalesSales.com, which is updated hourly, scours the Internet for online merchants offering deep discounts and specials on their products and services in over a dozen categories.

Navigation:

Shabang!
www.shabang.com

Shabang! features a comprehensive shopping directory
with product categories like Apparel, Personal & Gifts,
Electronics, Hobbies & Interests, Home & Office,
Major Purchases, and Services. Use their search
engine to search their affiliates for the merchandise
you want.

Navigation:

Shop4U
www.shop4u.com

Use Shop4U's shopping search engines to find the best
deals on the products you want.

Navigation:

ShopFind
www.shopfind.com

When you have something specific that you want to buy
online, start at ShopFind. This search engine searches
only those sites that allow you to purchase online.
Shopfind includes more than 3,000 online merchants,
and over 3,000,000 product pages from which you
can order.

Navigation:

ShopNow.com
www.shopnow.com

Explore ShopNow.com's directory of over 25,000 stores
to find all types of products.

Navigation:

ShopShop
www.shopshop.net

ShopShop is a search and navigational Internet
shopping directory that features the best sites on the
Internet, organized into more than 25 product
categories.

Navigation:

StoreSearch

www.storesearch.com

Thankfully, you won't find Ed McMahon presiding over StoreSearch. No, this site is an Internet shopping guide with a powerful search agent that helps you find everything you're looking for. There's also a comprehensive listing of product categories, stores, and major brands.

Navigation: 👍

TechShopper

www.techshopper.com

TechShopper, from CMP's TechWeb, can help you research and purchase hardware and software for your PC.

Navigation: 👍

WebMarket

www.webmarket.com

WebMarket searches the top online stores to bring you the best prices. Product categories include Apparel, Books & Stationery, Computer Hardware/Software, Consumer Electronics, Department Stores, Games & Toys, Gifts, Music, Movies & Videos, Office Supplies, Outdoor & Sporting Goods, and more.

Navigation: 👍

Yahoo! Shopping

http://shopping.yahoo.com

Yahoo!'s shopping directory features apparel, accessories, books, computers, electronics, flowers, gifts, health and beauty items, items for the home and garden, movies and videos, music, office supplies, sporting goods, and more.

Navigation: 👍